# iPad® Apps
# For Kids
## FOR
# DUMMIES®

## by Jinny Gudmundsen

WILEY

John Wiley & Sons, Inc.

**iPad® Apps For Kids For Dummies®**

Published by
John Wiley & Sons, Inc.
111 River Street
Hoboken, NJ 07030-5774
www.wiley.com

For general information on our other products and services, please contact our Customer Care Department within the U.S. at 877-762-2974, outside the U.S. at 317-572-3993, or fax 317-572-4002.

For technical support, please visit www.wiley.com/techsupport.

Wiley also publishes its books in a variety of electronic formats. Some content that appears in print may not be available in electronic books.

Library of Congress Control Number: 2012951873

ISBN: 978-1-118-43307-2 (pbk); ISBN 978-1-118-43326-3 (ebk); ISBN 978-1-118-52545-6 (ebk); ISBN 978-1-118-52548-7 (ebk)

Manufactured in the United States of America

10  9  8  7  6  5  4  3  2  1

WILEY

# About the Author

**Jinny Gudmundsen** is a leading authority on children's technology, and especially apps for kids. For the past 12 years, she has been the Kid-Tech Columnist for *USA Today* and the 82 Gannett newspapers. She is a trusted guru of the best apps, video games, tech toys, websites, and virtual worlds for kids. Jinny also works for Common Sense Media, the nation's leading nonprofit source of children's media reviews. She was the founding editor of *Choosing Children's Software* magazine, which is now online as Computing With Kids (www.ComputingWithKids.com). Her work has appeared in the Los Angeles Times, ABC News.com, and the San Jose Mercury News. She has contributed magazine articles to *Child, Family PC, Your Family, Computer Source Magazine, On,* and many others. She has judged numerous app, video game, and toy awards. Jinny appears on national TV and radio as a kid-tech expert.

Jinny got her start in the world of children's technology during a time when she was taking a break from practicing law to be a full-time mom. When her son Ted was a preschooler, a start-up named The Learning Company asked Jinny if Ted could be one of their first kid-testers for what became the seminal software game called "Reader Rabbit." With this glimpse into the inner world of the then-nascent children's technology, Jinny saw the potential of technology to teach kids. She bought an Apple IIe, back when people thought that "IIe" meant it was a genetically modified fruit; and she jumped on the Internet before her neighbors deemed it safe. She helped to set up and build computer labs at every new school her sons attended and trained teachers on how to use software in schools.

While a Kid-Tech Columnist by title, Jinny has always considered her most important and best job to be the mom to sons Ted and Peter. Her sons grew up kid-testing their way through their mom's technology-rich life and their home was always the coveted place to play because the hottest kid tech arrived every day. With so much technology around when her sons were growing up, it was with great relief and pride that Jinny watched both boys head off to Princeton without wanting to take video game consoles with them. She firmly believes that using technology with kids is all about getting the balance right.

# Dedication

This book is dedicated to Dorothy Sands, my 92-year-old mother and personal editor. She has edited every page of this book (and all of my *USA Today* Kid-Tech columns for the past 12 years) with great aplomb, wit, and loving encouragement. I am inspired by the way she is always willing to embrace new ideas and technology. I couldn't have written this book without you, Mom.

I would also like to include my supportive husband Vance Gudmundsen, who, despite not owning an iPad, is willing to stop his own work to marvel with me when I find an amazing app for kids — enthusiastically providing the "oohs" to my "aahs." And finally, a big shout-out to my two sons, Ted and Peter, who continue to be "kid-testers" for all the technology that I explore; I treasure your support and feedback. If life is a game of Cut the Rope, you guys are the candy to my Om Nom.

# Author's Acknowledgments

I would like to thank my *USA Today* colleague and fellow *For Dummies* author, Marc Saltzman, for introducing me to the Wiley Publishing group. I would also like to acknowledge my good friend from college, Gail Hochman, a top-notch literary agent, who gave me great advice when I was negotiating this book deal. Thank you Gail — you're a real pro!

I greatly appreciate all the work that the folks at Wiley Publishing have done to help me to write my first *For Dummies* book. In particular, I want to express my heartfelt thanks to Chris Morris, my project editor whose calm wisdom and great insight made this project even more fun to write. I also want to thank Kyle Looper for patiently guiding me through the Wiley process. I'm grateful for the special skills of my copy editor Amanda Graham, for Kelly Trent's help with marketing, and for Chantal Kowalski and Aditi Shah, my publicity gurus. A special shout out to my technical editor and personal friend Liz Panarelli for her thoughtful suggestions and helpful discussions. You're the best, Liz.

Apple is blessed to have a top-notch public relations team, which has been helpful in sharing their special recommendations. I would like to thank Jenn Ramsey Newhart, Christine Monaghan, Ted Miller, Jennifer Bowcock, and Sarah O'Brien. To write the Special Needs chapter, I valued the sharing of expertise from Apple Distinguished Educators Marc Coppin and Luis Perez.

I am grateful for the support of Common Sense Media, and in particular Shira Katz for being a flexible manager and a supportive cheerleader. My editor at *USA Today,* Nancy Blair, also deserves mention for extending my weekly deadlines when book deadlines were looming. Thank you, Nancy!

I would also like to thank my mother, who is my personal editor for all the things I write. What a team we make Mom — let's do it again!

## Publisher's Acknowledgments

We're proud of this book; please send us your comments at http://dummies.custhelp.com. For other comments, please contact our Customer Care Department within the U.S. at 877-762-2974, outside the U.S. at 317-572-3993, or fax 317-572-4002.

Some of the people who helped bring this book to market include the following:

*Acquisitions, Editorial*

**Sr. Project Editor:** Christopher Morris

**Acquisitions Editor:** Kyle Looper

**Copy Editor:** Amanda Graham

**Technical Editor:** Liz Panarelli

**Editorial Manager:** Kevin Kirschner

**Editorial Assistant:** Leslie Saxman

**Sr. Editorial Assistant:** Cherie Case

**Cover Photos:** Background: © Goldmund Lukic/iStockphoto.com; image on screen: © James Thew/iStockphoto.com; icons: © Paul Pantazescu/iStockphoto.com. Image of iPad photographed by Wiley Creative Services.

*Composition Services*

**Project Coordinator:** Patrick Redmond

**Layout and Graphics:**
Andrea Hornberger, Erin Zeltner

**Proofreaders:** Cynthia Fields, Jessica Kramer

---

**Publishing and Editorial for Technology Dummies**

**Richard Swadley,** Vice President and Executive Group Publisher

**Andy Cummings,** Vice President and Publisher

**Mary Bednarek,** Executive Acquisitions Director

**Mary C. Corder,** Editorial Director

**Publishing for Consumer Dummies**

**Kathleen Nebenhaus,** Vice President and Executive Publisher

**Composition Services**

**Debbie Stailey,** Director of Composition Services

# Table of Contents

## Chapter 6: Book Apps: For Younger Kids .......... 56

## Chapter 7: Book Apps: For Older Kids .............. 70

## Chapter 8: Cars, Trucks, and Things That Go Vroom ....................................... 80

## Chapter 21: Music...............................................182

## Chapter 22: Puzzles............................................188

## Chapter 23: Road Trip Apps ...........................198

## Chapter 24: Special Needs ...........................204

# Introduction

The iPad is the most exciting platform that I have experienced in my 18 years of reviewing children's technology. At the time of publishing this book, more than 650,000 apps were available in the iTunes store with 225,000 optimized for the iPad. That's a lot of apps to sift through to find the best ones for your kids. That's where I come in.

As the Kid-Tech columnist for *USA Today* and the 82 Gannett newspapers, I've been reviewing children's apps since the first iPad was released in April 2010. Over this time I have downloaded and played thousands of apps. Every week I open up a new app that astounds me. I have never before seen such innovation in technology. Developers are trying amazing things, but for every gem I find, I've looked at tens, if not hundreds, of duds.

Writing this book allows me to share with you the best of the best — 225 apps that have blown me away, made my jaw hang slack with wonder, or sent me running to show it to whomever happened to be near, preferably a kid.

Because the world of iPad apps is so new, it feels like the Wild West of children's tech. Very little "sheriffing" is going on, and many apps that sound great for your child end up being not very good, or worse — totally inappropriate. Let me be your sheriff and your guide to the world of iPad apps for your children. My goal is to help you enrich your children's lives with this new and amazing technology.

## About This Book

The purpose of this book is to help you find great apps for your children. Kids have different interests than adults, and different ways they like to play. An app that appeals to your preschooler won't be of interest to your tween. If you have a son who loves things that go vroom, we both know he'll be more attracted to a puzzle app about trucks than one about princesses. Perhaps you want your kids to spend some time exploring academic subjects, but you know they'll protest unless the app is fun. This book helps you find the apps that make the learning process a blast.

# How This Book Is Organized

Other than the first chapter, which explains how to set up an iPad for kids and how you can find more good apps, the chapters of this book reflect the different ways you might find apps for your kids: by age, academics, and interest.

The book covers apps appropriate for kids ages 2 through 14. Although developers make apps for babies, the American Academy of Pediatrics doesn't recommend screen time for kids younger than 2. Some of the higher-age apps in this book can be enjoyed by older teens, but I didn't focus on them either because most teens want to select their own apps.

Because the apps created for young children are geared to very specific ages, I decided to write three chapters based solely on a toddler, a preschooler, and a kindergartener. The rest of the chapters in the book cover apps based on a topic; within those chapters, I review apps for kids of all ages. Five of the chapters focus on the academic subjects of Language Arts, Math, Reference, Science, and Social Studies. Labeled Learning Apps and then followed by the academic subject, those chapters contain a mix of formats from activities to games to books. However, even within the Learning Apps chapters, no app is dry and boring.

The book also has a very useful Appendix. In it, I have sorted all 225 apps into age categories. If you have a 7-year-old, turn to the Appendix and look under Ages 7–8; you see a list of 160 apps that are appropriate for your child. For parents of special needs kids, I have put an asterisk beside the every app in the book that may work well with your children.

# The Selection of Apps

How did I decide which apps made it into this book? I played and evaluated thousands of apps to narrow it down to the 225 that made it into this volume. I judged the apps on the following factors:

- ✔ **Fun:** This is the holy grail of rating factors. If it isn't fun, kids won't play it.
- ✔ **Education Value:** If kids can learn something while having fun, you get a two-for-one. That said, lots of apps have been included in the book solely on the criteria that they are fun. Education is a factor, but not a requirement.

✔ **Ease of use:** If kids can't figure out what to do, they'll press the Home button and move on to another app.

✔ **Appropriateness:** This is one of the most complicated rating factors, but a very important one. I look at:

- *Content:* Is it appropriate to the targeted audience? This covers many facets from what the app is trying to teach to the difficulty of game levels (does it ramp up too quickly?) to presence of controversial stuff like violence, bad language, alcohol, and sex. For example, I frequently see a preschool app (yes, "preschool" is in the title of the app) that contains material that's way too hard for 3- to 5-year-olds to do. I also see apps advertised for 4-year-olds that are sporting gun-carrying characters. Nope, not on my watch!

- *Advertising:* I am very intolerant of ads in apps for young kids. First, ads can expose children to products that are totally inappropriate for them. Second, young children don't yet understand marketing. They see the ad telling them to buy something and they respond by informing you that you MUST go get the advertised item for them. I look for apps with no or minimal advertising; and if it's there, I warn you of it.

- *Enticements to spend money within the app:* Several very popular apps didn't make it into this book because they spend a disproportionate amount of time trying to convince you to spend money. Magic Piano, a free app by Smule, used to be an interesting app about playing the piano. But now, it's all about buying or doing things to earn Smoola, a virtual currency that can cost real money. Likewise, I used to love the free app The Oregon Trail by Gameloft, but now you pay for it, and it still spends lots of time pushing you to spend more money. I didn't include either.

- *Bias:* Within the app. If I see stereotyping or other offensive ethnic, gender, or racial representations, I won't select the app.

✔ **Wise use of iPad technology:** It's not enough to merely transfer content to the iPad platform. I'm looking for apps that make full use of the iPad technology. That's why, in the book app chapters (Chapters 6 and 7), I don't include books without bells and whistles. If you know that you love a specific children's book and you want to buy the app version to read to your kid, go for it. However, I want to give you a list of the ones that are doing something special.

✔ **Value:** Is this app worth the amount they're charging for it? I frequently see apps that price themselves out of the market.

# Conventions Used in This Book

Whenever possible, I refer you to other sources that can be helpful. If it's a website, then it's shown using monofont typeface, `like this`.

To help you find the apps listed in this book, I am careful to make sure that the name is correct (in this crowded marketplace, some apps have the exact same name and vary by simply adding an exclamation point to the end); but I also provide you the name of the publisher so that you have a way to double-check that you're downloading the correct app. The prices listed are current as of the time of publishing, but this is an industry where prices change weekly. I also provide the cost in currencies of the United States, Canada, and Great Britain.

I have also tried to steer you to other good apps that I didn't have room to include. I provide the name and the publisher so that you can search for them in the iTunes store.

# Icons Used in This Book

Throughout this book in the left-hand margin you see little icons. They are there to alert you to special things. The icons used in this book are

This indicates something that may help you use the app in a way that may not be obvious to you.

Occasionally I mention something that you may want to retain, such as the name of a developer that's consistently creating great apps.

This icon appears frequently in this book. It's to alert you that the app has things in it that aren't child-friendly, such as ads, in-app purchases, links to the Internet or social media (Facebook, Twitter, and others), connection to social gaming networks, and other possible concerns. It doesn't mean that you shouldn't use the app with your child, it merely means that you need to monitor its use and explain the buttons that you don't want your child to use.

Occasionally I explain technical stuff or jargon that is unique to the mobile app world. When I do this, I place this icon next to that paragraph.

# Where to Go from Here

This isn't a book that you need to read from cover to cover. Instead, scan the Table of Contents and see what chapters interest you. You may want to start with Chapter 26 because all of those apps are free. And don't miss Chapter 27 because that chapter lists the best of the best: my favorites of all the apps I've tried. I sincerely hope you have as much fun exploring these apps with your kids as I did writing this book.

Occasionally, we have updates to our technology books. If this book does have any technical updates, they'll be posted at www.dummies-.com/go/ipadappsforkidsfdupdates.

# 1 Using an iPad with Kids

Before you simply hand your iPad over to your kids and hope for the best, you should first do what you can to make using the device as safe as possible. After all, you probably don't want your toddler to end up on the Internet, or your preschooler deleting all of your apps. This chapter outlines the best ways to keep your iPad — and your kids — safe.

After you have your iPad set up for kids, how can you find some good apps to place within it? The answer is obvious: You check out the other 26 chapters of this book! But because I also want to help you become a good app shopper for your kids, this chapter also introduces some great searching strategies.

## Setting Up the iPad

Apple has done a good job providing parents with options to control their child's iPad world. These options, found in the Settings icon of your iPad, are discussed in the next few sections.

### Password Lock

If you want to control when your kids play on your iPad, the easiest thing to do is make your kids come to you to unlock it. That way, you always know when they are using it. You lock your iPad by turning on the Password Lock feature, which you find by tapping Settings⇨General⇨Password Lock. Toggle the switch to turn the Password Lock to On. You then create a password. If you want to keep control, make sure your kids don't see you input this code. You set how quickly the Auto-Lock comes on if the iPad is idle and whether closing the cover triggers that lock.

 Another important option under Password Lock is Erase Data. Because your kids may try to guess your password by fooling around with the keypad, I recommend turning the Erase Data option off. If you don't, then after ten failed attempts at guessing your password, the iPad automatically erases your personal data.

### Restrictions

Restrictions are Apple's version of parental controls. To activate them, go to Settings⇨General⇨Restrictions, and toggle them to On. (See figure below.) You must create another password for these. The options you see will vary depending on which iPad you are using and the operating system you are running. With these restrictions in place, you can decide whether your kids:

- ✔ **Surf the web.** The browser on the iPad is called Safari.
- ✔ **Visit YouTube.** This is not an option if you're running iOS 6.
- ✔ **Use the camera.** This feature is not on the original iPad.
- ✔ **Communicate using FaceTime.** This isn't on the original iPad.
- ✔ **Go to the iTunes store.**
- ✔ **Use Ping.** Ping is a music social network. This option is unavailable in iOS 6.
- ✔ **Go to the iBookstore.** This is available only in iOS 6.
- ✔ **Install apps.**
- ✔ **Delete apps.**
- ✔ **Use Siri.** This option is only for iOS 6.
- ✔ **Download content.** Called Allowed Content under Restrictions, this setting allows parents to set the age appropriateness of the media their kids use. The options cover music and podcasts, movies, TV shows, and apps.

✔ **Make in-app purchases.** This one is important. Many free apps make money by offering players the option to spend real money on things used in the game. These *in-app purchases* are frequently confusing to kids who have difficulty distinguishing between buying things with in-game currency and buying them with real money. Such apps are known as *freemium* apps. Beware: kids have been known to run up hundreds of dollars of charges by playing these "free" apps.

If you opt to let your kids explore these freemium games, make sure the In-App Purchases option is off, or at least make sure that you set the password requirement to Immediately. Otherwise, if you enter your password and buy something for your child, he can then purchase more items without having to enter your password again for 15 minutes afterwards.

These settings are found under Settings⇨General⇨Restrictions⇨ Allowed Content. (Refer to earlier figure.)

✔ **Reveal their location.** This option is only for iOS 6. You find it under Restrictions⇨Privacy.

✔ **Make changes to accounts.** You do this by selecting Don't Allow Changes. With this, you can keep kids from adding, modifying, or removing e-mail, Contacts, and Calendars.

✔ **Use Apple's Game Center to play with others.** Because Game Center can match players who don't know each other, I recommend that you don't allow these options for kids. This is a service meant to be used by older teens and adults. Set Multiplayer Games to off if you don't want your kids to play with others.

## Using Guided Access

iOS 6 introduces a new way of controlling apps for young children and kids with special needs. Under Settings⇨General⇨Accessibility is a nifty new feature called Guided Access. While Guided Access is running, kids can't leave an app. This ensures your kids play only the app you selected (and that they can't end up re-routed onto the web or your e-mail application). It also allows you to confine touch input to certain parts of the screen or to turn off the ability to use tilt. After you have turned on the Guided Access option, you activate it by opening the app you want your kids to play and then triple-clicking the Home button. Kids can't leave the app until you triple-click again and then input a password.

# Creating folders

Moving apps for your child onto one screen makes them easier to find. The iPad has a cool way of letting you organize apps across its 11 different screens. If you touch an app until it starts to jiggle, you can then move it around on the current screen; or, by moving it to the side, you can transfer its location to another screen. You can also organize your apps while plugged into iTunes.

Another way to manage apps is to group them into folders. You create folders by touching an app until it jiggles and then dragging it on top of another app. The two now reside within a folder that you can name.

Folders are helpful to use with kids in two ways. You can put all of your apps for young kids on one screen (as explained above) with no folders, so they can access them easily; and then move your adult apps into folders and hide them several screens away from your child's apps. Older kids can create folders filled with their favorite apps. Then each older child in your family can have his own folder(s).

# Handing down an iPad

If you want to hand down your old iPad to your kids, remember to wipe it clean before setting it up for them. You do this by connecting it to iTunes and opting to configure it as new. This way, your e-mail, contacts, Netflix account, and other saved items won't be available to them. And then revisit the Restrictions section, earlier in the chapter.

# Protective covers

Sturdy as it is, an iPad is still a fragile device, especially in the hands of children. You should talk to your kids about the iPad's fragility. You may want to set rules about where they can sit while using it. (I know of one little boy who tried to take it into the bathtub with him!) Stress never to run while holding the iPad. Even better, consider buying a cushioned case to protect the iPad.

Cushioned cases are sold in retail stores, such as Best Buy, Target, and the Apple Store. You have a variety to choose from, including the M-Edge SuperShell (www.medgestore.com), which comes in a variety of colors and adds about 1 inch of shock-absorbing soft plastic. The M-Edge costs between $30 and $35, depending on your iPad model. (See figure below.)

# Finding Good Apps for Kids

Apple's iTunes App Store is broken into several different categories. The best categories for kids are Education, Books, Games, Reference, and Entertainment.

The publisher of an app creates the description of their app in iTunes. They assign the age category, but that isn't always reliable. They also post screenshots of what is inside the app.

The best kid's apps make a point of stating they don't do things like collect information, use analytics, or contain in-app purchases, ads, or links to other websites or social networks.

And pay attention to user reviews. If more than a thousand people say this is a great game by rating it five stars, chances are they're right. But does that mean the game is appropriate for kids? That's another matter. Read the reviews to see why the app is so popular.

User reviews are also good for figuring out whether an app has a bug. If so, wait for an update.

## Free versus paid apps

The adage about "nothing in life is free" applies here. If a publisher offers an app for free, the app is probably still making money for the publisher somehow. The few exceptions to this rule are apps developed by nonprofit organizations and foundations — such as Alien Assignment, created by the Fred Rogers Center at St. Vincent College, and good, free apps intended as advertisements for another product, such as LEGO Creationary.

The most common model is to monetize a free app by placing ads inside it. I hate this model because it exposes kids to a constant barrage of advertisements — ads they are too naive to understand and that can sometimes be totally inappropriate for kids (that is, too sexy or too violent). If parents want to download a free version of an app just to evaluate it, that's fine. However, if you like it, I recommend you spend the minimal amount to unlock the version that doesn't show ads.

Another free model is the *lite* or free version that offers a small sampling of the full app's contents. Some of these are good, but most have rampant ads encouraging you to buy the full version. Again, parents should first review these on their own before purchasing the full version.

The worst of the free apps is the freemium model, which I mention earlier in this chapter. Freemium apps, like Smurfs' Village and Tap Zoo, frequently end up in Apple's list of Top Grossing iPad Apps. How can that be, you ask, since they're free? Ahh, here's the catch: The game is fun only if you buy things inside the game. For Smurfs' Village, Smurfberries (the currency of that world) allow you to progress through the game faster and to play with the cooler stuff, but they cost anywhere from $3.99 to $99.99. In Tap Zoo, you can buy both stars and coins (the currency of this world) with real money, and a Trunk of Stars costs $99.99! I find this expense to be unconscionable—only apps for special needs legitimately cost this much. These games also let you earn currency by signing up for things that you may not want your kids doing — such as subscribing to Netflix or the Disney Movie Club or downloading other games.

You won't find any in my recommendations for freemium apps within this book. I don't recommend them for kids younger than 10. However, parents can talk with older kids (teens and tweens) about the ways these games are marketed to kids and make their own choices about whether to investigate these games. Parents can even use these games to teach budgeting, by providing a certain amount of money to be spent in the game. That way, the expenditures are preordained, and kids learn to weigh what they spend.

## *Privacy and safety issues*

I've included lots of warnings in my reviews of the apps in this book. That's because this is such a new industry, and app developers are still trying to figure things out. Unfortunately, while they are creating exciting apps for kids to explore, they are doing things that aren't safe for kids; so I call out the areas where you need to be vigilant. Here are the five areas of concern:

✔ **Integration with social networks.** Many apps made for kids now sport links to Facebook, Twitter, and the like. Because you have to be 13 to use those services, it doesn't make sense to clutter up a title page with those links, which take your child out of the app to a social network they can't (and shouldn't) be exploring. I have contacted numerous app developers while writing this book to suggest that they put those links under a child lock.

A *child lock* is a way of keeping kids away from information or links directed at parents. App developers have lots of creative ways to do this. I've seen apps have parents: tap five times in a row, use a combination of swiping, solve a math problem, and many others.

✔ **Integration of social gaming networks.** Apple provides Game Center as a way of connecting with others to play multiplayer games (as well as to post scores to public leaderboards and such). But there are several other gaming networks as well, including Crystal, Gameloft Live, OpenFeint, and others. These networks aren't meant to be used by kids, and most require you be 13 or older to sign up.

I suggest you not go this route until kids are 13. Some of these networks allow strangers to reach out and communicate with your child, creating a safety risk. If you decide to let your kids play on these networks, see whether you can set the profile to private so that your child can only play with people they actually know. Some games on these networks don't allow any communication between players, making it safe. Read the fine print before agreeing to let your child play.

If an app in this book integrates with a social gaming network simply as a way of sharing scores and leaderboards, I don't warn you. But parents, make sure kids who list their scores aren't using their real names.

✔ **Location tracking.** Many apps ask to track your location when they have no need for that information. Also, you don't want your kids playing social apps that reveal where they are to others. If you want to use great educational apps like Star Walk to look at the stars in your backyard, it needs your location to operate best. But an ABC app? Definitely not.

You can decide on an app-by-app basis whether to permit this tracking. You can toggle it under Settings➪Privacy➪Location Services.

✔ **Links to the Internet.** Many, many apps have buttons which, when tapped by little fingers, open the Safari browser and take your child out of the app and onto the Internet. From my point of view, this is a no-no. Again, I would urge developers to put those links under a child lock.

✔ **Purchase links.** Many apps want you to buy stuff. From in-app purchases (see earlier discussion in the section "Free versus paid apps") to links to buy other apps, these links are disruptive to kids because they take them out of the app and ask them to make decisions that aren't appropriate. The best apps hide these links under child locks or put them into places that kids won't find easily. In this book I warn you if a purchase link takes you out of the app.

# Other useful sources for finding apps

Although I hope this book keeps you and your kids going for quite some time, I recognize that the industry is moving quickly. Here are some other resources for quality reviews:

- **My Kid-Tech column on USAToday.com** (www.usatoday.com/tech/): Look online under the Tech section to find my weekly column — I frequently review new apps. This column appears in some Gannett newspaper print editions, but usually only online for *USA Today*. You can also find my reviews on my own site at www.ComputingWithKids.com. I charge $20 for yearly access to a large database of reviews and delivery of a weekly e-zine to your e-mail inbox on Friday nights.

- **Common Sense Media** (www.CommonSense.org): This is the largest nonprofit reviewing site of children's media, and has a channel dedicated to reviewing kid apps. Their focus is on educational apps, but they cover the gamut. (Disclosure: I work for this group in addition to writing the *USA Today* Kid-Tech column).

- **Digital Storytime** (www.digital-storytime.com): This is a site that focuses on reviewing children's book apps. Written by Carisa Kluver, a mom and an educator, she really knows her stuff.

- **Kirkus Book Review** (www.kirkusreviews.com/book-reviews/ipad): This site has a separate section reviewing children's iPad book apps. I typically agree with their selections of the best — the ones that earn their coveted Kirkus Star.

- **Blogger Stuart Dredge at The Guardian** (www.guardian.co.uk): Dredge writes about all kinds of apps and his insights on kid apps are on the money.

- **Autism Apps by Touch Autism** (http://touchautism.com): From within this free, excellent resource app, you can find recommended lists and reviews of apps for kids with special needs.

# 2 Age Collection: Toddlers

## Moo, Baa, La La La! – Sandra Boynton

$3.99 US/$3.99 CAN/£2.49 UK, Ages 2–4, Loud Crow Interactive Inc.

My kids loved Sandra Boynton so much that we decorated one of their bedrooms with wallpaper featuring her cartoons (and matching sheets)! Boynton is known for drawing adorable animals doing silly things. In this adaptation of her beloved board book, you meet some animals and hear the sounds they make, such as a cow saying "Moo." Into this established routine, Boynton throws in some crazy pigs that like to sing. Instead of saying "Oink" they say "La, La, La." From here, hilarity ensues; and in this case, much of it is a result of the interactions that your toddler has with the book. When kids find that the dogs aren't barking, they are gently coached to "pull back" on the springy animal, which barks as it shoots across the page (leaving its collar behind!).

It's the pure whimsy portrayed by the animations in this book that make it a joy to read. The words highlight as read, and they repeat if you touch them. The narration is spot-on, as is the gentle musical accompaniment. Don't miss this one; it creates terrific together-time with your toddler.

**Best For:** Toddlers who are ready to giggle. I wouldn't suggest this book app right before nap or bed-time.

# Balloonimals HD
$2.99 US/$2.99 CAN/£1.99 UK, Ages 2–5, IDEO

If you're like me and not very good at blowing up balloons, you'll appreciate how easy this app makes creating colorful, adorable balloon animals with just the swipe of your finger. To start, select a colored balloon, and then swipe sideways to blow it up. When your toddler tickles the balloon with her fingers, the balloon magically forms into an animal shape. Your little one will delight in seeing a dog, a lion, a kangaroo, a snake, or even a T-Rex or a unicorn, take shape out of the balloon. But the fun doesn't stop there — tap the newly formed creature, and it animates and makes a sound. Tickle a different part of it, and it wiggles in a different way. When you're ready to create a new balloon, tap a button at the top of the screen and the balloon slowly inflates until it pops (you don't see it; it just makes a sound and disappears).

This app is fun for toddlers because it lets them help you create animals. The animals are adorable and silly, so kids are likely to start giggling. And when you touch them, the Balloonimals do funny things — the fish blows multicolored bubbles and the little joey jumps out of its mom's pouch. You can even take a photo of your creations, and they appear in the photos folder on your iPad (which means you can e-mail or print them).

**Best For:** Kids who like surprises. Note that when the balloon contorts into an animal shape, the app produces screeching sounds like the ones you'd hear when twisting a balloon in real life. So if your little one is sound-sensitive, turn down the volume on the iPad.

## Coloring Farm Touch To Color Activity Coloring Book For Kids and Family Preschool Ultimate Edition

$1.99 US/$1.99 CAN/£1.49 UK, Ages 2–3, Eggroll Games

With this app, your toddler can create simple drawings featuring farm animals. As they explore twelve different scenes, kids can touch parts of black-lined objects to instantly fill them with color. When you touch the farmer's face, it fills with color, but then something surprising happens — he grows a beard! Likewise, when you touch the pocket of his overalls, a mouse pops out just waiting to be filled with color. The other scenes include sheep, ducks, cows, horses, chickens, and an apple tree that grows apples to pick.

By playing this app with your toddler, you can help increase his vocabulary as well as his understanding of farms and the animals that live there. It's also a great way to start talking about colors. This app instantly provides a sense of accomplishment with its simple touch-to-create-color play pattern. Plus, each scene contains some hidden silliness for your little one to find. For example, in the duck scene, when you tap to color the mama duck, three tubes appear in the pond. Tapping the breathing tubes reveals three baby ducks wearing snorkels. It's hilarious and adorably cute!

The title page has an ad for more apps from this developer that leads your toddler out of the app.

**Best For:** Toddlers just learning about farm animals. This app instantly fills in drawings at the touch of the finger, but note that a child can't choose a specific color. Still, at this young age, children will be pleased with the sense of accomplishment the app provides.

# My Mom's the Best
$3.99 US/$3.99 CAN/£2.49 UK, Ages 2–4, Snappyant

This simple book app is filled with illustrations of baby animals interacting with their moms. Before seeing an animal pair, you hear the baby telling you what it likes best about its mom. Then a surprising and often humorous animation occurs. For example, for the little animal who likes the way its mommy hugs, the animation is a big brown bear squeezing her cub very tightly. For the animal who likes how his mom teaches him to dance, you see a silly, green frog kicking out her legs — swipe over the baby and it does a pirouette.

Expect your little one to want to read this book app over and over and over again. My favorite shows a mommy hippo teaching her baby how to hula-hoop. The app also has a fantastic narrator, simple navigation, and good background sound effects.

**Best For:** Very young children. This is an excellent first app for baby.

# Uncolor for iPad
$0.99 US/$0.99 CAN/£0.69 UK, Ages 2–3, ChristyBrantCo, LLC

Meant to be explored by a parent and toddler together, Uncolor encourages young kids to touch the all-gray screen. When they do, the gray disappears, revealing a cute, colorful animal. Then an animation plays. For the lion, a bee buzzes around the screen. For the hippo, a bird hops across its back.

Uncolor is a great way to introduce your toddler to cause and effect. When they touch the screen, they see something happen. If they keep touching, they're rewarded with adorable animals doing fun things.

This app provides parents with lots of teachable moments. I suggest you create a game by asking your child to predict who's hiding under the gray. The app does helpful things like show an owl and then turn the scene to night so that the owl can hoot. This gives you a chance to discuss how some animals are nocturnal.

**Best For:** Parent and toddlers to explore together. It's a fun way to get to know animals.

# PICTURE BOOK FOR KIDS - Touch & Listen

$1.99 US/$1.99 CAN/£1.49 UK, Ages 2–3, Wombi Apps

When my sons were toddlers and just starting to talk, I used to take photos of things and place them into small photo books to help them learn new words. This app does the same thing. Using high quality photos (or drawings if you choose), the app presents 72 different objects along with the sounds they make. The objects are separated into the following six categories: wild animals, farm animals, vehicles, musical instruments, tools, and special sounds.

Kids see 12 objects on the screen. When your child touches one, the screen transforms into a full-screen photo of that object. A narrator says the object's name, and then the animal or object makes a sound. The name of the object is shown on the bottom of the screen in tiled letters, and when kids touch the letters, the voice speaks the name again. Touching the photo returns your child back to the selection of another of the 12 photos. Kids access the six categories by touching icons on the bottom of the screen. This app also has a Guess the Sound game in which kids hear a sound and are shown four pictures. They try to guess what made the sound. The game can also ask kids to find an object as well as a sound.

What I like about this app is that it's the perfect learning app to teach toddlers vocabulary. The speaker announces the objects in a clear and friendly voice. The photos are stunning; and there are three different photos per object. These different representations rotate each time you touch them.

The app gives parents lots of control over what and how things are presented. If you want drawings instead of photos, you can set it up that way. If you don't want to show the word, it doesn't have to appear. You can even use this app to introduce kids to words in different languages because it offers six languages besides English. This is a great addition to any toddler's app library.

**Best For:** Toddlers just learning to talk. Use this app to help kids increase their vocabulary and understanding of the world.

## Old MacDonald HD - by Duck Duck Moose

$1.99 US/$1.99 CAN/£1.49 UK, Ages 2–6, Duck Duck Moose

This app turns the classic children's song into an interactive experience on the iPad. With bright, bold artwork, kids get to meet the animals and vehicles found on Farmer MacDonald's farm. Although the animals make the traditional sounds of a "moo-moo here" or a "quack-quack there," this isn't your traditional rendition of the song. In this version, friendly alien spaceships appear, and the cows do silly things like back flips.

To get youngsters giggling, most of the animals do funny things when touched. For example, one of the pigs busily paints a picture of the farmer. The sheep disco-dance. You can slide your finger across the tractor to start a trip around the farm. But this tractor is driven by a cow! You even get to meet a bear — a Teddy Bear, that is — who says "growl-growl." But he is held by a little girl and has a helium balloon attached to his leg so he can float. It's kooky and great fun!

This delightful app can be sung in five languages, or you can choose to listen to a cello, violin, piano trio, or a kazoo. The app even lets your child record herself singing. In between all of the laughter, your kids can learn to identify the animals found on a farm and hear the sounds they make.

**Best For:** Toddlers and preschoolers. Choose this version because it creates zany fun for kids and parents alike. Parents: don't miss the cow holding the "Moo Yorker" magazine!

 The Itsy Bitsy Spider HD - by Duck Duck Moose is another song-based app from this developer that's very well done.

# Pat the Bunny

$4.99 US/$4.99 CAN/£2.99 UK, Ages 2–4,
Random House Digital, Inc.

Dorothy Kunhardt's award-winning children's book transfers magnificently into the digital world. Because the original book is all about touching different materials within the pages of the book, this electronic version also celebrates the need to touch things. This delightful book presents 14 different situations for toddlers to explore. Starting with a game of peek-a-boo with a little boy named Paul, your child plays by reaching out to touch the cloth hiding Paul's face. Paul responds by lifting the cloth and showing a silly facial expression. Your toddler can also help ducks to swim and flowers to grow by sprinkling them with a hose. They can break a piñata, catch butterflies, and much more. This is one of the absolute best apps for toddlers! Every detail has been carefully thought out to respond perfectly when touched by your child. The scenes are not crowded, and the items to touch wiggle. The narrator gently suggests things for your child to try. One of the best interactions happens when your child is told to look into a mirror. The camera function of the iPad turns on, and when your child brings her face to the mirror, she sees herself!

In addition to reading and playing within this book app, kids can also paint the 14 pages of the book. Painting is as simple as placing your finger on the screen. Confetti appears where your child touches as the black and white scene slowly fills with color. Toddlers "color" the page by moving the finger around to the unpainted areas. The effect is quite magical. **Best For:** All toddlers. This is a must-have app for this age category.

# Make Me Smile!
0.99 US/$0.99 CAN/£0.69 UK, Ages 2–4, Third Bird Party!

In this app, your child makes friends with and helps ten unhappy monsters. The app starts with a big toothy monster growling at you as if he's angry. If your child touches anywhere on the screen, the monster is instantly comforted and becomes happy. He giggles in a child's voice, and as your child repeatedly touches the screen, he starts to dance and giggle even more. The next monster is sad, fighting back tears. Again, tapping the screen brightens up his mood. And additional taps are rewarded with new expressions of happiness. Kids cycle through different monsters that all need comforting by swiping along the bottom of the screen or touching the arrow keys.

Teaching empathy in this manner is fabulous. But the magic of this app is found in what it creates for the parents. The app has a special setting that secretly turns on the front-facing camera and takes photos of your child reacting to the monsters. Seeing your child's emotions displayed in a series of 10 to 20 photos, taken in a sequence from reacting to a sad monster and then joining in the happiness by giggling, is priceless.

Parents have an option to purchase 10 additional monsters for $0.99. If your child is enjoying playing with the first 10 monsters, these additional ones are equally as cute and more diverse.

**Best For:** Toddlers. This app is a great conversation starter to talk about feelings. Use the photo mode to capture both you and your child's facial expressions so that you can talk about them.

# The Going to Bed Book - Sandra Boynton

$3.99 US/$3.99 CAN/£2.49 UK, Ages 2–4,
Loud Crow Interactive Inc.

Ten adorable animals need your toddler's help getting ready for bed. In addition to reading a charming story, this app can also teach your child about bedtime routines.

Kids meet ten animals who live together on a boat. They are just starting to get ready for bed. They take a bath — all together in the tub. Kids help them by turning on the water and popping bubbles that appear. Next, the animals need help hanging up their towels; but when your toddler tries to help, he ends up hanging up the elephant and the lion too. It's hilarious. The routine continues with putting on pajamas, brushing teeth, exercising, heading off to bed, and then turning out the light. Your child can make something silly happen during each of these steps, including turning on the hot water to steam up the screen during tooth-brushing (so you have to wipe it off) and pulling down a cord to turn off the light, only to discover that the pig is dangling from the cord! Don't miss filling the night sky with stars on the last page — just tap the dark-blue sky.

You have two choices: Read it yourself or listen to the narrator. Either way, animations are available, and the words highlight and are spoken when touched. As with the other Sandra Boynton apps (Moo, Baa, La La La! or Blue Hat, Green Hat, elsewhere in this chapter, and Barnyard Dance in Chapter 6), narrator extraordinaire Billy J. Kramer drolly reads this story. Gentle piano music accompanies the bedtime routines. And although this book app will get your little ones giggling, it isn't meant to be as silly as some of Boynton's other apps. It provides a relaxing, humorous read for the end of the day.

**Best For:** Teaching toddlers about going-to-bed routines. Read this one right before bed.

# One Rainy Day: A Read-along, Play-along Story about Colors for iPad

$3.99 US/$3.99 CAN/£2.99 UK, Ages 2–4, mytales digital

In this combination book app and play center, kids hear a story about Duck, a duckling who loves to play in the rain. This baby duck lives in a house and can talk. Duck puts on his favorite red boots to go out in the rain and grabs his orange umbrella. The story introduces a new color on each page by Duck meeting a green frog, splashing in blue puddles, watching pink worms, and so forth until the rain stops. This story ends with Duck looking out the window at a rainbow shimmering with all the colors he just learned.

In addition to this simple but sweet story that's quite effective at introducing colors to your child, the app also reinforces these new color concepts with a straightforward drawing activity and play area. The four coloring pages from the book can be filled by touching one of ten colored drops on the bottom of the page, followed by tapping the area on the picture to make it fill. In the play area, the app asks your child to drag to Duck specific colored objects found in the story. For example, when asked for the pink worms, you have to choose among worms that are pink, red, blue, and green.

This is a great app for toddlers because it focuses on teaching kids colors. During the story portion of the app, it doesn't distract kids with unnecessary animations — the only movement is the rain falling inside the app. The rest of the interactivity comes from touching Duck to hear him talk to you, and from touching the colored items in the scene, which tell you their colors. The play area also keeps things simple, asking toddlers to touch and drag a requested colored item. It is all done in a very supportive tone.

**Best For:** Toddlers who are just learning about colors.

# Peekaboo Barn for iPad

$1.99 US/$1.99 CAN/£1.49 UK, Ages 2–3,
Night & Day Studios, Inc.

This was one of the first peek-a-boo apps to appear in the iTunes store, and to this day, it remains one of the best. This is the flagship app in Night & Day Studios' series of Peekaboo apps. Two more are reviewed later in this chapter.

The app does only one thing: It presents a bouncing red barn that sends out animal sounds. When your toddler touches the barn, the doors open and the camera zooms in to reveal a cute farm animal. The animal makes its sound, and then a voice tells you the animal's name as the words appear simultaneously onscreen. This cycle starts over again with a different animal hiding until your child has played with all 12 animals.

I recommend that this be one of the first apps you use with your toddler. It offers an almost irresistible way to teach your child about cause and effect. The wiggling barn beckons kids to touch it; and when they do, they learn to identify farm animals and the sounds they make.

I like that parents have to double-tap to activate the Options button. Parents can select what voice is heard. It can be an adorable child or an adult's voice in English or in Spanish. Plus, you can even record your own voice for kids to hear! You can purchase additional languages. The home page has an ad for more apps, but it's behind a parental lock so little ones can't accidentally tap their way out of the app.

**Best For:** First-time iPad users. This is a great toddler app.

# Peekaboo Forest

$1.99 US/$1.99 CAN/£1.49 UK, Ages 2–4,
Night & Day Studios, Inc.

From the makers of Peekaboo Barn, this app moves the game of peek-a-boo into the woods. In four different seasons and locations, it lets kids locate animals hiding in the woods.

In and around a tree stump in the winter, kids play peek-a-boo with a weasel, a frog, and a mouse. In spring, kids move into a forest to find a turtle, a butterfly, and a bee. Summer shows a tree sporting a hollow where a squirrel lives. A deer and a woodpecker also appear. In the fall scene, kids hunt for glowing eyes around a woodpile at night to find a family of raccoons. They also meet a fox, a chipmunk, and a skunk.

Like Peekaboo Barn, this app teaches young children that when they touch the screen, something happens. In this app, kids see part of an animal or a shaking leaf. If they respond by touching it, toddlers are rewarded with meeting the animal, hearing its sound, and learning its name.

This app provides options for which voice your child hears and language.

**Best For:** Toddlers and preschoolers. The seeking is more sophisticated here than in Peekaboo Barn.

# Peekaboo Fridge

$1.99 US/$1.99 CAN/£1.49 UK, Ages 2–4, Night & Day Studios, Inc.

This is the newest entry in the Night & Day Studios' Peekaboo series, and this time your toddler is opening a rattling refrigerator. Inside, your child meets hilarious animated foods that have attitude! The carrot makes a crunching sound as it poses with its red shoes. The cheese looks debonair with a mustache, and the strawberry sports long eyelashes. These anthropomorphized foods are adorable!

Although the shaking fridge isn't as welcoming as the red barn in Peekaboo Barn, the contents more than make up for it. These foods are a riot to get to know. Parents have the option of turning off the name so that they can ask their child if they know the hiding food.

**Best For:** Toddlers and preschoolers just learning their foods. The animated foods are a hoot.

**Blue Hat, Green Hat - Boynton**
$3.99 US/$3.99 CAN/£2.49 UK, Ages 2–4,
Loud Crow Interactive Inc.

Created by beloved author Sandra Boynton for the express purpose of eliciting belly laughs from little kids, this silly book app follows the exploits of four animal friends. The elephant, moose, and bear are busy showing readers how to get dressed in colorful clothing, while their buddy, the turkey, is a little slow at figuring things out. The friends put on their pants: the elephant's are yellow, the bear's red, and the moose's green. But when you look at what the turkey is doing, he has his blue pants on his head. This creates the book's repeating refrain of "Oops." By the end of this charming story, the turkey finally manages to get all of his clothes on correctly, just when he and his friends are going to the pool. So instead of wearing his swimsuit, the turkey jumps in the pool fully dressed — Oops!

This hilarious story is a great way to introduce toddlers to clothing and colors. To reinforce colors, the words on the page actually change color to reflect the color of the clothing the character is wearing. And the interactive bits are so much fun to explore. Touching each of the characters results in a giddy animation, but touching the turkey results in zaniness. My favorite is when the turkey is wearing his shoe on his head, and instead of moving it to his feet, he tries to walk on his head! Touching the word Oops results in clothing chaos, with items falling everywhere.

**Best For:** All toddlers. It's a raucous romp.

 If you enjoyed this book app, check out Barnyard Dance - Boynton, reviewed in Chapter 6 and Moo, Baa, La La La! - Sandra Boynton, and The Going to Bed Book - Sandra Boynton both earlier in this chapter.

# Peek-a-Zoo HD - by Duck Duck Moose

$0.99 US/$0.99 CAN/£0.69 UK, Ages 2–5, Duck Duck Moose

You will see many apps in this book by Duck Duck Moose. They are fantastic children's app developers, and this one is no exception. The app starts by showing a parade of animals. When tapped, each animal faces your child and says its name. The name cleverly incorporates the animal type. Kids meet 17 animals, including Caitlyn the Cat, Ellie the Elephant, and Skylar the Skunk. Each animal is voiced by a child.

Next, using the animals they just met, kids play a series of identifying games. For example, they may be asked to touch a specific animal or find the one that's doing or feeling something specific. With eight or so animals on the screen at one time, kids are asked to find the animal wagging his tail, or the one that's sad, or the one that's facing backward. They also hunt for actions such as winking, waving, yawning, or even sleeping. Some of the games involve identifying attire, such as sunglasses or a bow tie.

What makes this app so special is that it teaches young children about emotions and actions. As your child plays with these brightly colored, friendly animals, she is learning to look for details and clues. The setting is upbeat as jazzy music plays in the background. When exploring this app, kids never hear that they have made the wrong selection; rather, the animals make sounds or just talk to them. When your preschooler does find the correct animal, it moves to the middle of the screen and makes a fun sound.

**Best For:** All preschoolers. This app is unique because it teaches kids about emotions as well how to observe and find details.

# 3 Age Collection: Preschool

## AlphaTots
$1.99 US/$0.99 CAN/£0.69 UK, Ages 3–5, Spinlight Studio

AlphaTots is the gold standard of ABC flashcard apps. With bright bold graphics, it presents your preschooler with both the upper- and lowercase of a letter and announcing its name and the sound it makes. Then the fun begins as the app reveals a hands-on minigame using an item that starts with that letter of the alphabet. And boy, are these minigames creative!

Some of these minigames involve *kicking* (for the letter *K*) a soccer ball into the net while avoiding a moving goalie. For the letter *B,* you get to drag six pieces together to *build* a robot. The letter *S* is a *stack*-the-rings puzzle, *P* lets you *play* musical instruments, and *J* has you *joining* some railroad tracks. These sparkling minigames cleverly reinforce the alphabetical concepts being taught, and they provide great motivation to play this app over and over again.

The app also sings the alphabet song and has an activity that reinforces the letter order.

**Best For:** Preschoolers learning the alphabet.

# it's a small world
$3.99 US/$3.99 CAN/£2.49 UK, Ages 2–5, Disney

Based on the famous ride in the Disney Parks, this app takes your children on a virtual trip around the world. Showcasing kids from different countries, the app subtly delivers the message that although we all look different, we all share similar emotions and needs. It sends a charming but powerful message about accepting each other.

Presented as a hot air balloon ride, the app lets your kids join five other racially diverse children on a trip around the world. Over the 15 constantly changing landscapes, the app shows children from around the world as the balloon visits the African plains of the Serengeti, the windmills of Holland, the Great Wall of China, the snowy climes of Russia and Japan, and many other places. Players see kids in kilts, kimonos, and sombreros. Your child sees kids paddling Venetian gondolas and kids sitting next to a camel in a desert.

This app doesn't have a story line, just beautifully drawn scenes where every touch makes some small animation happen. In addition to real world scenes, the app also contains fun, fanciful things like mermaids and flying carpets.

The small world presented in this app feels big indeed. And it shares big ideas by simply having the international kids say one powerful word in a scene, such as "hope," "care," or "explore." It reminds us that we share "just one moon" and "one golden sun," and that a smile is the universal message of friendship. Near the end, the app showcases 16 multinational kids together in one tree, where each says "hello" in his own language. The last scene ends spectacularly as your child touches the sky to produce fireworks, while the theme song plays as a sing-along. It is magical!

This app can be enjoyed by kids as young as 2, but the sweet spot is really ages 3 to 5. And of course, it can be enjoyed by anyone who has taken the Disney ride for which it's named. If you're like me, I feel like I miss so much during the ride because I can't control the speed. Here, you have complete control of how long you linger on a page.

**Best For:** All kids and kids at heart. This delivers a compelling message about accepting others.

It's a small world. After all.

# Fish School HD – by Duck Duck Moose

$1.99 US/$1.99 CAN/£1.49 UK, Ages 2–5, Duck Duck Moose

The designers at Duck Duck Moose are fantastic children's app developers, and this one might be my favorite of their apps. By playing with fish, kids are introduced to ABCs, 123s, shapes, colors, differences, matching, and the ABC song. Preschoolers simply touch the screen, and a school of adorable-looking fish swims into formation. For ABCs, the fish start by forming the letter *A*. Then, when you touch the screen, a new group of fish immediately swims in from the side to form *B*, and so on. The schools of fish also form into shapes and numbers. For colors, the screen fills with different-hued fish. When you touch one, all like-colored fish magically appear while the announcer names the color. In the differences game, your child hunts for the one fish that's different from the rest. For matching, kids play a concentration game where they tap on 2 of 16 identical fish to see if the fish hiding under them match.

Your preschooler won't be able to resist these brightly colored, friendly fish. They'll want to keep touching the screen to see what these silly fish do next. The app is careful to present learning opportunities, including showing an object that starts with the letter the fish are making. Mozart's classical music accompanies many of the games. This app is simply swimmingly sensational in every way.

**Best For:** Preschoolers beginning to learn letters and numbers; however, all preschoolers can enjoy this app because it also has matching and find-the-differences games. Don't miss this nautical delight.

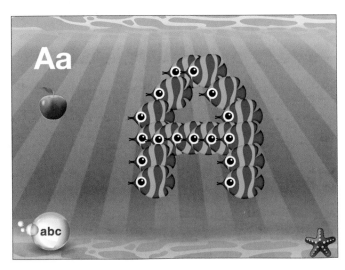

# Elmo Loves ABCs for iPad
$0.99 US/$0.99 CAN/£0.69 UK, Ages 3–5, Sesame Street

Elmo of the *Sesame Street* TV show stars in this preschool app that's all about learning the letters of the alphabet — both uppercase and lowercase — as well as the letter sounds. Elmo appears in the middle of the screen in full animated glory. He talks directly to your preschooler as he introduces the alphabet. The letters appear on the frame that surrounds Elmo's video, and Elmo encourages your preschooler to touch one. When your child touches a letter, a video plays that introduces that letter. Then your preschooler can select one of three objects that starts with that letter, and again, a fun video plays about the selected object. For example, select *M*, and the choices are mouse, mountain, and milk; your youngster can watch videos relating to each.

This app also teaches kids how to draw the letters. Kids can follow dotted lines with their finger on the screen. They can also play fun hide-and-seek games to find the three objects associated with each letter; they may have to bat balls around, pop balloons, or wipe off water droplets to find the hidden objects underneath. The app also has four different ABC songs, including my favorite, the one featuring Disco Grover!

This excellent preschool app makes it easy for youngsters to learn letters. Plus, they can play the app by themselves and won't feel alone because Elmo is right there to cheer them on.

**Best For:**
Preschoolers who are learning their ABCs. If your kids watch *Sesame Street,* they will recognize the format and immediately feel comfortable. Even if they don't know Elmo, this app is a winner.

 If you would rather try before you buy, check out Elmo Loves ABCs Lite for iPad. It gives you the first three letters for free.

# Monkey Preschool Lunchbox
$0.99 US/$0.99 CAN/£0.69 UK, Ages 3–5, THUP Games

By helping friendly, animated monkeys pack their lunch boxes, kids learn preschool skills. These primates are picky, so kids need to choose things like purple vegetables or fruits that start with the letter *K*. Some monkeys only like foods that come in pairs, so kids play concentration-type games to find the foods that match. Other monkeys want to pack only the fruit that is different from the rest. In all, the app offers seven different preschool games, covering the early learning concepts of colors, numbers, alphabet sounds, shapes, large and small, same and different, and spatial reasoning needed to put together easy jigsaw puzzles.

These monkeys are adorable, but a little demanding. They indicate whether kids are right or wrong by hilarious and charming facial expressions and gestures. If your child chooses incorrectly, the monkey shakes his head and frowns. But when your child is correct, the monkey gets excited and jumps up and down, making noises.

This app scrolls through the seven different minigames, so kids constantly see new and different learning opportunities. The experience is upbeat and fun so that kids never feel bad about selecting incorrect answers. The app constantly loops the seven activities, which means there is no way for kids to just play their favorites. The app does stop periodically to award kids with stickers.

**Best For:** Preschoolers who are learning colors, numbers, the alphabet, and shapes. The silly monkeys make learning fun.

# Farm 123 ~ StoryToys Jr

$1.99 US/$1.99 CAN/£1.49 UK, Ages 3–5,
StoryToys Entertainment Limited

When my children were learning to count, I looked for creative ways to reinforce the concept. We counted steps, we counted Cheerios, we even counted the whiskers on our cat! This app is an adorable farm story that makes learning to count fun.

Presented as a digital pop-up book, Farm 123 introduces your child to Farmer Jo. She needs your child's help counting her animals. Farmer Jo shows her animals by revealing a different animal and a new number on every new two-page spread. Your child counts one cow, two horses, three sheep, and so on until they reach ten hens. When you first turn the page, the animals pop up just as in a real pop-up book. But then the magic starts as the animals move around when touched. As your child uses her finger to count each animal, a number appears over it, and Farmer Jo speaks the number. After your child is finished counting, the animals do something silly, like jump over the moon (the cow) or spring onto a trampoline (the three sheep).

What I like about this app is that your child can touch the animals in any order. The app keeps track of the ones counted by shading them just a bit. On the bottom of the page, a virtual abacus appears where beads slide into place, reinforcing the concept of the number's value. I also like that the animals make realistic sounds.

In addition to this counting activity, the app has seven other counting games, which range from playing peek-a-boo to sponging off dirty animals. In each, Farmer Jo helps your child count each animal along the way. Very young children can watch the app in an autoplay mode where the pages turn automatically — but even in that mode, your child can still touch the screen to animate things, rewarding little fingers for their efforts.

**Best For:** Preschoolers beginning to learn how to count.

A free version of this app, which offers the complete story experience but just one of the seven games, is available; but it has ads on the first page for other books by this publisher and an in-app purchase screen to purchase the remaining games.

# Bo's Bedtime Story

$1.99 US/$1.99 CAN/£1.49 UK, Ages 3–5, Heppi

Bo is a little giraffe who needs help going to bed. Through ten different scenes, kids learn Bo's bedtime routine and, in the process, practice early learning skills of sorting, color recognition, matching, counting, listening, and fine motor control.

Readers start by helping Bo put away his toys and sort the pile into three different bins. Next, they help Bo put his dirty clothes in the hamper and his boots on the shelf. During bathtime, kids count rubber duckies and scoot the bathtub around so that the drops of shampoo dripping from the top of the screen fall onto Bo's head. Kids can help Bo dry off by tapping water droplets, brush his teeth by moving his toothbrush, sort his colored pajamas into matching pairs, direct his bear through a maze, catch letters falling off the ceiling so that he can read a bedtime story, and count kisses so he can fall asleep.

Bo is adorable and makes a good role model for how to follow a bedtime routine. I like that this app looks for little ways to reinforce learning, including identifying his body parts as kids wipe off the water droplets. And each of the ten activities are fun and varied.

Bo also stars in another app about dinnertime routines called Bo's Dinnertime, which is equally fun, endearing, and educational.

**Best For:** Preschoolers learning to follow a bedtime routine. By helping Bo the giraffe go to bed, kids learn how they, too should follow a routine.

# Pepi Bath

$1.99 US/$1.99 CAN/£1.49 UK, Ages 3–6, Pepi Play

Teaching preschoolers about hygiene is one of those key things that we parents need to do. This app can help.

Kids start by deciding whether to play with an adorable girl Pepi or an endearing boy Pepi. With Pepi, kids explore four different hygiene tasks: brushing your teeth, going to the toilet, taking a bath, and washing clothes. At each location, kids play by handing Pepi items or helping her do things like brushing her teeth.

While at the sink to help Pepi brush her teeth, you can also help her wash her hands, comb her flyaway hair, and cut her nails using nail scissors. Brushing teeth is as simple as rubbing the toothbrush back and forth until Pepi's teeth shine. In the bath, kids can drop in bubble bath, scrub her feet, and wash and rinse her hair. While Pepi is on the toilet, kids touch her belly to make Pepi grunt. Kids hear typical going-to-the-bathroom sounds, and need to hand Pepi toilet paper, flush the toilet, and spray air freshener. The washing clothes routine involves placing Pepi's dirty clothes in the machine, adding soap, and then hitting the start button. When Pepi's clothes are clean, players hang them up to dry.

This may sound rather boring, but because Pepi is so expressive and responds to the player's every action, it really isn't. She wrinkles her nose when you spray air freshener and contorts her face when trying to go potty. Pepi is both silly and serious, and always polite and appreciative. Pepi's routines might not completely mesh with what you're teaching your child, but that's okay because the point of the app is to show your kids that other children also have routines. Playing this app can serve as a springboard to talking about how what you do in your house may be different from what Pepi does.

**Best For:** Young children beginning to learn how to take care of their own hygiene. By helping Pepi learn routines, your kids might be more receptive to learning their own. This is a simple and fun way to motivate kids to follow hygiene routines.

# Dr. Panda's Hospital - Doctor Game For Kids
$1.99 US/$1.99 CAN/£1.49 UK, Ages 3–6, TribePlay

If your child likes to "doctor" stuffed animals, dolls, and — of course — you, then this is a cute app to download. It's also helpful to play before your child's next doctor's appointment.

Kids take on the role of a doctor tasked with healing eight adorable but sick animals. They treat animals for stomachaches, eye and ear infections, broken bones, problems in the mouth, bumps on the skin, and even give shots. From within the hospital waiting room, players select an animal to help. The scene then changes to a hospital bed where the miserable animal awaits. You can make the patient happy temporarily by changing the bed linens to look like a red roadster, a princess bed, or a bed of daisies. Touching the bed-ridden animal leads to an interactive medical game. For the bear with an eye infection, you put medicine drops in his eyes, watching as they change from red to white. You heal the monkey by realigning his broken rib bones.

What's fun about this game is that the ailments of the animals vary. The first time you see the monkey, he might have broken ribs; but the next time he visits you, he's got chicken pox. Kids get to perform some realistic actions, such as pumping up the blood pressure sleeve or delivering a shot (and putting on a Band-Aid, of course!). Some minigames aren't realistic though, and are just for fun. Kids earn stickers for healing patients.

The home page has a button that advertises other apps by this developer, but it can be disabled with the "For Parents" section.

**Best For:** Kids who like to pretend to be a doctor, or children who are afraid of going to the doctor. By putting kids in control, they might become more comfortable with what happens when visiting the doctor.

If you're looking for more pretend-doctoring apps, check out Toca Doctor HD from Toca Boca.

# iWriteWords (Handwriting Game)
$2.99 US/$2.99 CAN/£1.99 UK, Ages 3–6, gdiplus

With this app's adorable little crab teacher, your preschooler will want to practice writing ABCs and 123s. An outline of a letter appears onscreen, and then a red crab marks the spot where you start to trace the letter. He throws down some colored dots, which are numbered for you to follow. The crab attaches itself to your child's finger — cute! — so he, too, draws the letter or number. Also fun is that your preschooler hears percussive sounds every time he correctly passes over a dot. If he veers off the path, he hears a squeaking sound, and the exercise starts over. When your child is done, a voice announces what he drew and then cheers. This app also has options to write easy words, as well as numbers and upper- and lowercase letters.

From within the iPad's Settings app, you can adjust options for use, including font, right- and left-handedness, specific letters to practice, how much help is provided onscreen, languages, and more.

The adorable crab provides great motivation to trace letters. Each completed letter or number falls to the bottom of the screen; by tilting the iPad, you can make the letter or number slide into a spinning hole in the corner to disappear. This hole is a favorite feature for many kids.

**Best For:** Children who need practice writing their letters and numbers.

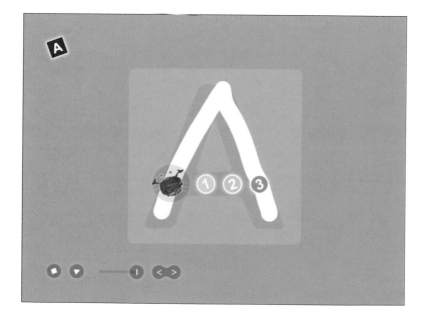

## ABC ZooBorns
$2.99 US/$2.99 CAN/£1.99 UK, Ages 3–7, Peapod Labs LLC

More about animals than ABCs, this app uses an ABC grid format to introduce kids to baby animals. What is magical about this app is that it features over 100 videos showing baby animals in the zoos and aquariums of the world. Kids also see adorable photos and can play 50 activities that involve touching the screen.

By selecting an alphabet letter from a grid, kids see different animals whose names start with that letter. Kids can hear the animal's name and some facts, see numerous photos of the animal by swiping sideways, and sometimes play a clean-the-screen game by using their fingers to erase an overlay covering an image of a baby animal. Letters spelling an animal's name appear on the bottom of the screen; when touched, they lead to other animals that start with that letter.

The photos of baby animals are enchanting, but the videos — a baby seal starting to nurse, lion cubs learning to swim, and a baby rhino trying to keep up with its mother when she runs — really get you hooked.

Note that this app needs an Internet connection to run the videos, some of which originate from YouTube.

**Best For:** Kids learning about animals. This app teaches kids about 50 animals, and it associates their names to the letters of the alphabet. Kids also learn interesting animal facts, which are spoken aloud.

 If you like this format of introducing kids to new concepts, the ABC series of apps from Peapod Labs also covers other topics, such as music, household objects, vehicles, food, wildlife, and sports.

# Over in the Ocean: In a Coral Reef

$4.99 US/$2.99 CAN/£1.99 UK, Ages 4–7, Dawn Publications

This app combines an exercise in counting with an introduction to creatures of the sea. You can explore it in three ways: Read to Me, Read to Myself, and Sing to Me. Each page starts with the words "Over in the ocean" and then introduces a mother sea creature and her brood. Starting with one baby octopus, then two baby parrotfish, three baby clownfish, and so forth, the story continues until it reaches ten — an old father seahorse and his ten seahorses. In a sing-song narration, your child joins in the fun by tapping on the babies to count and animate them; for example, the seahorses flutter, and the two parrotfish grind their teeth.

This simple story/song introduces counting to young children. But it is the artwork in this app that changes it from being just another counting book into something special. All of the illustrations are created using polymer clay. Also, the story ends with a fun, hidden-objects puzzle in which your child finds all of the babies talked about in the story. The last part of the app is dedicated to showing real photos of the sea creatures along with facts. This app is a two-for-one: counting plus marine biology.

**Best For:** Children who are learning to count and kids interested in science — in particular, creatures that live in the sea.

Over in the ocean
Where the sea grasses grew
Lived a mother parrotfish
And her parrotfish two.

"Grind," said the mother.
"We grind," said the two.
So they ground on the coral
Where the sea grasses grew.

# 4 Age Collection: Kindergarten

## Bugs and Buttons
$2.99 US/$2.99 CAN/£1.99 UK, Ages 4–7, Little Bit Studio, LLC.

This app delivers 18 different games that teach kids sorting, counting, letter recognition, alphabetical order, pattern recognition, path-finding, and much more. To play these games, kids touch virtual tarantulas, bees, ants, dragonflies, butterflies, ladybugs, roaches, and fireflies.

In one of the games, kids pick up the bugs by pinching the screen and sort them into jars. In another, they draw a path through a maze for an ant to follow. By tilting the iPad, your child controls a butterfly's flight path. Also fun is the activity that lets you use a slingshot to fling bees into a flower. Kids can play tic-tac-toe with a dragonfly and place colored buttons in patterns.

Kids can jump directly into the games they like, or they can let the app control the order in which they play the games. What I really like about these activities is that they have levels that adapt in difficulty, depending on how your child is doing. If they start to get too hard, and your child isn't successful, the game brings the level down. If your child is breezing through, the level gets harder.

I also really like that the Information button on the main screen has a child lock on it. A parent has to answer a math equation before you can get to the screen that allows you to rate this app or e-mail the developer.

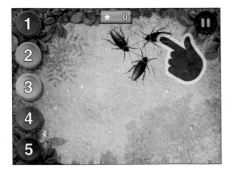

 Parents can control the game's settings not from within the app, but by going to the general iPad settings and then searching under Apps for this title.

**Best For:** Kids who are getting comfortable with the alphabet and counting. If your child is afraid of spiders, bees, or other creepy crawlers, this might not be the best app for them.

# Bob Books #1 – Reading Magic HD

$3.99 US/$3.99 CAN/£2.49 UK, Ages 5–7, Learning Touch

My younger son Peter learned to read using Bob Books. This app uses the same method found in the books, but adds animation into the learn-to-read experience.

Featuring a simple drag-and-drop interface, kids learn how to connect letters and sounds, sound out simple words, and then spell those words. With more than 12 pages of illustrations, kids learn 32 words. The pages can be explored on four levels of difficulty.

Kids learn to read by spelling the names of characters and other key-words presented on the pages and hearing the words sounded out. On Level 1, when kids touch a character or item in the black and white illustration, the app zooms in and shows how to spell the item or name by presenting it underneath the image but shaded lightly. Letter blocks appear jumbled on the page. As kids drag each letter to the shaded space to fill in the name, the app pronounces the letter's sound. When all of the letters are in place, the app slowly sounds out each letter in a row and then says the name. The item being spelled fills with color and appears that way when the picture zooms back out to the whole page. When kids have spelled all of the main words on the page, the app reads the sentence, the whole picture fills with color, and the characters ani-mate. It's a fun reward for learning to read the page.

Level 2 requires that kids slide the letters into order from left to right. Level 3 has kids spell the words without visual hints. And Level 4 adds extra letters to the page so that kids have to pick out the correct letters for the word.

The idea of starting with a stark, black-and-white line-drawing that fills with color and animation when you learn to read the sentence on the page is simply brilliant. It motivates kids to learn to read. And the four levels help kids gain confidence in the reading process.

If you like this app, the next stage is Bob Books #2 – Reading Magic HD, which is reviewed in Chapter 15.

**Best For:** Kids who recognize the letters of the alphabet, and are ready to move to the learn-ing-to-read stage.

Dot has a hat.

# Bugsy Kindergarten Math

$2.99 US/$2.99 CAN/£1.99 UK, Ages 5–6, Peapod Labs LLC

Bugsy is a cute little hamster with a big appetite. His favorite hangout is the inside of a refrigerator, but he also likes to go shopping at the grocery store. As kids play with Bugsy, he teaches them about numbers up to 30, comparisons in quantities and numbers, tracing of numbers, patterns, addition and subtraction up to 20, and number relationships.

While shopping, Bugsy asks kids to find food items for his cart. He may request that they select from two groups of watermelons by asking for the group that has more. Or he may want to know how many molds of Jell-O are on the shelf. If kids aren't sure, they can touch each item, and it counts aloud and shows each number. After several of these kinds of questions, where each one is working on a different math skill, Bugsy hits the checkout. He asks kids to select a nice food item. With that new food item in tow, Bugsy returns to the inside of his refrigerator to play. Kids discover that Bugsy can do silly things with food, such as jump on the Jell-O as if it were a trampoline or use the banana as a sled. Bugsy even dances.

This is a targeted math app with a sweet central character who makes exploring these math drills fun. The app self-adjusts, depending on how your child is performing. Kids hear all of the instructions and can use onscreen math manipulations to help figure things out.

Parents can control which math topics they want their kids to explore. If you register the app, it sends you progress reports via e-mail.

REMEMBER

If your kids like playing with Bugsy, he also stars in Bugsy Kindergarten Reading.

**Best For:** Kindergarteners. It helps make learning math fun.

# Kindergarten Reading – by Duck Duck Moose

$1.99 US/$1.99 CAN/£1.49 UK, Ages 5–6, Duck Duck Moose

This phonics-based program is all about playing with animals at the zoo. To learn the letter sounds for consonants and vowels, kids participate in games with the different zoo animals. The penguin wants balloons that have words that start with the *H* sound. The giraffe likes to eat the letter *P*, whereas the monkeys are interested in collecting all the *G* words from the ants carrying words on leaves. Kids move the requested items to the animals to collect stars. Stars are the currency in this game, and they can unlock more phonics-obsessing animals to play with. When they interact with the flamingos, kids help them by rearranging their order so that they can spell words.

Duck Duck Moose produces some of the most outstanding children's apps on the market. With this one, they have upped their game in terms of graphics. The animals are bold and bright and a riot to interact with. If you don't give them what they want, they may turn their head and give you attitude or worse — fall asleep. Cute! As kids collect animals, they can play with them by making their own zoo scenes.

And parents, this app has a Parent Reporting section that informs you how your child is doing and which letter sounds your budding reader has mastered.

**Best For:** Kindergarteners. These adorable animals make learning to read feel like a trip to the zoo — balloons and all!

## Bugs and Bubbles
$2.99 US/$2.99 CAN/£1.99 UK, Ages 5–7, Little Bit Studio, LLC.

My two sons loved bubbles; one was mesmerized by watching them float, and the other couldn't wait to pop each one. This app takes children's natural affinity for touching and popping these transparent marvels and turns it into meaningful play. Bubbles (and sometimes bugs) are the focus of 18 different games that teach a wide variety of early learning skills, including colors, counting, letters, patterns, shapes, sorting, balance, size and quantity differentiation, and even a little physics.

Kids can jump into this app in two different ways. Pushing the Play button leads to a mode where the app decides the order of the games. Pushing the Explore button lets kids select the game they want to play. The games are divided into three stages by difficulty.

Games in the first stage are as simple as sorting bubbles based on color. In the second stage, kids pop bubbles with matching letters or numbers inside. More sophisticated games populate the third stage, including a version of Connect Four using bubbles, a scale-balancing game, and one that tests your memory.

This app is carefully put together so that your child experiences success. It automatically adapts the difficulty to your child's skill level. Most of the instructions are visual and spoken, so nonreaders can see and hear how to play. Within a given game, your child plays through multiple levels that introduce new challenges, so things stay interesting. Kids can earn achievement stickers as they play, and the app can handle more than one profile. It even remembers where your child was the last time he played.

In addition to a great play design, the visuals of this game are outstanding. Set in and around a Bubble Factory, the warehouse background gives the game an interesting aesthetic. Encasing realistic-looking bugs inside the bubbles is also fun. As your child plays, he hears more than 50 minutes of gentle music.

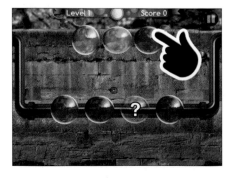

 If this app is a favorite, check out its companion app, Bug and Buttons, reviewed earlier in this chapter. It's from the same developer.

**Best For:** Both boys and girls ages 5–7. Younger kids can play and enjoy the Stage One games, but many of the other levels may be too tough.

# Memory Train

$1.99 US/$1.99 CAN/£1.49 UK, Ages 5–10, Piikea St. LLC

Kids climb aboard a moving train with an adorable elephant named Spacey. While on their way to the circus, they pass lots of geometric shapes, numbers, and strangely dressed animals. The idea of this app is to recall the details of the items you pass. The geometric shapes are colored and have different facial expressions. Likewise, animals and objects shown have different attributes.

Through ten progressively harder levels, players practice using their short-term memory. At first, the challenges are as easy as remembering the color of a large square. But as the game progresses, you're asked to remember a detail from two differently colored geometric shapes. Perhaps it was the color of the first object, or maybe whether the second circle was smiling or frowning at you. By the end, the game tests your ability to recall three objects at once.

The elephant makes a lot of noise but never speaks. He just shakes his head if you're wrong or nods if you're correct, and dances if you're correct several times in a row. If you're nailing each answer, the train speeds up, but flub an answer, and the train slows down. The game presents the memory questions as a visual with three possible choices, and the wrong selections disappear when you select them.

This is a simple but ingenious way to create a memory game. The app is set up as if you're looking out a train window as it passes by things, making you feel as if you're going on a journey with the elephant. The app keeps track of how well you do by awarding you colored peanuts. Four different players can try it out, so whole families can give it a go.

**Best For:** Kids who enjoy a challenge. This makes memory recall a competitive game, but one that's fun to play.

# 5 Art

## Draw and Tell HD – by Duck Duck Moose

$1.99 US/$1.99 CAN/£1.49 UK,
Ages 2–7, Duck Duck Moose

Of all the drawing apps reviewed in this chapter, this is the best one for young budding Picassos. It gives kids two options: Draw on a blank sheet of paper or fill in coloring pages by touching the page. The art tools are intuitively displayed along the edge of the screen and include crayons, pencils, and paintbrushes. You can also paint with patterns, draw with stencils, use a glow-in-the-dark crayon on a black background, and place stickers inside your artwork. For the coloring pages, kids tap to select a color or pattern and then tap to fill an outlined area. Kids can also select a rainbow crayon that randomly assigns colors.

Another great attraction of this app is its Tell feature. After your children finish creating, the app provides a way to record their voices as they talk about their paintings. If the drawing includes stickers, kids can move them around to create animation as they speak. The self-created animation and the storytelling can be played back as a video and saved within the app or sent to the iPad's photos folder. From there, a parent can e-mail the artwork or video (or send it to YouTube).

**Best For:** All young children. Toddlers will like the coloring pages; older kids will enjoy telling a story about their drawing.

# Draw Along with Stella and Sam
$1.99 US/$1.99 CAN/£1.49 UK, Ages 3–6, zinc Roe

Your kids join Stella and her little brother Sam in coloring and decorating shapes, which magically come to life within a short animated story. The app presents ten shapes to color, including a frog, a flower, a rocket ship, a butterfly, a bird, and more. The paint program keeps things simple, offering only 12 colors, using either a pencil, a crayon, a marker, or nine patterned stamps. You can even take a photo using the iPad's camera to use as stamps, so your child can color using a stamp of your dog, your grandma, or even your refrigerator.

When your child finishes decorating a shape, Stella tells Sam a cute anecdote about the shape; and your child's drawing is incorporated into a short video that acts out the fanciful thing that Stella told Sam. For example, with the rocket ship, kids watch as their decorated rocket ship blasts off on its way to dunk a cookie in the Milky Way!

This is a great first drawing app for preschoolers. Its clean interface, with few options, makes it simple for young children to use. The app produces good-looking results because kids can't color or decorate outside the lines. And the reward for finishing an object is exciting — watching your rocket take off is, well, a blast! During the reward video showcasing your artwork, kids can push buttons to save the video or a photo of the video to the iPad's photos.

The relationship between older sister Stella and her younger brother Sam is supportive and loving. If your kids enjoy playing with these characters, you might want to consider the some of the other Stella and Sam apps by zinc Roe.There are several.

**Best For:** Preschoolers who are hesitant to make their mark in the art world. This app gives the reluctant artist a reason to explore color and stickers.

# Nick Jr Draw & Play HD
$6.99 US/$3.99 CAN, Ages 3–8, Nickelodeon

If your kids are fans of Dora the Explorer, Diego, Team Umizoomi, and the Bubble Guppies, this drawing and art center will be popular in your house. With Dora talking to your kids along the way, this art app offers players lots of ways to get creative. Featuring an excellent drawing program with intuitive painting, coloring, and drawing tools, the app also offers coloring pages (which automatically keep kids' strokes within the lines) and a magical collage maker.

Lots of apps provide drawing and coloring, but this app's cool extras set it apart from the others. Among the collage-maker tools, kids have 15 items to add to their pictures; and when they do, the items make sounds. Add confetti, for instance, and you can use it as a stamp or draw with it as if it were ink; do so and the app makes the sound of a birthday-party horn. In addition to regular paint options, this app provides kids with magical art tools, including tops that splatter ink, magic wands with ink that animates on the paper, fireworks that explode into the image of a favorite character, surprise blocks that open up to reveal a short animation, and bouncing balls. If kids add stickers to their drawing, the stickers animate when touched.

I also like that this app offers guided activities by presenting a Picture Idea gallery. If a drawing in the gallery looks interesting, Dora explains how you can re-create it. You can even take a photo of your pet, place it as a background, and then add accessories — cute! Kids can save their work to an in-app gallery, or in the iPad's photo storage.

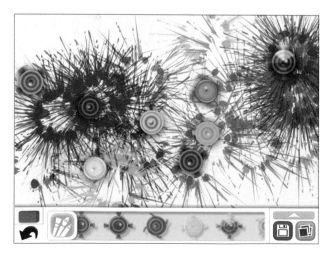

 Kids can also send their artwork to others, using e-mail and Facebook, but parents can turn off that option using the Settings button inside of this app.

 **Best For:** Fans of Nick Jr television shows. This app makes creating art with Dora fun and full of whimsy.

# Faces iMake – Right Brain Creativity
$1.99 US/$1.99 CAN/£1.49 UK, Ages 4 and up, iMagine machine LLC

This app encourages your kids to create faces, using everyday objects. Ever think of making broccoli into a nose? How about using apples for eyes? You can make fanciful faces with everything from food to musical instruments to toys and lots in between. Think of this app as a virtual collage-maker that is chock full of whimsy.

You start by choosing the color of your background and then selecting the outline of a face. Next, you pick items from collection folders found at the edge of the screen. Touch the folder to expand it, and then you can scroll through it by swiping. You can choose from the following collections: food, toys, music, candy, kitchen, tools, school, buttons, and letters. There is also an option to shoot photos of your own objects and import other photos into the app.

This app contains wonderful tutorials in the form of YouTube videos. It also has an inspiration gallery that serves to provide kids with ideas; to which kids can add their own creative touches. The app comes with its own funky music, but you can choose to add your own.

This interface is one of the best in the iTunes market. It is so simple that preschoolers can have success by themselves. And for kids who are older, the app also provides sophisticated tools, such as the ability to make one object go behind another and the option to create a mirror image of objects. This is a great way to expose kids to the concept that objects can represent ideas.

Faces iMake has recently added a new FaceWorld feature where users can share their creations with others and download faces made by others and modify them. I will talk about this more in Chapter 27.

**Best For:** Kids ages four and up and their families. This create-with-objects app can help get the creative juices flowing for the whole family. How about asking each family member to create a self-portrait?

# Drawing Pad

$1.99 US/$1.99 CAN/£1.49 UK, Ages 4 and up,
Darren Murtha Design

Drawing Pad is a full-fledged traveling art studio for your kids. They draw by touching a finger on the blank screen. But this is where the fun comes in — their fingers can become all sorts of art tools from paintbrushes to chalk to crayons to colored pencils and more. Your kids will enjoy the wide selection of stickers that can be sized using pinch-and-pull with two fingers. They can change the background by selecting different colored papers or by importing a photo.

This drawing studio works well across a range of ages. For preschoolers, it provides a simple way to draw with crayons or markers. They'll get a kick out of the special roller pens that create a pattern of hearts, bubbles, stars, or dots. Unlike other art apps geared specifically for young kids (such as Draw and Tell HD, reviewed earlier in this chapter), this app has no fill option so kids will color areas manually. Drawing Pad provides sophisticated tools that allow subtlety for those seeking more options. Artists can add depth to the color by repeating applications, blend colors using a special tool, place stickers in the background to draw on top of them, and use multiple mediums within one drawing to get just the effect they want. I really like this app's ability to let users create in landscape or portrait mode, depending on how you turn the iPad.

You can save your work to a special in-app gallery, which allows you to come back and work on your artwork at your leisure. You can also save your work to the iPad's photos or send it to an AirPrint-compatible printer.

Unfortunately, this app also has less kid-friendly options for saving artwork, including Twitter, Facebook, and e-mail. The e-mail option can be turned off by going to iPad's Settings icon, and then looking under Apps and selecting Drawing Pad. There you can also opt to turn off the in-app store that sells add-on coloring books.

**Best For:** Older kids looking for an art program with depth.

# SpiroDoodle
$0.99 US/$0.99 CAN/£0.69 UK, Ages 5 and up, AI Vector LLC

Did you grow up playing with a Spirograph? I played with it for hours, as did my two sons. Now there is a digital version of that classic toy, and it's just as captivating!

The app opens with a round drawing space and two slider bars, as well as a rainbow circle of hundreds of colors from which you can pick. The vertical slider adjusts the width of the line you're drawing. The horizontal slider lets you control the number of connected lines you draw, from 1 up to 30. For special effects, you can turn on a mirror mode so that the line you're drawing is mirrored with a second line. The app also allows you to activate a paint-bucket mode that turns off the lines and lets you fill in with color the shapes you have drawn symmetrically. This app even has a button that randomly generates colors every time you touch the drawing circle. If you don't like the effect of what you've done, you can use the Undo button to remove up to ten steps. And when you get a drawing that you like, you can save it to your photos and then share it from there.

This is one of those apps that the longer you play it, the more you discover. The lessons about symmetry are exciting to explore. Try turning on and off the mirror mode, adjusting the number of lines, choosing when and how much to fill, and varying the thickness of the lines — all factors that greatly affect your outcome.

**Best For:** Kids old enough to appreciate the nuances of what is happening here. Although kids as young as three can play, I recommend using it with older kids who can appreciate the math involved in creating this kind of art.

**iLuv Drawing Animals – Learn how to draw 40 animals step by step**
$2.99 US/$2.99 CAN/£1.99 UK, Ages 4–8, MyVijan LLC

Choose this drawing-lessons app for your young artist. It shows kids how to draw 40 different animals, ranging from cats and dogs to bears and whales. Kids learn to draw by tracing dotted lines shown in gray, step by step. A voice-over explains what to do for each step. When kids are done, they can color in the drawings, add backgrounds and even stickers, and then save them to an in-app portfolio, or send them via e-mail. Kids can return to a drawing in the portfolio to keep working on it.

This app makes the drawing process simple to understand, and its undo and coloring options are easy. I really like that it has a fill option for kids who want to splash color onto big areas.

  Kids can connect to your e-mail to send their finished drawings. Also the More Apps button leads kids out of the app into iTunes.

**Best For:** Younger kids who need a confidence boost about how to draw. It's also fun for kids who love drawing.

 **How to Draw – Full Version**
$1.99 US/$1.99 CAN/£1.49 UK, Ages 6–12, Mind the Kids Ltd

This drawing-lessons app is a little more complicated than iLuv Drawing Animals, so choose this one for kids ages 6 and up. Instead of tracing dotted lines (as you do in iLuv Drawing Animals), here you copy strokes, but the strokes are shown only very quickly. The 12 items you learn to draw — cat, dump truck, robot, and more — have a fair amount of detail.

Don't get me wrong, this is a nifty drawing app, but it's designed for older players. Your paintings are saved in the iPad's photos — this app doesn't have an in-app portfolio. The narrator and the art style are a little cheeky, making it a fun environment in which to explore art. The art tools are rather limited, but the results are impressive.

 The home page has a button taking users out of the app to iTunes.

**Best For:** Older kids looking to hone their drawing skills.

## MoMA Art Lab

$4.99 US/$4.99 CAN/£2.99 UK, Ages 6 and up, MoMA,
The Museum of Modern Art

The Museum of Modern Art in New York City provides interactive spaces known as MoMA Labs for kids and families to make art together. With this app, the museum shares some of the concepts and activities that it offers in these labs and evolves them into a virtual modern art creator.

The app opens with a terrific tutorial that can be spoken aloud or read. Kids see a white workspace for building art. Unlike traditional drawing apps that display art tools in the tray below the canvas, this app's tray is full of interesting geometric and funky shapes. You can drag these shapes to the canvas and color, size, and rotate them as you desire. If you change your mind, you can easily delete a shape by dragging it off the workspace. The tray also offers a line-making tool. Kids can change the background color (all are vibrant), save their creations to an in-app gallery, or delete their work.

The real gold of this app is that it offers stimulating ideas and activities inspired by famous art. The app introduces kids to the work of famous artists such as Henri Matisse, and then offers a special activity to create art based on his work. For Matisse, kids use virtual scissors to cut out shapes to use in their art. In an activity based on the work of Elizabeth Murray, they assign noises to portions of a painting so that running a finger over the artwork creates a sound composition. This app even has a cooperative art activity for a family to try in which each person draws a different part of the piece.

MoMA Art Lab creates one of the most creative and inspiring experiences that I've encountered since the iTunes store opened. The tools are easy to use and produce fascinating artwork. The six activities based on the work of real artists make brilliant use of the iPad.

**Best For:** Kids and adults, regardless of whether they're interested in art. Actually, this is a great app to explore for kids who don't like art. It makes modern art accessible.

# Auryn – Van Gogh and the Sunflowers

$3.99 US/$3.99 CAN/£2.49 UK, Ages 6–11, Auryn Inc.

This book app, written by Laurence Anholt, teaches kids about the life of painter Vincent Van Gogh and introduces them to the famous painter's artwork. The story focuses on a little boy named Camille, who meets the artist when Van Gogh stays with Camille's family in a village in France. Van Gogh paints portraits of Camille and members of his family. He also paints the sunflowers that Camille picks for him. Although Camille's family befriends Van Gogh and sees the beauty and talent in his paintings, many people in Camille's village ostracize the painter for his odd behavior and bold painting. By reading this story, kids can learn the importance of accepting differences in others.

I am very impressed with the way this app incorporates Van Gogh's real paintings and lets kids see them close up. At various times in the story, you can tap on a painting to go to a virtual museum showing ten paintings by Van Gogh. Within this museum, you can examine the painter's work and read and hear facts about the artwork's subjects.

Also exciting is the unusual way this book app animates its characters. The first few characters in the book appear as though they are in a pop-up book — turning a wheel or pulling a flap makes them move and jiggle. The later illustrations don't move until you tap on them

and enter the Armature Game mode. In this mode, kids see underneath the paper to the gears and mechanisms that make a character move. If kids tap again, the mechanisms spring apart into a puzzle where kids must slide the pieces back into position in a limited amount of time. When the puzzle is solved, the characters appear to animate when viewed within the story. In all, there are 19 of these Armature puzzles, playable on three difficulty levels. Kids can also use a simple art program to repaint the characters.

**Best For:** Kids interested in learning more about Vincent Van Gogh and his art. This art history app smartly weaves together a good interactive story, a 3D virtual art museum, fun engineering puzzles, and the ability to repaint the characters.

## PlayART by Tapook

$3.99 US/$0.99 CAN/£0.69 UK, Ages 6 and up,
Tapook Publishing

This collage-making app divides the artwork of five famous artists — Van Gogh, Monet, Klee, Cézanne, and Rousseau — into usable bits and then lets you arrange them on a canvas to create your own master-pieces. Think of it as an irresistible art masters' mashup.

You can put together elements from several different paintings by the same artist, or you can save elements from different artists to My Favorites, which then lets you mix and match elements from all five artists within your own creation. I had a great time creating a vase filled with sunflowers from Van Gogh, water lilies from Monet, a weird red circle on a stick from Klee, turquoise fronds from Rousseau, and an upside-down pear from Cézanne. Channeling my inner Klee, I added eyes and a pomegranate nose to the Van Gogh vase. My tour de force is shown in the figure on this page.

Fanciful musical sounds play when you place the parts of classic artworks onto your own canvas, adding to the whimsy. You can save your creations to your own gallery, sign them as if you were famous, and even come back later to edit.

PlayART is a very well-designed app. It's easy to jump into because it starts with an excellent video tutorial. It also has a help area. In addition to being an inspiring and fascinating way to explore art, this app is also educational. This app has five interesting videos — one about each artist — narrated by children. The app includes a museum for each artist, filled with six works that you can enlarge for a closer look. I like that the name and location of each piece of art is shown, so you can discover the current location of the painting.

This app has a Facebook option for sharing, which parents can disable in the iPad general settings.

**Best For:** All kids, teens, and adults. Kids interested in art will enjoy the educational videos, and kids with little or no interest in art just might be intrigued by this easy-to-use art creator.

# 6 Book Apps: For Younger Kids

## Barnyard Dance – Boynton

$3.99 US/$3.99 CAN/£2.49 UK, Ages 2–4, Loud Crow Interactive Inc.

"Stomp your feet! Clap your hands! Everybody ready for a Barnyard Dance!" So begins this bouncy musical version of the classic Sandra Boynton board book for toddlers and preschoolers. Accompanied by upbeat banjo music, this simple book app shows farm animals joining in a traditional square dance. A cow plays the fiddle, pigs twirl, bunnies bounce, and ducks strut — all to the barn-dance caller's directions. As your kids make the barn animals dance and sing by tapping or sliding their fingers across the page, expect your whole family to start toe-tapping, body-bouncing, and maybe even do-si-doing.

The animations are simple but inventive. Tap a page filled with little chicks, and the whole lot scrambles around while chirping. Draw a circle around a pair of pigs, and they dance round and round. Also good is the scene where the animals promenade two by two; if you tap on them, they make their true animal sounds, so it's a great way for kids to learn. This book app is an upbeat musical romp that's a hoot to explore. Yee-haw!

**Best For:** Young children who are still learning about animals and the sounds they make.

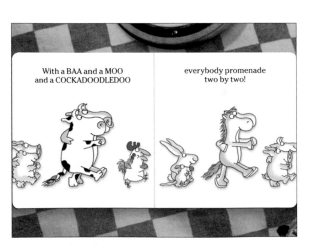

With a BAA and a MOO and a COCKADOODLEDOO

everybody promenade two by two!

# A Present for Milo: A Touch-and-Surprise Storybook

$5.99 US/$5.99 CAN/£3.99 UK, Ages 2–5, Ruckus Media Group

This high-energy, entertaining book app is in a category all alone for delighting children. It presents the most interactive environment of all the book apps reviewed in this book. Don't be put off by its higher price — it's worth it.

The app presents a story about Milo the cat chasing a mouse. Their madcap chase leads them under the sofa, across a piano, up and down stairs, through the kitchen, down hallways, and into other places found in this house. Each page shows the chase, accompanied by narration and wonderful sound effects involving a kazoo, cymbals, drums, triangles, and other fun noise-makers. As the duo turn the house upside down, each place they pass through offers your child wonderful opportunities to explore. Tap on a toy spaceship, and a little mouse appears within and blasts off. Tap on a lamp, and the room goes dark except for the illuminated Milo and the mouse. Find more than 125 animations by tapping on the 80+ objects in this house. Some of the cutest appear only after you've touched the same object once or even twice. The story ends with a big surprise that's sure to have you and your child laughing.

Written, illustrated, and read by Mike Austin, this book's narration is wonderful. When you pair it with whimsical animations and a wide range of funny sound effects, this app creates a rich playground for kids to explore. Even though this app was originally published in 2010, it still remains unsurpassed by others for its clever use of animation.

**Best For:** Young children who enjoy stories with a rambunctious nature. The story is so simple that even 2-year-olds will enjoy it. Don't read this one right before nap or bedtime, though, since it's likely to jazz your kids up.

Under the sofa

# Nighty Night! HD

$2.99 US/$2.99 CAN/£1.99 UK, Ages 2-5, Shape Minds and Moving Images GmbH

This enchanting story isn't an adaptation from a printed book; rather it was created specifically for the iPad, and it shows! Oscar-nominated animator Heidi Wittlinger masterfully creates a simple tale for toddlers about helping seven little animals settle in for the night. As your little one visits each animal, he interacts with it by touching it. When your child decides that the animal is ready to sleep, he can turn off the light in its enclosure and then watch as the animal closes its eyes. The narration is performed by actor Alistair Findlay, who has a deep, melodious voice that perfectly complements this gentle story.

For the illustrations, Wittlinger combined paper cutouts with other 2-D illustrations. Using sweeping, animated visuals, you visit a farm nestled at the edge of a town. The overall affect is of a beautiful rural setting at night. Each animal responds to your child's touch, and repeatedly touching an animal produces a different animation from the same hotspot.

In addition to modeling good behavior about how to settle and go to sleep at night, this app also teaches toddlers about the sounds that farm animals make. You will hear a dog, a pig, a sheep, a cow, a duck, chickens, and some fishes. Plus finding the light switch for each will be a fun hunt for your toddler. The app offers three more types of animals (cats, a pony, and a rabbit) as an in-app purchase for $.99 which, if purchased, seamlessly appear within the story.

**Best For**: Bedtime reading. This story app is a perfect way to end your child's day.

# Auryn HD – Teddy's Day
$4.99 US/$4.99 CAN/£2.99 UK, Ages 2–6, Auryn Inc.

In this story about a little girl who wonders what her Teddy Bear does all day when she's gone, your kids get swept into the story because they're in on the bear's secret life. The little bear is careful not to show anything to his little-girl owner as she schemes to trap him into revealing his secret life. But he willingly plays with you when she's not looking. The result is a darling story filled with fun, interactive bits. When the little girl cannot see (and when you help by tapping Teddy), Teddy jumps on the bed. He also dances with a doll friend, and even squirts paint on the screen, which you wipe off with your finger. In one hilarious scene, your tapping on highlighted spots results in Teddy popping out of cupboard when his little girl is looking elsewhere.

This app waits a few seconds after narrating a page to highlight where you should touch. This lag lets kids enjoy the watercolor illustrations before interacting and provides them a way to try to find some of the animations on their own.

The magic of this book comes from the way the app cleverly invites you to participate in the story. Tapping on crayons and paper in one scene leads you to a a blank page with a simple drawing program. Your creation magically appears in the next scene as a drawing taped to the little girl's wall. It's empowering. Kids can also put together a puzzle from right inside an illustration.

**Best For:** Little kids who love their stuffed animals. Because the book is read by a darling little-girl voice, young girls will identify with both the Teddy Bear who is trying to keep his secret as well as the little girl protagonist who is trying to find out the truth.

I love my teddy bear!

Does he sit upon my pillow...
not make a single sound?
Or does he jump upon my mattress,
running all around?

# The Monster at the End of This Book . . . starring Grover!

$3.99 US/$0.99 CAN/£0.69 UK, Ages 3–7, Sesame Street

This is one of my all-time favorite book apps (and even one of my overall Top Favorite Kid Apps, as you see in Chapter 27). Starring cute, furry, old Grover, this is an app in which kids join Grover in reading a book that scares him — because there is a monster at the end! The app re-creates the beloved *Sesame Street* book, but enhances it with Grover's highlighted narration and hilarious animations as he tries to keep your child from turning each page.

What makes this app so much fun is that Grover pleads, begs, and cajoles your child not to turn the page, but kids will want to anyway to see what happens next. As they keep turning, kids experience Grover's creative solutions to keep them from turning the page, including tying the pages together, nailing them together, and building a brick wall. Your child will have fun undoing each obstacle that Grover constructs. For example, tickling Grover makes him let go of the rope tying the pages together. Who can resist tickling cute, loveable Grover?

This book app is the perfect blend of a great story with hilarious animations. All of the interactions serve to draw your child deeper into the fun that's a part of reading this book. Your child and Grover have a delightful surprise at the end.

**Best For:** Muppet-loving youngsters. It's also a great book to read with kids who have fears — including fears of monsters under the bed or in the closet.

If you love this book app, try out the sequel called Another Monster at the End of This Book...starring Grover & Elmo!, which I review in Chapter 20.

# Pete's Robot

$2.99 US/$2.99 CAN/£1.99 UK, Ages 3–8, Heartdrive Media LLC

Don't be put off by this book app's surprisingly simplistic drawings. Within its juvenile, cartoony world beats a heart worth exploring — a robot's heart, that is. This story follows the construction of a robot by little Pete, who forgets to install the machine's "heartdrive." With this obvious metaphor for the importance of feelings and being kind to one another, the story takes your kids on a madcap adventure with Pete and his little dog, Spot. Readers help Pete put together the robot, chase after it when it's wreaking havoc, and celebrate its kindness when it's properly outfitted with the all-important heartdrive.

The interactions in this app are what make it so good. With just a tap of the finger, kids can change Pete's expressions. By swiping your finger, you make time pass as Pete and Spot wait for the robot parts to be delivered to Pete's mailbox. Swirling the robot's eyes on a psychedelic background drives home the robot's craziness. When the malfunctioning robot grabs the mailman's pouch, shaking the iPad sends mail careening around the screen. Pressing on the robot's head makes its arm slowly ratchets its way to a mailbox. At the end, when the robot is whole, Pete, Spot, the robot, and others form a band, and your child can touch the musicians to turn their music-making on and off.

Your kids can read the story to themselves or choose from three different narrators. Unfortunately, the words do not highlight when read aloud. (Highlighting words makes it easier for kids learning to read to follow along.)

The first and last pages have links to the publisher's website, as well as to Twitter and Facebook.

**Best For:** Kids who enjoy wacky, high-energy stories. The visual style of this app, as well as the audio accompaniment, is high octane — things flash and blare. It's a great story for daytime reading, but it won't help little ones settle in for sleeping.

# Miss Spider's Tea Party
Free US/CAN/UK, Ages 3–8, Callaway Digital Arts Inc.

This app was released on the day that the first iPad became available in April of 2010. It was awe-inspiring then and still is today. Although a lot of innovation has occurred in book apps since its release, this app's brilliance has stood the test of time.

With this app, David Kirk's classic children's book about a lonely vegetarian spider, who has trouble convincing insects to trust that she won't eat them and to become her friend, becomes so much more than a book. Kids can watch an animated movie, which looks like a Pixar production, while the words are read and highlighted. Alternatively, kids can opt to have the book read aloud while they play with the characters in the illustrations. Tap on a caterpillar, and it counts its curling-up exercises. Touch Miss Spider, and she repeats or expands on what she said on that page. Things sparkle and glow and respond to your child's touch.

But that's not all. Kids can also color the pages from the book, put together jigsaw puzzles, and play concentration-type matching games featuring characters from the book.

Accompanied by gentle, lyrical music, the app offers kids a heart-warming tale of friendship. In addition to inspired rhyme, the story introduces kids to counting, as Miss Spider tries to make friends with sets of bugs. On the page where she tries to invite seven butterflies

to tea, the insects are camouflaged in a bouquet of flowers. As kids touch them to count them, they flutter. This app even lets you zoom in to the illustrations, something I wish more book apps would do.

**Best For:** Families to watch and read together. The combination of a top-notch story, an outstanding reader, and incredible animation make this book app a wonder to behold!

# Cinderella – Nosy Crow animated picture book

$5.99 US/$5.99 CAN/£3.99 UK, Ages 3–8, Nosy Crow

This version of the classic fairy tale keeps the story intact but updates the setting to modern times. The stepmother and stepsisters are still mean and demanding, just without as much rancor. And the prince likes Cinderella because she is nice (not pretty) and wants to know if he can text her.

Although iTunes has tons of Cinderella apps, this is my favorite because this version involves your child in the storytelling and it uses technology in cool ways. In each scene, after the words highlight and the narrator finishes, the characters on the page talk directly to you, asking you to do things like help put a log on the fire. Touch the stepmother and she makes cruel comments. And when the fairy god-mother needs help collecting things from the garden to transform into Cinderella's carriage and horses, you are her go-to helper. You find the pumpkin, the mice, and so on.

Tech-wise, the app does things you don't often find in other apps. For example, if a mirror is hanging on the wall, your child sees her own reflection in that mirror! This cool feature involves the app using the iPad's forward-facing camera. Also, you can choose the color of Cinderella's ball gown, and that color appears throughout the story.

**Best For:** All kids. This app makes the Cinderella fairy tale relevant to today's times. It offers three ways to explore it, so pre-readers or readers can enjoy it.

Hmm, I'm just going to change the colour.

# The Three Little Pigs–Nosy Crow animated storybook

$5.99 US/$5.99 CAN/£3.99 UK, Ages 4–7, Nosy Crow

A modernized version of the classic fairy tale, this interactive book app is also tamer than the original because none of the pigs is eaten by the big, bad wolf. The book tells the story of three little pigs who leave their parents' home to construct their own houses: one made of straw, one made of sticks, and one made of bricks. A big, bad wolf, who arrives in a catering van, tries to eat the pigs. The wolf, with your child's help blowing into the iPad's microphone, huffs and puffs to blow down the flimsy houses of straw and sticks. But the house of bricks stymies the wolf. The two now-homeless pigs escape the wolf and congregate in the house of bricks. There the pigs cleverly stop the wolf's attempt to enter their home via the chimney by placing a boiling pot of water at the end. Scalded but alive, the wolf shoots back out of the chimney in defeat.

This book app has all of the components that make a good book app: a classic fairy tale told with good narration while the words highlight as read; options of how to experience the book (narrator reads, your child reads, or your child listens and plays at the same time); gorgeous illustrations; a unique musical identity for each character; and clever ways to interact within the story. It's the latter — the interactions — that make this book app so fabulous.

On every page surprises await your child's touch. When you interact with the characters, they talk to you, moving the story forward. But

you can also do silly things like make the wolf turn somersaults in the air. Some of the scenes are fully animated, which means they look like you're watching a video.

**Best For:** Both boys and girls. This book is particularly good for kids who like to look carefully at each illustration because it has clever collection elements, such as finding a cute spider on each page.

# How Rocket Learned to Read – by Tad Hills

$4.99 US/$4.99 CAN, Ages 4–7, Random House Digital, Inc.

A little black-and-white dog named Rocket stars in this storybook app. Rocket meets a little yellow bird who decides to teach him to read. When Rocket shows no interest in learning the alphabet, the little bird draws the reluctant Rocket into her learn-to-read project by reading a book about a dog who lost his bone. Before Rocket knows it, he's entranced by the story and wants to learn to read. As Rocket learns to read, so too does your child.

On each page, kids can tap, tilt, swipe, and blow to make subtle things happen on the page. For example, touching a sleeping Rocket makes his tail wag. Kids can even use their fingers to trace letters of the alphabet as they help Rocket draw letters in the snow. Also, kids can explore two games that further their learning to read.

This excellent book app offers two ways to read it: Watch and listen as words are highlighted while read aloud by the fabulous narrator, Hope Davis; or read it to yourself with the ability to touch any word and hear it spoken. This latter option provides a great way for kids to get help when they're first learning to read.

This may be my favorite book app for kids ages 4 to 7 because it conveys the importance of learning to read in a way that hooks even the most reluctant reader. This book app faultlessly integrates a cozy, feel-good story with illustrations and light animations that tug on your heartstrings; and it has a narrator who is pitch-perfect. Download this one for sure!

The last page has links to Facebook and Twitter.

**Best For:** Kids who are reluctant readers. It's also perfect for kids who are just learning to read or have recently learned to read. Kids will identify with Rocket's journey to learn, and it may help make their own reading journey easier.

At last the little yellow bird appeared. "Hello! How wonderful to see you in class," she chirped. "I can tell by your waggy tail that you are well rested."

# Dragon Brush
$2.99 US/$2.99 CAN/£1.99 UK, Ages 4–8, Small Planet Digital

Based on a Chinese folk tale, this book app follows the life of Bing-Wen, a young rabbit-like boy who loves to draw. Because his family is too poor to afford art supplies, Bing-Wen uses a stick to draw dramatic paintings of dragons in the dirt. One day, after helping an old woman, she gives him a special magical paintbrush that makes his drawings come to life. Bing-Wen wants to use the brush to draw things that will help his community, but when the cruel, selfish emperor hears of the brush, he forces Bing-Wen to draw things just for him. Bing-Wen is cleverer than his emperor, however, and manages to use his brush to outfox the cruel leader.

Dragon Brush features a great interactive mechanism: It asks kids to swipe their finger over an area where Bing-Wen has drawn; and when they do, his drawings appear under their fingers. After uncovering a painting made with the Dragon Brush, the drawing springs to life. This involvement makes kids feel like they are a part of the story. Also good are the fantastic graphics, cute interactive bits, and fabulous musical accompaniment. Plus, kids can find special pots of paint throughout the book. These pots feature paint as iridescent as dragon scales, which can be used on the last page to paint original sparkling drawings.

**Best For:** All kids ages 4–8. The art creation within the book can be done by anyone — it just involves swiping your finger over the page. The book has an option to have it read to you (although the words do not highlight) or you can read it yourself. This book is a special delight for kids who love to draw because the magical paint pots that you find within the book create unusual glowing effects when used to create drawings at the end. These drawings can be saved to the iPad's photos and shared from there if you so wish.

But this didn't really work out the way he'd expected.

# Brave Rooney

$1.99 US/$1.99 CAN/£1.49 UK, Ages 4–8, Bacciz

My two sons went through a stage where they were always wearing capes and imagining they could fly. If your kid is into superheroes, read on. This clever book app is about a normal little boy named Rooney who is sent to the superhero school. Needless to say, he doesn't fit in. He can't fly, he can't put out a forest fire with his breath, and he can't stop a rock-slide with his strength. But one day Rooney discovers he can do something all the superheroes are afraid of — he can stand up in front of a crowd and read a poem he has written. This bravery wins the respect of the whole school, and Rooney finally fits in.

Every good book app has to start with a good story, and Brave Rooney excels at that. You can read the book to yourself or have the app read to you by the author of the book; and that narration is spot-on. The book has an index so your child can easily navigate to a favorite page. Lots of books have those options, but this app excels in the other extra options, including the ability to display the text (with highlighting as it's read), hide the text after the narration so that kids can enjoy exploring the scene, disable the interactions during narration (so kids don't get distracted), automatically turn the page, or turn the page by swiping (versus using arrows on the bottom of the page). The artwork has a comic-book feel to it, and the animation is plentiful but not overwhelming. Overall, this is a well-put-together app.

**Best For:** Kids who worship superheroes. Both girl and boy superheroes are represented.

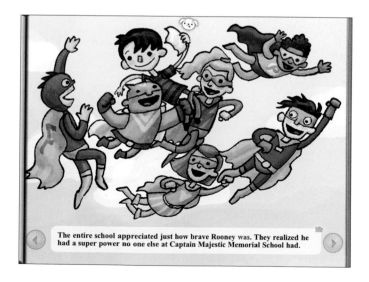

The entire school appreciated just how brave Rooney was. They realized he had a super power no one else at Captain Majestic Memorial School had.

# Leonard

$3.99 US/$3.99 CAN/£2.49 UK, Ages 4–8, Ink Robin, Inc

Leonard is a friendly little boy who's got a big imagination. When his family decides to move from the city to the countryside, Leonard is surprised that he can't seem to find any other kids to play with. While looking for friends in a variety of settings, Leonard's imagination keeps him entertained. He envisions a whale-filled underwater world while visiting a stream, visits outer space when climbing a ladder, and sees African animals instead of cows pasturing in the fields. Frustrated by not finding other kids, Leonard decides to build his own friend, in the form of a cardboard-box robot. When Leonard takes his robot to the park, he finally meets some other kids.

This book app delivers a charming story in its 18 pages, filled with neon illustrations on a black background. But what makes it stand out from other book apps is how your kids get to see inside Leonard's imaginings. Every time Leonard cooks up some wild fantasy, a thought-bubble located on a slider appears on the page. When your child moves the thought-bubble along the slider, he or she makes the scene change into an imaginary one. Then, your child can play inside Leonard's fantasy world. For example, touching the underwater scene makes all of the brightly colored fish swim toward your finger. Another neat feature is that a second reading of the book produces some new imaginings.

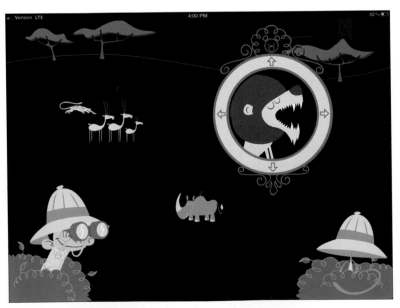

**Best For:** Kids who have vivid imaginations and love to live in make-believe worlds. This book app may appeal more to boys than girls because the main character is a boy who does things like squish bugs in one of the imaginary scenes.

# Auryn HD – Where Do Balloons Go? An Uplifting Mystery

$5.99 US/$5.99 CAN/£3.99 UK, Ages 4–8, Auryn Inc.

I still remember the heartbreak on my son Teddy's face when he accidentally let go of a prized helium balloon. I wish I could've played this fanciful app with him back then. It would've helped to ease the pain.

This book app transforms Jamie Lee Curtis's popular book *Where Do Balloons Go? An Uplifting Mystery* into a digital experience filled with delightful interactive surprises. Read by Jamie Lee Curtis, it explores the secret life of freed balloons. Do they have parties up in the sky? Do they make it into outer space? Can they read? Do they get a cold? The balloons come alive and talk, dance, grow bigger, get smaller, and of course, zip around the world.

Although Curtis's print book is both fanciful and thoughtful, the interactions in this book app create whimsy. Curtis embraces the addition of interactivity to her book, explaining that it's a "new overlay that doesn't disturb the preciousness of literature but enhances it."

The many interactive enhancements in this book app are very clever. Touching some balloons makes them expand. You can record your voice and hear it played back in a high pitch as if a helium balloon were speaking. On several pages, an electric fan icon is present. When you touch it, it attaches to your finger and you can blow the balloons around the page. On an outer-space screen, you can touch the stars to create a dot-to-dot picture. And at the end of the book, you can create and film your own play, using balloon characters as your actors. You can even design a balloon character that sports your photo on its round face. All of this interactivity fits seamlessly into this wonderful book app and makes reading and playing in it special.

**Best For:** Kids who love exploring the details of a book. With so many hidden surprises, it will take several readings before your child finds them all.

# 7 Book Apps: For Older Kids

## Three Little Pigs and the Secrets of a Popup Book

$3.99 US/$3.99 CAN/£2.49 UK, Ages 7–12, Game Collage, LLC

This version of the fairy tale is a digital pop-up version that has unique x-ray goggles to let kids see behind the illustrations to understand how the gears and levers would work to create the pop-ups.

Because it targets an older audience, this version has no narration. Also, it's based on the classic, more grisly version in which the first two pigs are eaten by the wolf and the tale ends with the third pig eating the wolf.

Download this app to let kids explore how pop-up books are made. By touching the x-ray glasses in the top-left corner, the colorful illustrations become black and white and reveal how the wheels, gears, and levers all work together to make the pop-up animate. It's fascinating to explore.

**Best For:** Kids age 7 and older who are interested in mechanics and how things work. Although the illustrations don't focus on the grisly aspects of this tale, the story does; so wait to introduce this version until kids are old enough to take it in stride.

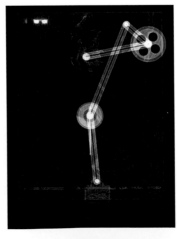

# Wild About Books

$4.99 US/$4.99 CAN, Ages 5–8, Random House Digital, Inc.

Told completely in rhyme, this book app is an adaptation of an award-winning children's book by Judy Sierra, illustrated by Marc Brown. Molly McGrew, the bookmobile librarian, mistakenly drives her transient library into a zoo. She decides to teach the animals to read and lures them into loving books by reading them such classics as Dr. Seuss's books, *Harry Potter*, Nancy Drew's mysteries, *The Wizard of Oz,* and *Goodnight Moon*. The animals display a voracious appetite for good books and eventually many become authors themselves. The story ends with Molly building the animals their own Zoobrary.

Several aspects of this book app contribute to its appeal. It uses colorful language with clever phrasing and alliteration. Every time you turn a page, the illustrations spring from the page, filling in from the foreground, then the middle, and then the background, as if each page were a diorama. But even better, by tilting the iPad, the background sways while the foreground stays in place, creating the illusion of 3D. Kids can find secret animations or extra dialog by tapping. Penguins flip, animals stampede, and a cheetah reads to you from her manuscript. Librarian Molly succeeds in making the zoo animals wild about books, and this app may have that effect on your child, too.

**Best For:** Kids who are already reading. The language of this book is sophisticated and it references many books appropriate for kids older than preschoolers.

# Bartleby's Book of Buttons Vol. 1: The Far Away Island

$0.99 US/$0.99 CAN/£0.69 UK, Ages 5–10, Octopus Kite

This book app represents a new kind of virtual pop-up book made specifically for the iPad. It stars Bartleby, a dapper man who searches the world looking for unusual switches, knobs, and dials to add to his unique button collection. In this first book in the series of Bartleby iPad books, your child joins the intrepid collector on a trip to a mysterious island to search for a new, rare button.

Although the story is a simple adventure tale, this app is special because each page contains a complex puzzle that can be solved only by flipping switches, turning dials, sliding slides, and pushing buttons. For example, as shown in the figure below, to get Bartleby's car to the ship's dock, you must figure out the order of switches to flip and buttons to tap so that Bartleby's car stops at a railroad crossing, the stoplight changes from red to green, and the car travels the correct direction at each intersection. The app purposely doesn't provide you any hints; so trial-and-error is the key, as is keen observation.

**Best For:** Kids who love puzzles. These puzzles can't be skipped, which means the story won't move forward until you solve the conundrum presented on each page. Choose this app for kids who relish thinking challenges! This is a good book for a parent and younger child to explore together.

TIP

If you like this book app, you'll also enjoy its sequel: Bartleby's Book of Buttons Vol. 2: The Button at the Bottom of the Sea. It has all new puzzles and another fun adventure.

# The Fantastic Flying Books of Mr. Morris Lessmore

$4.99 US/$4.99 CAN/£2.99 UK, Ages 5 and up,
Moonbot Studios LA, LLC

This is one of the most magical book apps in iTunes. By combining a moving story with unbelievable graphics and film clips and then layering on innovative interactions, this book app takes storytelling to new heights.

Written and illustrated by William Joyce, the app tells the story of a young, book-loving man who gets transported to a new wondrous land via a tornado. In this new land, books are alive and can talk and fly. As Morris makes friends with these fantastical animated books, he becomes the caretaker of them and their home — a library. In turn, the books take care of him and teach him a very important lesson about life: Everyone's story matters. Morris ages while staying with the books, but every day he writes the story of his life; and when he reaches the last page of his book, he decides it's time to move on. When leaving, Morris gifts his own book to his dear book friends at the library. Shortly after that, a little girl arrives at the library, and Morris's book flies over to her to become her friend.

The story and video sequences are based on a film that won the 2012 Academy Award for the best animated short film. This is a poignant and moving tale. Its presentation on the iPad is nothing short of masterful. Each page contains something intriguing to do, whether it be swirling clouds to create a tornado, restoring a stormy sky to sparkling blue, or creating music by helping the books fly into the library.

This story about the transformational power of books and the circle of life will likely resonate with you and your child long after you've closed your iPad cover. This is the first book I recommend whenever I am asked for advice about the best apps for the iPad.

**Best For:** All families to sit and enjoy together. Adults will appreciate it on a different level than kids, and it may be even more powerful for them.

It was then that Morris Lessmore would once again write in his own book. He wrote of his joys and sorrows, of all that he knew and everything that he hoped.

# The Witch With No Name HD
$4.99 US/$4.99 CAN/£2.99 UK, Ages 5–10, SlimCricket

Within minutes of starting this app, I knew I was experiencing a rare treasure. This app's visual style is stunning, displaying a 3D world filled with animation rather than static pages. Presented with an original musical score and fully voiced characters, this app is more of an interactive movie than a static book. In addition, you can read the words or have the app read them to you (but the words aren't highlighted).

When you first meet the Witch With No Name, her neighbors fumble to greet her with silly nicknames. Annoyed, the witch responds to these greetings by turning each of her neighbors into animals. Upon arriving home, the witch's pet bat berates her for behaving so badly. The witch decides to rediscover her name so that she can fit in better with her neighbors.

Kids join the witch on her quest to find ingredients — a giant's nose hair, an elf's smelly sock, firefly juice, and a concert of farts — to make a potion to reveal her name. To obtain each ingredient, kids play a game. These games include sorting, tossing, collecting, and rhythmic touching. They can be played on three levels of difficulty.

This adventure is exciting for kids because the locations they visit are filled with interesting, magical things to see and touch. The Giant is a whole ecosystem himself with plants and animals living in his socks and his beard! To find the elf's smelly socks, kids sort through gross but hilarious items strewn around the elf's home.

The book ends with your child selecting a name for the witch and recording it using the iPad's microphone. The app magically takes your child's recording and changes the voice (but keeps the name you created) so you hear different characters speak in their own voices the name your child selected! That technological feat is impressive.

- Batina, I'm back.

The title page contains links to the developer's website and Facebook page, and it links to Twitter.

**Best For:** All kids! This jaunty tale is delightfully magical, with just the right mix of silly and gross witchy things.

# Unwanted Guest

$6.99 US/$6.99 CAN/£4.99 UK, Ages 7 and up, Moving Tales Inc

In this traditional Jewish folk tale, written by Jacqueline O Rogers, kids meet an old man who is so poor that he is forced to sell his personal possessions. Sitting in his dilapidated and neglected house, the man fails to notice that an unwelcome visitor has snuck into his home. Hiding in a dark crevice is the unwanted guest called Poverty. Shown at first as merely naked bony limbs, the gaunt and angular body grows bigger as the old man gets poorer. Poverty eventually grows so large that it occupies the house and pushes the old man outside. This rude awakening motivates the old man to revaluate his life and come up with a new plan. With new resolve and hard work, the man makes enough money to repair his home. In the process, the man is able to drive Poverty from his house.

This book app delivers one of the most powerful storytelling experiences that I've discovered on the iPad. The app doesn't do it with imaginative interactivity; rather, it moves you by how it presents its potent story. Using mostly grayscale images presented as moving 3D animation, the starkness of the scene makes the old man's situation feel palpable. You watch as a camera skims over the scene in 360 degrees, sweeping you into the setting. The soulful violin music helps create the feeling of helplessness. And the metaphor of the naked Poverty with his emaciated limbs sticking out of the house makes you feel the old man's despair. The words form on each page from letters falling individually from the top of the page, as if they too have been swept into a maelstrom by the presence of Poverty. These words are read by a brilliant narrator who modulates his voice with just the right amount of regret and eventually pride for what the old man accomplishes.

**Best For:** Children ready to tackle heavier topics such as the ups and downs of life. This book app is great for rereading because the images change from viewing to viewing. It uses randomly selected alternative views when presenting its evocative images.

 If you like this book, try Pedlar Lady and This Too Shall, two other magical folk tales from Moving Tales Inc.

# Oz for iPad

$0.99 US/$0.99 CAN/£0.69 UK, Ages 8–13, podotree, inc.

This app isn't based on the movie *The Wizard of Oz,* but rather on L. Frank Baum's original novel. Spanning 79 pages, this book has a fascinating presentation that frequently has the reader tilting, tapping, swirling, and doing other actions to make things happen on the pages. Some pages are filled only with words, though others present an illustration with which to interact. Many combine both.

The reason to download this book app is because it has a spectacular visual and interactive presentation. The artwork is unusual, using brown ink drawings and watercolors to create an old-fashioned look. Among other book apps, the interactivity here — whether you're oiling the tin woodman or throwing a bucket of water on the Wicked Witch of the West — is fresh and exciting. These interactions vary greatly, and many are quite creative, including a page where the Wizard presents each character with his basic desire. The scene starts with the Scarecrow getting his brain, but if you tap him, one of the other characters magically appears instead and the story changes to talk about the new character. You control when the Tin Woodman, the Lion, and the Scarecrow hear about their futures.

The writing and narration are just okay; the narrator uses a weird cadence and a few sentences have poor grammatical construction, but the story is a good one. Plus, in this version, none of the characters is scary, not even the flying monkeys.

**Best For:** Older kids who can handle the vast amount of reading. This is a fun app to check out after watching the famous movie; and it will give families things to compare. Parents might want to lead a discussion about the two versions, how and why are they different.

# Middle School Confidential 2: Real Friends vs. the Other Kind

$2.99 US/$2.99 CAN/£1.99 UK, Ages 8–14, Electric Eggplant

This is the second in a series of book apps written for tweens and presented as graphic novels. You needn't have read the first one to enjoy this second one. Although the first app in the series, Middle School Confidential 1: Be Confident in Who You Are, is good and worth downloading, this second book app is even better.

Focused on a group of six friends attending middle school, the book explores issues surrounding friendships. Broken into 8 chapters and spread out over 38 pages, the book presents real-life situations, such as what to do if a friend has an eating disorder, what to do if a friend is using you, how to resolve disputes between friends, and other important topics. Periodically, between chapters, kids can take quizzes that help them reflect on the issues that are presented in the story. In one called Do You Make Snap Decisions?, the quiz presents a series of scenarios and asks if you would make a decision about someone, for example, if she wears a strange shirt or plays a tuba.

This book app does a great job of creating compelling and interesting characters who speak authentically about social problems that are common and relevant to this targeted audience. The combination of watching others your age struggle and resolve real issues and then asking you to think about and respond to personal questions in quizzes helps tweens to reflect and learn from others. It also provides them with a framework of how to resolve conflicts with their friends and can provide them confidence that they too can handle tough social situations.

**Best For:** All middle school students and kids in upper elementary school as well. This is a group of six friends you hope your kids find in real life.

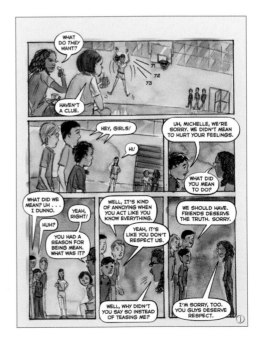

## The Artifacts
$1.99 US/$1.99 CAN/£1.49 UK, Ages 8 and up, Slap Happy Larry

This mesmerizing book app for older kids is a transformative tale about how the experiences of childhood shape us into the adults we will become. The story follows a boy named Asaf who loves collecting things. To him, his collections contain wondrous artifacts and fine art found in the discarded items of others. To his family, however, his room is filled with junk. When the family moves to a new house when Asaf is 13, his parents declare "No more collections." This abrupt change in Asaf's life, just as he is entering his teen years, initially makes him resentful and withdrawn; but it results in motivating him to explore his own imagination and the world of books. As Asaf grows and adjusts, he spends more time reading, learning new words, and writing. He eventually learns how to harness his love for collecting and transforms it into a love of gathering new thoughts, concepts, and vocabulary so that he can explore bigger ideas.

Although the underlying story has deep themes, your child's interaction with this book app yields a series of eclectic and marvelous happenings. Each page of this book has something unusual or fascinating to explore. Early on, you touch the screen to discover what Asaf is collecting. His empty bookshelf fills to overflowing the more you tap. When angst-filled Asaf is first exploring his imagination, your tapping captures shadows of objects or things that wiggle furiously when he pins them onto a clothesline in his mind. You release the shadows by tapping, and watch them slowly dissolve into wisps of black smoke. While Asaf is imagining

adventures, you help to navigate his bed floating over the ocean during a storm. This book app does a great job of taking kids on a fascinating interactive journey that also makes them think about deeper philosophical questions. It's extraordinary!

**Best For:** Tweens and teens who are struggling with leaving childhood behind. This book app is even wonderful for adults to explore.

# The Voyage of Ulysses
$4.99 US/$4.99 CAN/£2.99 UK, Ages 10 and up, Elastico Srl

Kids go adventuring with the famous Ulysses in this shortened retelling of Homer's epic poem, *The Odyssey*. This book app presents the highlights of Ulysses's 20-year adventure, starting with the Trojan War, followed by encounters with the Lotus-Eaters, the Cyclops Polyphemus, Aeolus, Circe the Sorceress, Calypso, Princess Nausicaa, and eventually making it back to his home of Ithaca. Kids help Ulysses sail through the treacherous waters where the Sirens beckon and the six-headed monster Scylla threatens. Upon arriving home, Ulysses must win back his beloved Penelope in a bow-and-arrow contest before happily reuniting at the end.

This book app is special because it lets kids participate in Ulysses's adventures. They touch the side of the Trojan Horse to open it and tap again to release the soldiers. When the story tells of storms sending Ulysses's boat off course, readers take their finger to slide the storm over the ocean and see the rain fall. They create the tracks in the sand to meet the Lotus-Eaters. When fighting the lure of the Sirens' song, kids can spin the water underneath Ulysses's boat to make the music more vibrant and intense. And when Ulysses finally escapes Calypso on a raft, the app invites readers to navigate through the ocean by tilting the iPad. Kids even win the contest for Penelope's hand in marriage by tilting the iPad at just the right time to make the arrow fly through the obstacles. Kids bring the star-crossed lovers together for a kiss at the end.

In addition to all of this great interaction, the book is read by a talented narrator and accompanied by a varied musical score. One extraordinary feature is the book's navigation: You can scroll through pages, of course, but more magical is selecting a spot on the map and watching Ulysses's boat travel there! Another great feature is the ability to pull up extra information boxes, which impart information about Greek myths and history.

**Best For:** Kids who enjoy adventures involving giants, heroes, magic, and myths.

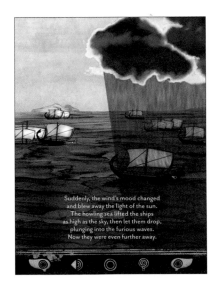

Suddenly, the wind's mood changed and blew away the light of the sun. The howling sea lifted the ships as high as the sky, then let them drop, plunging into the furious waves. Now they were even further away.

# 8 Cars, Trucks, and Things That Go Vroom

## Apps Covered in This Chapter

- Wheels on the Bus HD
- Bizzy Bear Builds a House
- Trucks HD – by Duck Duck Moose
- Cars in sandbox: Construction
- My First App Vehicles
- Happi Full Throttle
- Car Toons! HD

## Wheels on the Bus HD

$1.99 US/$1.99 CAN/£1.49 UK, Ages 2–5, Duck Duck Moose

The classic "Wheels on the Bus" song comes to life in this app. Kids start the song by simply swiping across the screen; when they do, the school bus starts rolling forward. Each new stanza of the song is shown as its own interactive page. When the doors of the bus go "open and shut," your child uses her finger to perform the opening and shutting, and she can even tickle the bird standing inside the bus. When the song comes to the wipers going "swish, swish, swish," your child's finger makes that motion happen on the windshield; and when she does, it actually clears the rain while the eyes (headlights) of the bus watch you work. It's adorable. This version has even added some original stanzas, such as "The baker on the bus says 'Have some cake.'"

The doors of The BUS go opeN aNd shu...

The clean, crisp graphics and interactivity of almost everything in the scenes make this app wonderfully engaging. Plus, kids can change the performer of the song so that it's played in different languages, by a violin, a kazoo, or even your own child's voice.

**Best For:** All toddlers and preschoolers. If you've got a little one who loves buses, download this one because this bus is alive and full of fun animal friends.

# Bizzy Bear Builds a House
$3.99 US/$3.99 CAN/£2.49 UK, Ages 2–4, Nosy Crow

Your truck-loving little one will wiggle with pleasure when exploring this app. Kids join Bizzy Bear when he visits a construction site and they help him run the machinery that's being used to build a house.

The app invites your child to help Bizzy Bear as he performs a variety of jobs at the construction site, all using big machinery! Your child directs Bizzy to dig a deep hole using a digger, scoop up sand with a front loader, lift other workers using a crane, dump gravel while operating a dump truck, and move bricks using a load lifter.

By interacting with the other characters building the house, kids learn what each machine does and how it helps in the process of building a house. They also learn about other jobs in the process. In some scenes, they can do other things in addition to helping Bizzy Bear, including painting a fence. Because Bizzy Bear is new at this, kids learn along with him.

All this playing with machinery takes place in a book app format. The words of the simple story about how to build a house can be set to highlight as read. However, much of the talking between characters is not part of the story. Rather, the characters glow with a blue dot when they have things to say, and tapping on them allows them to speak in kid voices. This method of involving your child in the story works well to keep him engaged in what the app has to offer. And letting preschoolers control the big machinery by tapping it or moving it around in the scene is sheer brilliance.

**Best For:** Kids who love visiting construction sites and run to put their toy hard hat on first thing in the morning. This app lets them take their big truck fantasies to the next level.

## Trucks HD – by Duck Duck Moose
$1.99 US/$1.99 CAN/£1.49 UK, Ages 2–5, Duck Duck Moose

For your youngest vehicle enthusiasts, this app offers five simple activities involving different cars and trucks. One is a virtual car wash. Before cleaning up a car, kids get the pleasure of making it dirty by driving it through a mud puddle. In another activity, kids choose a sharp object, then watch a car run over it and blow a tire. A tow truck arrives and takes the car to the repair shop. At the shop, kids help fix the tire by raising the lift, choosing a new tire (you can select some funny options, including one with a monkey's face on it), lowering the lift, and then driving the repaired car out of the garage. The activity involving garbage trucks has kids sorting garbage into three containers: recyclables, trash, and compost. Another activity takes place at a construction site, and kids get to control a dump truck and a front hauler. The last activity is a parade filled with 12 vehicles, including a fire truck, a police car, and a mail truck. Tapping these vehicles produces an appropriate sound.

All of these activities, except the garbage-sorting one, are simple enough for a toddler to perform because they involve only touching on the vehicle. The activities teach kids the order of things, whether it's washing, rinsing, and then drying a car, or that the dump truck can't keep dumping until the front hauler has taken away some of the pile created by the dump truck. The garbage-sorting activity is a little more sophisticated, but it's set up so that you can't put the garbage in the wrong bin.

**Best For:** Toddlers who can't get enough of things that go vroom. Older preschoolers and kindergartners will likely think that they don't have enough to do in this app.

# Cars in sandbox: Construction
$2.99 US/$2.99 CAN/£1.99 UK, Ages 3–7, Thematica

This app turns your iPad into a virtual sandbox filled with eight construction vehicles. Each vehicle has a mission for your truck-loving kid to explore. With the grader, your child can start up the truck, move it sideways, and lower its blade so that it can push balls into a canister that's farther down in the sandbox. After you move the five balls into the canister, you earn a star for each one contained. With the crawler-mounted excavator, you move six marbles from a pile to a container. Similar missions involve using a dump truck, dumper, tractor, telescopic handler, loader, and a crane.

This is construction-zone heaven for vehicle-crazy children. Your child has to have some dexterity to figure out how each vehicle works. Experimenting with tapping on and around the vehicle leads to success. You can even open the doors of each vehicle, toot its horn, and turn on its lights. Moving a vehicle is as easy as touching it on the front to move forward and on the rear to move backward, but tilting the iPad also works. If your child is puzzled by what to do with a given vehicle, step-by-step instructions appear in the background as hand-drawn illustrations.

There is a button on the Home screen where one tap takes your child out of this app and to the iTunes store to see other apps created by this publisher.

**Best For:**
Kids who love construction sites and the vehicles that work there. This virtual sandbox combines open-ended play with some goal-based missions.

# My First App Vehicles
$1.99 US/$1.99 CAN/£1.49 UK, Ages 3–6, appp media

For vehicle lovers in preschool and kindergarten, this app provides three different activities — all filled with cars, trucks, rescue vehicles, and even a spaceship! In the first activity, kids can build eight vehicles by matching the fronts and backs in a vertical scrolling game.

With the second activity, kids tilt the iPad to roll a marble into holes to make a vehicle do things like turn on a flashing light or send street-cleaning brushes twirling. The last activity is a puzzle where kids can assemble vehicles that have two, four, six, or nine pieces.

These cartoony graphics create funny sequences, including an elephant driving the street-cleaner truck or a cow driving the tractor, and a silly clown toots his horn to encourage your child's success.

Some parents will want to know that the puzzle of the race car driver shows him holding a bottle of champagne. Although he is not drinking it, it is there.

**Best For:** Car enthusiasts in the preschool range.

# Happi Full Throttle
$1.99 US/$1.99 CAN/£1.49 UK, Ages 4–7, Serendipity

Kids: Start your engines! This app puts your child behind the virtual dashboard of four different vehicles. Using the iPad's camera to capture the real world around your child, the app then displays that view as if it were the view from a dashboard. Kids can drive by moving the iPad around in the air from a stationary position or by turning around in an office chair. If you have a protective cover on the iPad and/or you feel your kids are capable of walking with the iPad while playing, they can pretend to be driving as they walk around to change their scenery.

Your child can drive a fire truck, a sports car, a police helicopter, and a submarine. The iPad shows the dashboard of each and provides appropriate buttons for kids to explore driving, honking, wiping, blinking, diving, sending pings underwater, and more. When piloting the submarine, they can even use a periscope.

**Best For:** Kids old enough to hold the iPad responsibly as they turn around to explore their environment while they "drive." This is a cool use of augmented reality.

# Car Toons! HD

$1.99 US/$1.99 CAN/£1.49 UK, Ages 8 and up, FDG Entertainment

The Car Toons, a fire truck, an ambulance, and a police car, star in this physics puzzler. Their job is to bump a marauding gang of mobster cars off the road — literally. To restore order to this anthropomorphic town of vehicles, the Car Toons deliver over-the-top justice in this series of more than 100 puzzles. Presented with slick cartoon graphics, the motorized heroes deliver hilarious one-liners and clever solutions to ridding the roads of the black, sinister baddies.

The player's role is to help pull off the wild, Rube-Goldberg-type solutions presented in every puzzle. Each puzzle shows baddies perched in precarious positions — at the edge of a bridge or in the corner of a parking garage on top of a tall building — where, if a Car Toon can get to them, it can ram them over the edge and send them to the junkyard. The good news is that you have crazy contraptions and superpowers at your disposal. You may be able to run into a giant hammer so that it pounds down on a barrel of explosives parked next to a bad-boy truck. Or, by double-tapping the screen, you can make the ambulance jump up to a ledge to dislodge a giant wheel. As the wheel careens down a track, it triggers the remote to a trap door that sends the baddie falling down to the land of crushed vehicles.

These puzzles are inventive, charmingly wacky, and completely engrossing. I love this app because the characters are so much fun to interact with and the puzzles encourage kids to conduct experiments. Tapping a vehicle starts it moving and tapping it again makes it stop. Many of the puzzles involve timing your taps so that the vehicles stop at just the right time.

On the title page, the app does offer players the ability to get help with a tricky level by buying, via in-app purchase, tow trucks that solve a given level.

**Best For:** Car-loving kids who enjoy playing with wacky contraptions.

# 9 Co-Op and Multiplayer

## OLO game
$1.99 US/$1.99 CAN/£1.49 UK,
Ages 4 and up, Sennep

This is a great game for families to play together because it's simple to learn and provides fast-pace, action-like gameplay. Your iPad screen becomes a divided court of two colored rectangles with end zones on each side. You launch your discs from your end zone hoping that they stop in your colored rectangle on the opposite end of the court. Combining aspects of shuffleboard and Nok Hockey, the object of the game is to have the most discs in your scoring rectangle when you and your opponent(s) run out of discs to shoot. Like shuffleboard, you can spend your turns knocking your opponents out of their scoring zones. And like Nok Hockey, you can use the sidewalls to ricochet your discs into position.

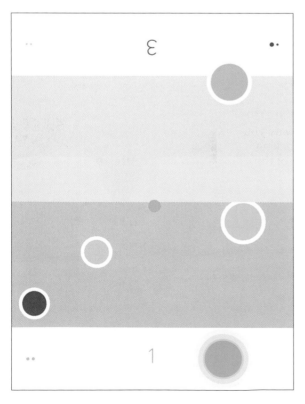

Playable with two or four, this turn-based game has a score that's in constant flux. Players fling discs over the surface in hopes of foiling their opponents while simultaneously scooting their own discs into scoring position. It's a wild raucous game that all ages can enjoy.

 The game can be played online using Game Center.

**Best For:** Families looking for madcap fun. The game can be entertaining for all skill levels.

# Marble Mixer for iPad

$1.99 US/$1.99 CAN/£1.49 UK, Ages 4 and up, GameHouse

Here's a fun multiplayer app that the whole family can play. It's simple enough for preschoolers, but still fun for older kids and even adults. Part of the reason that this game has such great appeal is that it involves flinging marbles!

The app has three different game variations. Each can be played with up to four people. If you're playing by yourself, the computer can control up to three other opponents; but the real reason to download this game is to play it with someone else. The game mechanics are the same in each variation — you use your finger to flick marbles from your designated corner onto the game board to score points.

In the variation called Monster Picnic, the center of the iPad turns into a rotating green-and-orange monster with a cute (not scary) mouth that opens and closes. The goal of the game is to flick as many of your colored marbles into the open maw before the time runs out (sort of like the board game Hungry Hungry Hippos). In the Space Mania variation, the board looks like a rotating ringed target with a hole in the center. The rings are numbered, and marbles landing there get the corresponding points. But if you knock your opponent's marble into the center hole, you get 25 points. The game has 3 rounds of 60 seconds each, with an unlimited number of balls. The calmest of the three variations is Table Tactics. The game board is again a moving target with a hole in the center; but this time, you take turns shooting a total of ten marbles. This way you can be strategic about knocking your opponent's balls out of the scoring rings.

This is a great addition to any family's library of game apps to play together. It's known as a *huddle game* because you all crowd around the iPad and play together at the same time.

The home page has buttons for More Apps, Facebook, and e-mail — none can be hidden.

**Best For:** Families looking for fun games to play together on one iPad.

**UNO HD**
$0.99 US/$0.99 CAN/£0.69 UK, Ages 5 and up, Gameloft

Uno is a card game about matching colors and numbers. It's easy to learn, so kids as young as 5 (or younger if they know their numbers) can join in, but it's also fun for older kids and parents. It was one of the first card games my family played together, and a favorite whenever the grandparents were around.

The app has three modes — Quick Play, Single Player, and Multiplayer — but I included it in this chapter because it can be played with up to four people huddled around one iPad. The object of the game is to be the first to play all your cards from your hand. You get rid of your cards by matching either the number or the color to the card on the discard pile. You can also play action cards that affect the color or direction of play. If you don't have a card to match the discard pile, you must draw.

Uno HD is one of those games that transfers seamlessly to the iPad. This version is fun because it has upbeat, techno music playing in the background if you want; or you can choose music from your iTunes collection to listen to. It also has great sound effects, especially for the action cards.

 This app connects to the Gameloft Live gaming center. That service allows you to befriend strangers and communicate with them. I would not recommend using this service with your kids. Have them play with real people in the same room or with computer-generated opponents instead.

**Best For:** Families looking for a fun card game to play on the iPad.

# Pictureka! for iPad
$4.99 US/$4.99 CAN/£2.99 UK, Ages 6 and up, Electronic Arts

This app brings the popular seek-and-find board game to the iPad. Up to four players can enjoy it on the same iPad, passing it around when it is their turn to play. The board is full of wacky cartoon characters and objects. To win, you must be the fastest to find objects on the board.

Although the app has a solo Adventure mode that's fun, I'm recommending this app for its Versus Mode so that siblings or whole families can play together. In this mode, a player rolls the virtual dice by tapping on a cup or shaking the iPad. The dice determine if you get a green, red, or blue mission card. Green cards challenge you to find a certain number of objects in 30 seconds — such as "two men with beards." The red cards let you bid against the other players to see if you can find the greatest number of a specific object. The player who bids highest gets to play that round even if it isn't his turn. The blue cards pit players against each other in a competition to see who can find an item the fastest. Each player gets a crack at the board. The game is over when a player completes 6 cards.

The crazy, fast-paced music, the whimsical drawings, and the wild sounds that blare each time your avatar appears, all contribute to a circus-like silliness. You sort of expect a big-footed clown to appear at any moment. Like most seek-and-find games, this one makes you think about words and classifications in different ways. When asked to find four transportation vehicles, for example, kids discover that a witch on her broomstick qualifies!

The home page has all sorts of buttons you would rather your kids didn't see: a More EA Games button, a scrolling newsfeed about other EA games, and a push for you to sign up for the Origin game network to unlock the Quick Game Mode. Don't do it; it isn't worth it. And the Origin network leads your kids to social networking via Facebook, Google, your contacts, or with others on Origin.

**Best For:** Families who enjoy hidden objects and seek-and-find puzzles — now you can play those in a competitive game setting.

# Blokus HD

$0.99 US/$0.99 CAN/£0.69 UK, Ages 7 and up, Gameloft

Mattel's popular board game transfers flawlessly to the iPad. The game's excellent tutorials quickly teach kids how to play this strategy game about placing 21 geometric pieces on the board before the space runs out. This game can be played alone against fake players controlled by the app, but it really shines when played with others sharing the same iPad.

In the multiplayer mode, you can play with two, three, or four players. You can also play using one iPad, multiple iPads over local Wi-Fi, or online using Gameloft Live service; but I don't recommend the latter option for young children. Within the multiplayer mode using one iPad, you can play four different ways, so the app offers families lots of fun options to explore.

This is one of my family's favorite games to play huddled around one iPad. It's great for kids because it teaches them strategy. To be good at this game, you need to study the board and place your pieces in ways that block your opponents. As with all good board games, the rules of this one are simple, but the play gets complex as more players get involved. A game with four players takes 20–40 minutes, but the app can remember your game if you have to stop in the middle.

**Best For:** Families that like playing strategy games. This version of the game is a great way to learn to play because its tutorials are so helpful and it flashes spots on the boards where you can place your pieces.

# Carcassonne

$9.99 US/$9.99 CAN/£6.99 UK, Ages 8 and up, TheCodingMonkeys

Transferring the classic board game of the same name to the iPad, Carcassonne is a fabulous multiplayer game about building a medieval community. The gameplay involves placing 72 tiles on a grid so that you build an old-fashioned world filled with roads, cities, cloisters, and farms. You earn points whenever you complete building something onto which you've placed a follower, or *meeple*. The strategy comes in deciding where you place the tiles and your seven meeples so that you garner the most points possible.

This version allows you to play alone, but it's most fun when played with up to five players who take turns passing the iPad. You can also play against computer-generated players of different abilities. For younger children, you can set options to make placing tiles easier and the strategy for scoring not so difficult to understand.

This is an intriguing game to play as a family. I really like the actor-voiced tutorial as well as the well-written manual. The lyrical, classical-guitar music in the background adds to the feeling of playing a gentle board game. Younger kids will like this game because they get to create a community; and older kids and adults will enjoy it because there is complex strategy involved in placing tiles and your limited number of followers.

This game can connect to Game Center and has a chat function to communicate with other players. I would suggest not using this feature with kids.

**Best For:**
Families looking for a way to use the iPad to create a Family Game Night. This game is simple to play, but has deep strategy.

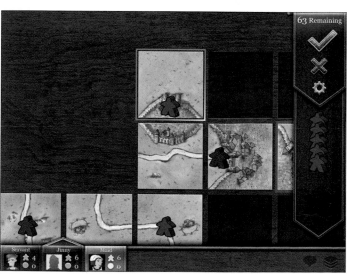

# 10 Creativity, Storytelling, and Journaling

## Apps Covered in This Chapter

- Shake-N-Tell
- Doodlecast for Kids
- iDiary for Kids: journaling platform for writing & drawing
- Toontastic: Play, Create, Learn!
- Happipets
- The DAILY MONSTER Monster Maker

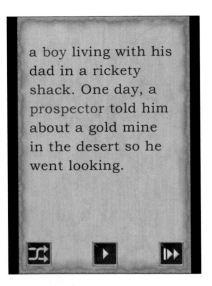

a boy living with his dad in a rickety shack. One day, a prospector told him about a gold mine in the desert so he went looking.

## Shake-N-Tell
Free US/CAN/UK, Ages 3 and up, Your Name In Cows

This is a free app to download for your parental toolbox. It provides parents who are in an I-am-so-tired-I-can't-think state of mind with some much-needed creative juice to entertain their little ones with an original story at the end of a long day.

Shake-N-Tell gives you story ideas that are filled with wonderful characters, settings, and plot twists for you to use and embellish. The app even encourages your original contribution by putting certain words in red ink so you know to use a silly voice or add descriptions or a funny sound. Although this app can provide you with scaffolding, it's up to you and your child (include them in the process for more fun) to come up with the details, sounds, gestures, and plot twists. This app is a tool to help you and your children become great storytellers.

If you don't like a suggested scene, tap a button to shuffle to a different scene. And you have the option of telling a long or short tale by using or ignoring the fast-forwarding button. These story starters are fabulous, and a lifesaver on those days when you're feeling drained.

 You can purchase optional in-app content, including the ability to record and save your story ($0.99). You can also buy three additional story packs for $1.99 each, covering ghosts, princesses, and outer space.

**Best For:** All families. Give your storytelling a boost.

# Doodlecast for Kids
$1.99 US/$1.99 CAN/£1.49 UK, Ages 3–14, zinc Roe

My sons' paintings were always full of stories. Many times their imaginative tales took longer to tell than they did to draw. With this app, you can capture both the drawing and the storytelling in one place and turn the whole thing into a movie to cherish and share.

Doodlecast provides your kids with 11 visual prompts, such as water drawn across the page or simply a mouth with big teeth. The visual is accompanied by a verbal prompt so that your child might hear: "What's happening in the water?" For those who want only a verbal prompt, the app also provides 12 spoken prompts, including "yucky," "wet," and "happy." Kids also have the option of simply using a blank page. To start, kids select their paint from a small color palette and begin drawing. If they don't talk or sing as they're creating, you may want to encourage them to do so by asking questions, because the app records both sound and motion. When they're finished, storytellers tap the purple triangle to activate the Done button. The movie screen then appears and shows the painting being created step by step while also playing all the recorded sounds. Watching the creative process replayed is magical for both you and your children!

The app provides about three minutes of video per picture, but kids can hit a round red button to pause if they need to take a break. If kids change their minds, the Eraser button makes it easy to remove something and redraw it. You can save the movie to the iPad's photos and then share and watch it from there.

As much as I adore this app, it has a few troublesome features. The first time it starts, it prominently displays an ad page promoting other apps from this publisher as well as an entreaty to set up a YouTube account. You can disable this ad and in-app messages by tapping on the i button in the upper-left corner; however, the button to set up YouTube remains in the upper-right corner of the home page.

**Best For:** Encouraging kids to create and share their own stories. Doodlecast makes the process of storytelling easy, and the results are so spectacular you'll want to share them with grandparents and other family members.

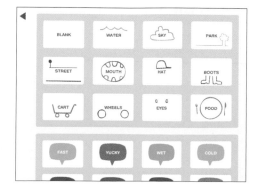

# iDiary for Kids: journaling platform for writing & drawing

$1.99 US/$1.99 CAN/£1.49 UK, Ages 5–13, Tipitap Inc.

This app gives kids a way to create a password-protected journal into which they can write, draw, and store photos. With writing prompts for reluctant journalists, an address book, and a scrapbook section, this is a robust tool for fostering self-expression.

After kids design their cover, create a title, and choose a theme, they can go within the journal to start expressing themselves. The intuitive interface makes it easy to enter a journal entry, start a scrapbook, and create an address book.

The journal is the main focus of this app. It allows kids to type (or write with their finger) a date-stamped entry, and then add stickers, drawings, and photos. The maximum pages allowed for a day is three. If they wish, kids can share their entry by e-mailing it, saving it to the iPad's photos, or printing it using an AirPrint-compatible printer. Kids access the creativity tools on the side of the journal page. They can use markers, pencils, or crayons and select any color by using an intuitive color wheel. Unfortunately, these creativity tools aren't available in the scrapbooking feature — that area stores only photos taken from your camera roll to which you can add captions.

This journaling app has a slick interface that's easy to understand. It also has a great help section explaining all aspects of the app. If you open the journal to write and you don't do anything for a few minutes, an icon pops up onscreen which, when tapped, provides you with verbal prompts for writing subjects, such as "What's your favorite food and why?" or "The perfect day at the beach?"

**Best For:** Kids wanting to explore journaling and to express themselves through private writing.

# Toontastic: Play, Create, Learn!
Free US/CAN/UK, Ages 5–10, Launchpad Toys

Toontastic is an app that teaches kids how to tell a story under the guise of having them create cartoons. The app provides a step-by-step process of how to make a cartoon using intuitive tools. Similar to putting on a puppet show, this app allows kids to tell a story by moving stickers around on the screen. Narration and self-created animation are combined into a short cartoon movie. The end result is a professional-looking video, complete with a title page, author acknowledgement, and background music. What's most amazing about this powerful tech creation tool is that it's free!

By following the steps set forth in this app, kids learn that a cartoon is made up of a series of animated scenes that tell a story. The app explains that cartoons have a story arc, and then it takes kids through the following five steps to create their own cartoon: setup, conflict, challenge, climax, and resolution. Kids create five frames, one for each of these steps, but can add more if they want.

I love that this app accommodates all levels of creativity. For the reluctant narrator, the app has characters to use and premade scenes (castle, underwater shipwreck, outer space, and so on). For the children who have the gift of storytelling, this app provides the tools to create heroes and heroines plus their own scenery. By leading kids through the process of telling a story, adding background music, and then rolling all of the individually created frames together, this app produces a great-looking cartoon. Kids can save it in the app, or with your permission, decide to share it with the world via Toontastic's own ToonTube, where they can also watch cartoons made by kids from around the world.

This app's capability to break down storytelling into digestible bits is what makes it so remarkable. With its scaffolding, all kids feel good about creating a story, and the result is a great-looking, polished presentation. Kids will feel proud of their work because by following the steps in the app, they've learned how to tell a good story.

The Toontastic's Toy Store has in-app purchases to buy new playsets. Some are fun!

**Best For:** All kids! It's free and fabulous — what are you waiting for?

# Happipets

$1.99 US/$1.99 CAN/£1.49 UK, Ages 6 and up, Happi

Kids create animals and beasts by using the letters found in the creatures' names and combining them in unique ways so that the combined letters look like the creature. Funky versions of alphabet letters become building blocks in this creative playground. Some letters have stripes; others are covered in dots; some have bony ridges, eyes, and other affectations that help them look like animals or creatures.

This isn't an app meant to teach the alphabet. Rather, it's an app for older kids who are looking for a fun and new visual playground. The app offers three ways to explore alphabet art: play using the letters found in real animal words, explore making beasts from made-up names like Delipolk or Souot, and create your own beasts using over 140 embellished letters. In the first two, when kids select an animal or beast word, it moves onto the play space where kids can enlarge, rotate, and move the letters around to create an animal. By pushing the Help button, kids see what the animal or beast is supposed to look like — but only for a brief few seconds. When you resize and rotate a letter into the correct position, it clicks into place. And when the puzzle is complete, the animal makes a sound, and a backdrop appears. Tapping the i button reveals fun facts about the real animals and silly ones about the beasts.

These animal alphabet puzzles are challenging but greatly satisfying when you complete them. By having the solution flash onscreen for a brief glimpse when kids push the Help button, they have to use quick observation and memory skills to figure out how to solve the puzzle. The open-ended creation area is also great fun. With no restrictions, kids can enjoy exploring how they want to combine the crazy-looking letters to create new creatures with silly names.

 Kids have an option to share their creations on Facebook or using e-mail.

**Best For:** Artistic kids who enjoy a challenging puzzle and playing with new ways to create animals.

# The DAILY MONSTER Monster Maker

$0.99 US/$0.99 CAN/£0.69 UK, Ages 6 and up, DailyMonster.com

This app sparks kids' creativity simply by presenting an ink splat. But kids can create amazing things using that splat! The app provides kids (and adults) with a delightfully wacky set of parts to add to your ink splat to turn it into a monster. The images on this page are hilarious examples of ink monsters that my family made using this app.

When kids first start the app, they see a canvas and one black Tap to Blow the Ink button. So starts your adventure in making ink monsters. If you don't like that randomly generated splat, you can start over. Next, the fun begins when a Parts file arrives onscreen and opens to reveal many different, whimsical, inky eyes. In addition to eyes, parts are sorted into five other categories of mouths, arms, legs, accessories, and bodies. You simply drag parts to your ink splat to bring it to life. Additional tools let you flip the parts, move them back or in front of the splat, delete an item, undo up to five steps, add a talk bubble, take a photo of your creation with you by its side, and save.

What makes this app magical is that it teaches kids that they can create something recognizable by starting with something abstract. I like that the developers don't muck up the interface with too many bells and whistles. They make the process of creating a great-looking monster easy by presenting a well thought-out and intuitive interface. Kids just drag the body parts to the ink spot to add. As kids try things out on their inky splat, other ideas flow naturally as the monster starts to take on a life of its own. What whimsy! What fun!

 **WARNING!**

Kids can save to Facebook, Twitter, Tumblr, e-mail, and Zazzle.com.

**Best For:** All kids. You don't have to have an artistic bone in your body to be successful with this app. Anyone can be creative with these tools.

# 11 Dinosaurs

## Piece me DINOSAURS!
$0.99 US/$0.99 CAN/£0.69 UK, Ages 3–5, Fashionbuddha

Exhibiting bright and bold artwork, this collection of seven easy jigsaw puzzles lets your dino-loving pre-schooler put together an Apatosaurus, a Tyrannosaurus, a Stegosaurus, and so on.

Each dinosaur puzzle breaks apart with a tinkling sound, and the outline of each piece remains to help your child figure out where to place the pieces. When you tap a piece, it sticks to your finger so that you can slide it to its location. It makes a clicking sound when it snaps into place. The puzzles vary, but most have 7–12 pieces.

When you complete a puzzle, the friendly looking dino animates and makes a sound. A child's voice reads the name of the dinosaur as it appears on the bottom of the screen.

This app is a great way to introduce young kids to dinosaurs because they are cute rather than scary. The artwork is funky and exciting to look at, and kids can even tap a page to meet the artist. Puzzles like this are great for helping kids develop fine motor skills. The developers were careful to not make the puzzles too hard — all you have to do is get close, and the piece snaps into place. This no-fail environment guarantees your child's success.

**Best For:** Preschoolers who are interested in learning about dinosaurs and enjoy puzzles. These puzzles are appealing to both boys and girls.

TRICERATOPS

**Oh Say Can You Say Di-No-Saur? - All About Dinosaurs**
$5.99 US/$5.99 CAN/£3.99 UK, Ages 4–7, Oceanhouse Media

Dr. Seuss's famous cat (from *The Cat in the Hat*) stars in this interactive book app about introducing kids to dinosaurs. As part of The Cat in the Hat's Learning Library — a series that introduces kids to science — this app invites you to join The Cat, youngsters Sally and Dick, Thing 1, Thing 2, and the fish (all from the original *The Cat in the Hat* book) on a hot air balloon trip to find dinosaur fossils. In addition to discovering the bones of ancient reptiles and learning how archeologists work to put the bones together to create a skeleton, you also visit a virtual dinosaur museum.

What makes this app so good is that it combines learning to read with science concepts. By having the whole thing delivered by The Cat in rhyme, this virtual field trip feels wacky and fun. You can choose to have the book read aloud or read it to yourself. The book shows key scientific glossary words in bold type so that you can tap them to hear a definition. Each dinosaur has special facts that show up when tapped. Also, touch any part of an illustration and a word pops up onscreen to help early readers make a word-object connection.

Animated objects appear on each screen, and you can interact with them by tapping. It's a riot to send Thing 1 and Thing 2 zipping around the scenes. The book hilariously ends with The Cat showing you a new species of dinosaur: the Catinthehatosaurus!

**Best For:** Young kids who like to learn in a silly environment. It's perfect for the dino-loving child who is just starting to read because each word in the book can be tapped to hear it read out loud.

 If your kids like this app, they may also enjoy another dinosaur book app from the same publisher: Triceratops Gets Lost – Smithsonian's Prehistoric Pals ($2.99, ages 4–7).

With a club for a tail and a back full of **spikes**, this dino was strong— like an army **tank**. Yikes!

ANKYLOSAURUS

# Ansel and Clair: Cretaceous Dinosaurs

$1.99 US/$1.99 CAN/£1.49 UK, Ages 5–12, Cognitive Kid, Inc.

This is the second app created by the makers of Ansel & Clair: Adventures in Africa (Chapter 19), and like the first, it's fabulous!

Kids join cute alien photographer Ansel and his sidekick robot named Clair. The two are visiting Earth to learn about dinosaurs, so they've landed at a fossil-dig site in North America. The alien's spaceship has a special machine that can scan the dinosaur fossil and then transport Ansel, Clair, and your child back in time to see that dinosaur alive and in action.

At the dig site, Ansel and Clair meet Dr. Lindy Bones, who explains what paleontologists do and how to dig for fossils. He agrees to let Ansel and Clair borrow a fossil if they help him find one in the dirt. Kids take an elevator down to the fossil-site level and help Ansel and Clair dig for Cretaceous-period fossils by tapping and swiping the screen. When they find fossils, they put them back together in a jigsaw puzzle-like activity. With these fossil found and assembled, Ansel's spaceship can now travel back in time to the Cretaceous period.

This next part of the app is pretty thrilling. Kids see dinosaurs moving in the environment (T-Rex, Velociraptor, the newly discovered Kosmoceratops, and five others) and can select each one to learn more about it. After hearing Clair tell general information about a given dinosaur or landmarks in the environment, kids can opt for greater detail by touching a light bulb icon. If they do this, they earn a sticker for later creative play. Kids can also take a photo of each dinosaur for Ansel's Travel Log.

This app uses a clever device to spark your child's curiosity; it makes Ansel the curious one and Clair full of encyclopedic information. Ansel is able to ask questions that lead to information such as "Why did the Kosmoceratops have frills on its head?" The app even explores the theories of why dinosaurs became extinct. Plus, it creates funny situations, such as having the Kosmoceratops sneeze green snot on Ansel.

**Best For:** Dinosaur-loving kids, although this app's clever presentation of wrapping academic information in an engaging storyline may draw in kids who aren't already dino-crazy.

# The Magic School Bus: Dinosaurs
$7.99 US, Ages 5–9, Scholastic Inc.

For more than 25 years, Ms. Frizzle and her magic school bus have been wowing kids with outrageous field trips. With this app, your kids experience a virtual field trip with the beloved "The Friz" by using their iPad.

You join Ms. Frizzle's class as they turn their classroom into a dinosaur land. By tapping other students' reports or talk bubbles, you hear facts or what someone is saying. Unexpectedly, Ms. Frizzle announces that it's time to go on a field trip to a dinosaur dig. After stopping there, The Friz decides to activate the bus's time machine; and before you know it, you've traveled back in time to when dinosaurs walked the Earth. Various pages offer special digs that provide you with a hammer to break apart rocks and a brush to clean off the fossil bones you find. You then drag and drop the bones onto a skeleton to put together a dinosaur and are rewarded with a dino card full of information about the dinosaur you just dug up.

Based on the book *The Magic School Bus: In the Time of the Dinosaurs* by Joanna Cole and illustrated by Bruce Degen, this version is so much more interactive than the book. Packed full of information delivered in easily digestible bites, this book app just begs to be played over and over again. The app also has a fun arcade game about matching three or more dinosaur types to make them disappear from the constantly filling grid.

**Best For:** Older kids who are very interested in facts about dinosaurs and the time periods in which they lived. Although kindergarteners can navigate this app (most of the words and talk bubbles can be tapped to be read aloud), this app is so jam-packed with information that it works best with older kids who are more receptive to learning dino facts.

If your kids love The Magic School Bus, check out another excellent app called The Magic School Bus: Oceans (Chapter 18).

# Dino Discovery!

$0.99 US/$0.99 CAN/£0.69 UK, Ages 6–8, Robot Super Brain

In this app, your child joins Team K.I.D. on a mission to discover the location of some of the world's dinosaur bones. Kids start by selecting an avatar and then they're off to a continent of their choice to start their dig.

To dig, you play a logic game where the underground earth is represented as squares in a grid. After digging down one square, you must decide which direction to go next. Some squares appear as gray rock, which you can't penetrate with your shovel. Others are easy to dig through because they are brown dirt. At each juncture, you must decide which direction to dig next. The farther underground you go, the more of the squares you can see. Sometimes you see the outline of a fossil several squares away; however, rocks may be blocking your way, so you must plot a course around the rocks.

When you find a fossil, it may be a dinosaur footprint or an insect in amber. Occasionally, you find a big fossil, requiring further excavation. When this happens, the screen automatically turns to dirt, and your tapping brushes away the dirt to reveal fossils underneath. When you uncover all of the bones, you help reassemble the fossils to create a dinosaur skeleton. A shadowed picture of what the skeleton looks like appears, and you drag the found bones onto the picture until it's completed. Magically, a fully skinned dinosaur appears along with interesting facts about the reptile. The dinosaur turns into a sticker that you can then place on a prehistoric scene.

This app does a great job turning digging for dinosaurs into an inventive reveal-the-maze type game. The act of brushing off the dirt requires you

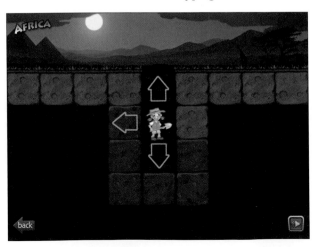

to use keen eyesight because you can see only small bits of the fossil bones. Assembling the fossils is fun because when they come together, they do so with a satisfying snapping sound.

**Best For:** Kids who are sort of interested in dinosaurs and can read. (This app's dinosaur information isn't read out loud.). The app focuses on presenting fun games that are dino-themed.

# March of the Dinosaurs
$7.99 US/$7.99 CAN/£5.49 UK, Ages 8–14, Touch Press

This book app takes you on a journey following two young dinosaurs. Scar, an Edmontosaurus, treks more than 1,000 miles to migrate from the cold arctic to the warmer climates found in the south. Patch, a Troodon, stays in the frigid north and must learn to survive the bitter cold.

Told by actor Kerry Shale, with text that highlights, the story is presented in 12 chapters, covering more than 65 pages. Filled with rich illustrations, the app also contains ten 3D animated dinosaurs that can be viewed at 360 degrees. These ten dinosaurs were created by the team that made the TV special *Escape of the Dinosaurs* for National Geographic.

As they take the journey with the two young dinosaurs, kids can imagine what it was like to have lived so long ago. They experience the hardships these dinosaurs survived and come away with a better understanding of the predator-prey relationships.

**Best For:** Kids who like dinosaurs and enjoy being entertained as they learn. This is a story with facts, not a factual reference.

# Britannica Kids: Dinosaurs
$4.99 US/$6.99 CAN/£4.99 UK, Ages 8–12, Encyclopaedia Britannica, Inc

When your kids need some concrete information about dinosaurs — perhaps for homework — reach for this app. It combines solid information with fun, interactive gameplay. You can access facts about 36 dinosaurs, view photos and videos, read articles about these giant reptiles and the time periods in which they lived, and test your knowledge with quizzes. But you can also learn by playing games like Memory Match (turn over cards to match dinosaurs pairs), jigsaw puzzles, Magic Squares (unscramble images of dinosaurs), and Brush Off (remove sand from fossils and then identify the type of skeleton).

**Best For:** Kids in grades 3–6 who are looking for credible information about well-known dinosaurs and who like to combine game playing with their learning. The app doesn't offer any pronunciations or reading aloud, so kids need to be strong readers.

# Inside the World of Dinosaurs - narrated by Stephen Fry

$13.99 US/$13.99 CAN/£9.99 UK, Ages 8 and up,
M5859 Studios Pty Ltd

Of all the encyclopedic dinosaur apps discussed in this chapter, this is the most exciting. Kids get up close to 60 dinosaurs that scientists, artists, and animators have re-created in loving detail. These dinosaurs move in 3D, can be rotated 360 degrees, and make sounds. Actor Stephen Fry does an amazing job inviting kids to explore further through his exciting narration, which totals five hours. Kids can also read articles about prehistoric life and famous dino hunters. For dinosaur-loving kids, this is a dream app.

The app offers a great navigation system, with easy access icons on the bottom of the page. You can simply flip through more than 280 pages of information, or enter through the index that sorts the information into articles, dinosaurs, and dinosaur hunters. Other entry points are by buttons at the bottom of the page that lead to time periods (Triassic, Jurassic, and Cretaceous) and one that takes you to an interactive timeline.

But the best part of this app is the dinosaurs in their full animated glory. Seeing 60 expertly modeled dinosaurs walking, roaring, and even fighting on your iPad is just amazing. They are colored, scaly, and breathtaking. Kids can use the reverse-pinch to zoom in and, although some are seen engaging in fights, no blood is shown. Each dinosaur comes with a fact file, so it's easy to learn about it at a glance.

This is my favorite dinosaur reference app. And although it's expensive, it's worth it.

**Best For:** Dinosaur lovers and haters. This app makes studying these ancient creatures so interesting that everyone looking at it can't help but become interested.

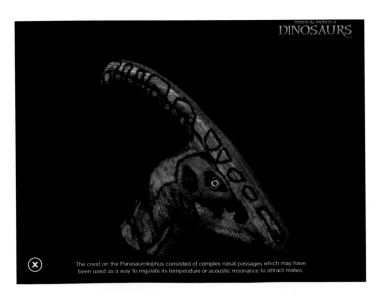

The crest on the Parasaurolophus consisted of complex nasal passages which may have been used as a way to regulate its temperature or acoustic resonance to attract mates.

# Ultimate Dinopedia: The Most Complete Dinosaur Reference Ever

$4.99 US/$4.99 CAN/£2.99 UK, Ages 10 and up, National Geographic Society

The most comprehensive dinosaur app in this chapter, this resource features more than 700 dinosaurs. By including photos, videos, an interactive dinosaur family tree, and read-aloud stories for 76 of the most popular dinosaurs, this app entices your exploration. Tap the screen, and navigation icons appear on the top of the screen. You can enter this reference from many points, including a table of contents, an interactive family tree showing the dinosaurs, an alphabetical index of dinosaurs covered, or by watching videos.

Seventy six of the most popular dinosaurs have an expanded dino profile page, which consists of a dino stats card, a fully voiced factual story about the dinosaur, a fun fact card, and picture information. Each dino stats card lists the name of the dinosaur, what its name means, the period in which it lived, where it was found, how many fossils have been found, its length, and an image showing the size relationship between a human and this dinosaur.

The artwork shown in this app is amazing. It includes videos of lifelike dinosaurs flying and fighting. By creating a story for each of the best known dinosaurs, you can't help but want to know more. With more facts just a tap away, you find yourself pushing the Fun Fact or the Dino Stats buttons. Plus, the app cleverly intertwines all of its information so that you can access it from many dif-

ferent entry points. If you're looking at the family tree and tap an interesting-looking dinosaur, the app whisks you to the Dino Profile page. If you're unclear how to pronounce a given dinosaur's name, you can tap to hear it spoken. I have trouble putting this app down because it's so compelling.

**Best For:** Older kids wanting to learn more about dinosaurs.

The photos and videos sometimes show bloody scenes where a dinosaur is shown eating another. For example, the Giganotosaurus profile picture shows the carnivore with bloody entrails dangling from its mouth.

# 12 Games: Angry Birds & Other Popular Games

## Apps Covered in This Chapter

▶ Bejeweled HD

▶ Angry Birds HD

▶ Where's My Water?

▶ Temple Run

▶ Peggle HD

▶ Cut the Rope HD

▶ Where's My Perry?

▶ Plants vs. Zombies HD

## Bejeweled HD
$3.99 US/$3.99 CAN/£2.49 UK, Ages 6 and up, PopCap

Bejeweled is the crown jewel of the match-three puzzles. Thousands of clones are out there, but this is the game that started the craze. The classic Bejeweled game is set on a grid filled with multicolored gems. Players swap adjacent gems to match three in a row by color. A matching row can be vertical or horizontal, but not diagonal. If you match more than three, you earn extra points and special gems. In addition to this classic mode, the game also provides players with four other modes. My favorite is called Butterflies, where you match fluttering butterfly gems to like-colored stones to release the butterflies from the board, saving them from being eaten by a menacing spider lurking at the top.

Players use keen observation skills when playing these match-three puzzles. When kids are first learning to play, they can benefit from turning on in-game help and auto-hints. This interface is clean and sparkling, and the puzzling is accompanied by serene music. Playing well — making numerous matches in a row and other achievements — earns special gems, such as a hypercube that clears the board of all similarly colored gems when activated. Kids can also earn badges for certain ways of playing.

 Under settings within this app, click "about" and deselect user-sharing so that PopCap doesn't collect data from your playing.

**Best For:** Kids who enjoy visual puzzles. This is a classic.

# Angry Birds HD
$0.99 US/$2.99 CAN/£1.99 UK, Ages 6 and up, Chillingo Ltd

Even if you're new to the iPad, you've probably heard of Angry Birds because it's now one of the most popular mobile games and a staple in conversational culture. This app has players using a slingshot to hurl angry birds at block structures built by egg-stealing pigs. The simple back story is that the pigs stole the birds' eggs. The vengeance these angry birds wreak is legendary and fun!

This game is a constantly updating series of puzzles involving flinging the angry birds at the pigs. The birds are placed into a slingshot one at a time, and you control the trajectory and the strength of the shot. These avian heroes vary in types, with some having special abilities that the player activates while they are midair. The pigs show up inside a wide variety of block structures, which vary in construction materials (including wood, ice, and rock). The challenge for each puzzle is how to use your limited number of birds to knock down the block structures to smash the bad pigs.

Kids learn about physics from figuring out how to knock down block structures. When meting out punishment to the egg-stealing swine, all you see is the block structures falling down on top of the pigs, causing them to disappear in an explosion. Kids experiment with trajectory, the force of gravity, and structural integrity of block structures as they repeatedly try a level to see if they can earn the coveted three stars. To succeed, kids need to use logic and skill.

 The app allows you to purchase a power-up called Mighty Eagle, which lets you power through a level. Costing $0.99, it has unlimited use, but can be activated only once an hour. It also opens up some new challenges.

 The game offers several other power-ups which are sold separately from the Mighty Eagle. But the settings options within the game allow you to disable these purchases by turning off the Power-up Shop.

 This app connects to Facebook and Twitter.

**Best For:** Kids (and their parents) who enjoy physics-based puzzles.

 If you enjoy these puzzles, three other apps are available. Angry Birds Space is fabulous and brings rotational gravity into the mix. Angry Birds Seasons themes its puzzles to reflect the most current holiday and Angry Birds Rio is tied to the movie *Rio*.

# Where's My Water?
$0.99 US/$0.99 CAN/£0.69 UK, Ages 6 and up, Disney

One of the top games in the iTunes store, this family-friendly puzzler stars Swampy the Alligator. A cute, toothy gator, Swampy is an outcast among the New York City sewer gators because he loves to be clean. But he needs your help to get his shower working. The other alligators don't understand Swampy's need for cleanliness and have been purposely wreaking havoc on the pipes. Swampy needs you to study the subterranean layers of the earth and figure out a way to use your finger to draw a path for the clean water to pick up his three favorite rubber duckies and then land in the pipe that feeds his shower.

The premise is simple, but these puzzles can get devilishly tricky as obstacles such as toxic ooze and expanding algae are introduced. Employing real-life water physics, kids use logical thinking and trial-and-error to solve these puzzles. Many times, you must act at just the right time to split the water into different paths or bring two divergent streams together.

Broken into themed chapters, this app has more than 200 puzzles that are inventive, brainy, and filled with humor. The amusing story is presented periodically between puzzles and features a female alligator named Allie, who sort of takes a shine to Swampy, and the alpha male of the sewer gators, Cranky, who is resentful of Swampy's human-like ways.

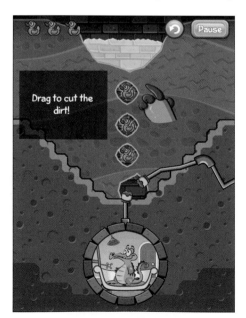

**WARNING!** The home page has direct links to Facebook and Twitter. This app also has in-app purchases to expand into different storylines and puzzle types. For example, Cranky has his own set of 85 puzzles. The first 5 are free, and the rest cost an additional $1.99 via an in-app purchase. See Chapter 1 to learn how to turn off in-app purchases if you're concerned.

**Best For:** Everyone. Young and old alike will be charmed by Swampy, and the puzzles get everyone thinking.

# Temple Run

Free US/CAN/UK, Ages 6 and up, Imangi Studios, LLC

This very popular, free app is known as an *endless runner* — a type of game featuring a character that starts running, and it's up to the player to keep him from harm so that he can keep running.

In Temple Run, you're the guardian of an Indiana Jones–type fortune hunter who has just grabbed an ancient artifact from inside a temple, triggering a horde of chimps to chase him. To keep this angry posse of primates from reaching your runner, you must swipe sideways at T intersections or turns, swipe up to jump, and swipe down to slide under things. You also need to tilt the iPad at crucial times to help your runner collect coins.

When (yes, *when* not *if*) you screw up, the game scores your distance traveled and coins collected, and awards you points for your performance. The game presents a series of challenges, such as running for more than 1,000 meters. The coins you collect can be used within an in-app store to purchase power-ups.

That in-app store also sells additional coins that you can buy with real money. To avoid your child making these kinds of purchases, remember to turn off in-app purchases in your Settings (see Chapter 1). This app also has ads and connects to e-mail, Twitter, and Facebook.

For such a simple concept, this game is surprisingly fun. It's one of those games in which you find yourself thinking that if you play it one more time, you'll surely beat your last try. Other than some quick decision-making and using fast reflexes, kids won't learn much from this game, but if you're looking for pure entertainment, this game delivers.

**Best For:** Kids who like frenetic gameplay. This game is all about responding quickly and appropriately to stimuli that flash across the screen.

# Peggle HD
$0.99 US/$0.99 CAN/£0.69 UK, Ages 6 and up, PopCap

PopCap's blockbuster title is a variation on pinball, where players launch metal balls into a grid of colored pegs. The goal is to hit — and therefore remove — all of the orange pegs in the grid. You have several balls to launch per round, and you control the direction of the ball's initial launch. As in pinball, the balls bounce off other pegs, earning points for each peg hit. Every peg touched by a ball disappears from the grid. The game ends when the last orange peg is hit, or you run out of balls. In the latter case, you have to replay the level to try to clear all of the orange pegs.

Although this premise is simple, the execution can get complicated because other pegs block your way to some of the orange ones. Sometimes, the different colored pegs have special properties, such as a green one that can release a second ball onto the grid when hit. Players can use bank shots, trying to angle the shot to reach an orange peg. Underneath the grid is a moving free ball bucket. If you time your shot (or more likely, if you're just lucky) so that it falls into the moving bucket, you get another free ball to launch.

The game has four modes of play. Adventure mode introduces you to the game and lets you learn by playing with ten different masters. When you clear levels in the Adventure mode, you can then revisit them in the Quick Play mode. The cleared Adventure mode levels are also available to play in Dual Mode, a game that pits you against a friend. You alternate with your friend to shoot balls onto the grid, and the one with the most points when the last orange peg is hit wins. Playing the Adventure Mode also unlocks the Challenge Mode filled with harder puzzles.

Although this game has a fair amount of luck to it, the longer you play, the more you understand that how you direct the ball matters. You use logic and strategy in how to approach each different Peggle board.

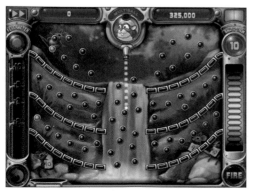

 The game has a store to purchase Peggle Nights, another version with 60 levels, where the first five are free and the rest costs $.99.

**Best For:** Kids who like games with lots of moving parts.

# Cut the Rope HD

$3.99 US/$3.99 CAN/£2.49 UK, Ages 7 and up, Chillingo Ltd

One of the most popular games in the mobile app world, Cut the Rope combines simple physics puzzles with an adorable mascot to create a winning combination that's hard to put down. Om Nom, the endearing, green monster who stars in the more than 300 puzzles, wants nothing more than for you to cut the rope that's holding the candy dangling above his head. You cut the rope(s) by swiping your fingers across the rope. In addition to getting Om Nom his candy, you must also collect three stars by swinging the candy over the stars' location before feeding the bonbon to Om Nom.

At first, the puzzles are pretty easy. Cut one rope, and the candy falls down, passing over the three stars on its way to Om Nom's open mouth. But the fun of these puzzles is that they get progressively harder. You face multiple ropes (some of which are stretchy), as well as constant, new environmental elements. A bubble might encase the candy, resulting in it floating up to reach a star. Can you pop it at just the right time to make it fall into Om Nom's mouth? You encounter blowers, magic hats, electrical currents, spikes, and much more.

Players can tackle these puzzles in many different ways. Because they're instantly replayable, some players won't want to move on until they've achieved the top score by collecting the three stars before feeding Om Nom his candy. Others are fine just getting the candy to Om Nom. In either case, players experiment with physics and timing to win.

For kids needing help, the app offers an in-app purchase of Super Powers as well as a key to unlock all of the more than 300 levels. If you've become a fan of Om Nom (it's hard not to!), you can download a sequel app called Cut the Rope Experiments, which also stars Om Nom, but this time a professor is involved and he's conducting experiments. Eeek! Read my review of this one in Chapter 27.

This app has ads for the sequel to the app, invites you to talk about it on Facebook and Twitter, and can connect to the Crystal gaming network.

**Best For:** Puzzle-lovers looking for amusing, brainy fun.

# Where's My Perry?

$0.99 US/$0.99 CAN/£0.69 UK, Ages 8 and up, Disney

Where's My Perry? is a spy-themed physics puzzler that uses all forms of water — liquid, ice, and steam — to solve over 100 levels of puzzles. Starring Perry from the *Phineas and Ferb* television show, this platypus is really a fedora-wearing, secret spy called Agent P. He had been called to headquarters for a briefing about the newest villainous escapades of Dr. Doofenshmirtz (Dr. Doof), but is stuck in the transportation tubes used to get to headquarters. The tubes are powered by generators that use water or steam, and Dr. Doof has mucked up the channels that allow the water to get to these generators.

In each of the puzzles, you use your finger to draw a path through the dirt for the water or steam to get to the generators. But you have to deal with Dr. Doof's obstacles, including lasers and such. One kind of laser can heat the water to turn it to steam. Another kind freezes water. The challenge is to figure out how to use all of these water-changing devices to your advantage. Instead of collecting three stars, as you do in most puzzle games, in this game you collect garden gnomes that are buried in the dirt. Collecting the three gnomes unlocks bonus levels and allows you to find top-secret collectibles.

Similar in style to the puzzles found in Where's My Water? (earlier in this chapter), these puzzles require thinking, planning, timing, and experimenting. The madcap secret agent theme contributes to the fun. Semiaquatic sleuth Agent P is a riot, and when you fail a level, Dr. Doof delivers a hilarious, sarcastic put-down. These puzzles get progressively harder, but if kids get stuck, they can skip a puzzle.

You unlock the next chapter of puzzles by earning a certain number of gnomes. If your child is struggling, you can unlock one chapter for $0.99 or all chapters for $1.99 via an in-app purchase.

Every time you finish a level, the app asks you to share your score on Facebook. The home page also links to Facebook.

**Best For:** Where's My Water? fans and kids who like fun, wacky physics-based puzzlers.

# Plants vs. Zombies HD

$6.99 US/$6.99 CAN/£4.99 UK, Ages 10 and up, PopCap

This strategy game features an unlikely set of foes: zombie-thwarting plants and the undead. Meant to be funny, not scary, this game is about keeping a hoard of advancing zombies from reaching your house by planting zombie-zapping plants in your front lawn. This type of app is known as a *tower defense strategy game,* and Plants vs. Zombies is the king of this genre.

The main Adventure mode challenges you to defeat the zombie hoards in 50 levels. The key to defeating the undead is your quick wits and speedy planting fingers. You start simply with some sunflower seeds (which produce sunlight, the currency in this world) and pea plants that shoot peas at regular intervals. As you work your way through the levels, you unlock more powerful plants, which can be planted when you've collected enough sunlight. The key to success is planning where on your grid-like lawn to plant your weapons-oriented plants. Some work well in tandem, so you learn to plant the Chomper (a Venus zombie-trap-like plant) behind the Wall-nut because it can reach around this obstacle-creating plant to munch down on unsuspecting zombies. While your plants get more powerful, so do the zombies, and that's what makes this game fun. It requires fast thinking as you fend off bigger bunches of stronger zombies. In addition to the main Adventure mode, you can play several other unlockable modes, including the super-difficult Survival Mode.

I am not much of a zombie fan, but I love this game just because it's done with so much tongue-in-cheek humor. The plant names are hilarious and clever — a Snow Pea plant, of course, shoots frozen peas! And the zombies are never frightening. Even so, because you're blowing them up (with potato mines, cherry bombs, and such), I put the age appropriateness to age 10.

The game contains a button that leads you out of the game to buy Plants vs. Zombies merchandise.

**Best For:** Kids who like fast action, zombies, and/or tower defense strategy games. Playing with these zombies produces undeadly laughter and giggles.

# 13 Games: Great for Kids

## Sprinkle Junior
$1.99 US/$1.99 CAN/£1.49 UK, Ages 4–10, Mediocre AB

Grab your hose and start sprinkling! Kids can do just that in this zany water-physics game, filled with 30 puzzles of fiery fun. Some aliens have crash-landed in a peaceful community, causing the fires to spring up. It's up to you to put the fires out.

Each puzzle opens with some fires burning and your hose nicely positioned on some scaffolding that you can raise and lower as needed. But barriers are in your way of shooting water on the fires. You must figure out what you can manipulate in the environment — either with your finger or by shooting water — to clear the way for the water to get to the fires. This app has no instructions and no time limits as you spray your unlimited supply of water. Sometimes just putting out the fire is not enough to complete the level, so you need to experiment with what else can be done in the landscape of the puzzle. For example, in one of the puzzles, after you put out the fires, you need to move ice cubes into a glass and fill it with water.

I love the open-ended feel of these puzzles for kids. With no time pressures, they can enjoy the exploration of these quirky, charming puzzles.

TIP ⌖ After your kids outgrow these puzzles, the same publisher offers Sprinkle, a more difficult, timed set of water-physics puzzlers.

**Best For:** Kids who love playing with the hose!

# Pajama Sam Thunder and Lightning

$4.99 US/$4.99 CAN/£2.99 UK, Ages 5–8, Nimbus Games Inc

Sam is a little pajama-clad boy who is afraid of violent weather. Tired of being scared during a thunderstorm, Sam decides to emulate his hero, Pajama Man, and dons a cape to become the superhero Pajama Sam. So starts this adventure game in which your child joins the emboldened Pajama Sam in confronting Thunder and Lightning, two charming old ladies he finds running the World Wide Weather factory in the sky. When talking to the weather ladies, Sam accidentally messes up the weather machines. Being a good and polite boy, he offers to help repair the machines. Kids adventure through the clouds filled with weather-making machines to find the four missing parts.

Originally a computer game, this game transfers well onto to the iPad. It looks like a Saturday morning cartoon that's fully interactive. In each scene, you have fascinating gadgets and gizmos to touch; and when you do, they come alive. But it's the adventuring that makes this game so good for kids. Everywhere Pajama Sam goes, he meets crazy weather characters with whom to talk. If Pajama Sam helps a character with his or her problem — such as finding canned sunshine to feed Sid, the snowflake inspector detector — the character helps Pajama Sam find one of the missing parts. Players also need to use keen observation skills to pick up items in the environment that may be helpful, such as a crowbar or a can of sunshine. You can also find puzzle pieces to collect.

Each adventure takes several hours to complete, but the app saves your progress. And this game is replayable because it has alternative parts to find. Kids will love helping superhero Pajama Sam overcome his fear of thunder and lightning; and perhaps, in the process, they will learn how to face their own fears.

**Best For:** Young kids who enjoy going on imaginative adventures. Pajama Sam is one of the best role models for kids because he's courageous, polite, kind, and respectful.

# Flick Champions HD
Free US/CAN/UK, Ages 5-up, Chillingo Ltd

For sport-loving kids, this app brings the heat in eight different sports. It starts with four games (basketball, tennis, hockey, and soccer), and has four more (golf, football, archery, and bowling) waiting to be unlocked. Offering intuitive controls that use the flick or slide of the finger, the app lets kids swoosh baskets, ace serves, and score hat tricks. They can play by themselves or locally against a friend to see who can score the most goals, touchdowns, strikes, holes-in-one, and bulls-eyes in both short exhibition match-ups and longer tournaments. They can even choose to represent a country in World Cup competitions. The blocky little athletes look like Lego characters and sport the colors of your chosen country as they amuse you with their antics.

This app shines because it gives your kids so many sports to explore and in ways that make them accessible for all ages. Kids as young as five can have great success at complex sports like soccer, hockey, and football because these sports are presented as arcade-style games. But older kids (and even adults) will find plenty of challenge as they try to "school" computer-controlled opponents in three levels of difficulty. To keep the app fresh, it periodically unlocks wacky variations and equipment. You can bowl with a Rubik's Cube, throw touchdowns using a jar of pickles, and even smack into your opponent's golf ball.

Kids earn points by playing the first four games. When they accumulate enough points, they can unlock the bowling, archery, golf, and football games. But the developer purposely set the points-bar high, hoping that most families will be willing to spend $.99 to unlock the games (via an in-app purchase) instead of spending hours of playing. Because it's a free app, that $.99 isn't a bad route to go to get eight good sports games from the get-go.

WARNING! This app can connect to the Crystal gaming network, but you have to be 13 to join.

**Best For:** Armchair athletes and families looking for an opportunity to get in some good-natured trash-talking.

# Bag It! HD

$2.99 US/$0.99 CAN/£0.69 UK, Ages 6 and up, Hidden Variable Studios

Who knew that bagging groceries could be so much fun? This game is about doing just that, except these groceries are alive! The eggs start quivering if you hold something heavy — like a watermelon — over their heads. And if you don't heed the visual cues, the foods are crushed, which means you lose points. Also fun is that some items like to be with each other. Pack the juice next to a carton of milk and you discover that you get a bonus because you packed sweethearts next to each other.

This game follows the earn-three-stars model found in a lot of other popular games, including Angry Birds and Cut the Rope (see Chapter 12). You need to experiment with packing the grocery bags to figure out what earns you the three stars. Some of the levels mix up the rules, such as having the goal be to smash as many foods as you can in a limited amount of time instead of carefully packing them. You have more than 60 levels to explore. The main game is called Classic, but a Multiplayer mode has recently been added. Direct your kids to the classic mode because it is about solving a series of progressively harder puzzles.

The multiplayer mode focuses on earning high scores to compare to others using Game Center or Facebook and thus is meant to be played by kids 13 and older. This mode involves purchasing power-ups and has in-app purchases of Gold Coins. It also rewards coins for doing things on Facebook such as "liking" this game. Remember to turn off in-app purchases in the iPad's Settings app and steer your kids to the classic mode instead.

These groceries have such cute personalities and varied preferences that it's hilarious to play with them. The classic mode is a great game for kids because it requires them to experiment to get positive results. This app has a lot of logical thinking going on behind all of the food silliness.

**Best For:** Kids who like to solve puzzles that involve trial and error. Although the early puzzles are pretty easy, they get progressively harder and require some sophisticated thinking that comes only with age.

**A Monster Ate My Homework**
$0.99 US/$0.99 CAN/£0.69 UK, Ages 6 and up, Geek Beach

This 3D physics game presents more than 100 puzzles in which you throw balls at geometric-shaped monsters. Sitting on top of a box, these monsters are hiding among your homework. The challenge is to knock off the monsters while keeping your homework on top of the box. Similar in format to the popular Boom Blox video game, kids need to rotate the scene to look at where the monsters are hiding in relation to the homework.

You throw balls by tapping on the screen where you want the ball to hit. Frequently, the monsters are lurking over or under the homework; so well-placed throws that keep in mind the physics of a situation provide the key to success. If you knock some of your homework off, you lose a star. The goal is to try to earn three stars per puzzle, but you can move on with earning one or two stars. It may take multiple tries before you succeed at the puzzle. The puzzles get progressively harder as you move from the first set of 20, designated as First Grade to those labeled Second Grade and beyond.

The monsters are so much fun to interact with because their eyes follow you as you rotate the scene 360 degrees. They playfully growl at

you and stick out their tongues. Don't be surprised when you hear them grunting when hit. Kids use trial and error plus reasoning to discover the best strategies to make the force of a ball move the monsters. Although kids may think that they're just having fun knocking down block structures, winning actually involves a fair amount of strategic reasoning.

 The home page has direct links to Twitter and Facebook. Grade Third and up can be unlocked via an in-app purchase.

**Best For:** Kids who like puzzles with a lot of action. Although the monsters never appear to be hurt, this is a game about hurling balls at the animated, blocky monsters.

# Munch Time HD

$1.99 US/$1.99 CAN/£1.49 UK, Ages 7 and up, Gamistry

In this physics puzzler game, you control a cute chameleon named Munch. In each of the 84 levels, your goal, after swinging by to pick up three stars, is to guide the hungry Munch to his favorite buggy lunch. Munch's sticky tongue, which acts like a grappling hook, provides the key play mechanic as you direct him to swing from one colored flower to another. However, Munch can stick only to flowers that are the same color as his skin. Luckily, being a chameleon, Munch can easily change color by munching on fluttering paint bugs.

Reminiscent of the Om Nom character (who stars in Cut the Rope — see Chapter 12) in his cuteness and constant need to eat, Munch is fun to play with because he's adorable. These puzzles require logical thinking and good timing to win. Tapping a flower when its petals are open allows Munch's tongue to attach to the flower; and tapping again in mid-swing allows him to keep sailing through the air in the direction he was swinging when you last tapped. You need to use this process to move him from flower to flower over the screen. Although you can unlock the next puzzle by merely collecting one star per puzzle, the win-three-stars mechanic encourages kids to try again to see if they can figure out how to get to all three stars.

With smooth music and a loveable main character, this game creates a gentler vibe than a game like Angry Birds (see Chapter 12), but the increasing difficulty and the variety of challenges makes it just as intellectually stimulating.

The main page has direct links to Facebook, Twitter, and ads for other apps by this developer.

**Best For:** Kids who love nature and gentler games. Munch delivers lots of lizard-swinging fun, without creating much of an adrenaline rush.

# Beat Sneak Bandit
$2.99 US/$2.99 CAN/£1.99 UK, Ages 8 and up, Simogo

If your kids like music and puzzles, this is the game for them. Bandit and his sidekick Herbie star as two thieves stealing to do good! Duke Clockface has stolen all of the world's clocks and stashed them away in his mansion. It's up to you, Bandit, and Herbie to sneak them all back. The gameplay requires that you use rhythm, stealth, and brains as you scour the Duke's mansion looking for clocks.

The game is presented in four chapters and a finale. Each chapter has ten regular levels that involve figuring out how to reach (and snatch!) a special flag-bearing clock. But extra clocks are in each level, and by collecting those, you unlock the harder bonus levels known as Shadow Mansion levels. Each chapter offers four Shadow Mansion levels.

A level looks like the inside of a dollhouse, with four floors of the house revealed. You play by listening to the beat of the funky music, and by timing Bandit's movements to that beat. When you tap the screen, Bandit runs in the direction he's facing until he hits something (the wall or a security guard, for example). You must ascend and descend stairs, avoid trap doors or fall through, miss spotlights,

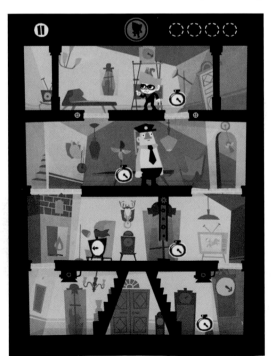

and avoid many other obstacles in the environment. You need to move when the security guard isn't looking; or the challenge may be to avoid the vacuum-buster that's trying to suck you up. The puzzles get progressively harder, and the game ends with a battle against the Duke himself.

Although these puzzles get difficult, the game offers you the ability to skip the level you've failed several times and come back later. This is a unique puzzle game in the sea of iPad games, and one that nicely combines great graphics, a fun use of rhythm, and interesting puzzle mechanics.

**Best For:** Tweens and teens who enjoy music and puzzles. Don't be surprised to see your kids' toes tapping and bodies grooving as they puzzle this one out.

# LEGO Harry Potter: Years 1–4

$4.99 US/$0.99 CAN/£0.69 UK, Ages 8 and up, Warner Bros.

Your child can become Harry Potter in this Lego-esque version of the events found in the first four books of J.K. Rowling's *Harry Potter* series. This adventure game lets you puzzle your way through 40 stunning levels of *Harry Potter* scenery and events. You meet and can even play with more than 100 characters, including Ron and Hermione. As Harry, you perform spells, duel, mix potions, and even fly on broomsticks. Because this is a Lego game, the world you explore is made of Legos. You collect lots of things within the game, but the most obvious are Lego bricks, the currency of this world. Also, because the cutscenes are acted by Lego equivalents of the characters, the scenes are always tongue-in-cheek, which makes them hilarious to watch.

*Harry Potter* fans will relish visiting all of the locations and scenes from the books and movies, including Diagon Alley, Ollivander's Wand Shop, Gringotts, Hogwarts, Hogsmeade, and more. Kids have to figure out which of the many characters in a scene can do the magic required and then switch between characters by tapping the head of the one they're currently playing. This game also offers a brilliant navigation system allowing you to control your character by simply having it follow your touches or by using a virtual D-Pad that appears on the bottom-left corner of the screen. Plus, you can see where you are in the level by using the map in the upper right. To talk to characters, you walk up to them and tap. The game sends you on many missions and it automatically keeps track of when you accomplish them.

This is the best *Harry Potter* app in iTunes. It's fascinating to explore, and it stays fresh by constantly introducing new environmental puzzles.

**Best For:** *Harry Potter* fans. Your wannabe magicians will be in Hogwarts heaven.

# Max and the Magic Marker for iPad

$2.99 US/$2.99 CAN/£1.99 UK, Ages 8 and up, Electronic Arts

This unique game pays homage to the classic children's book, *Harold and the Purple Crayon,* by creating a character named Max who owns a magical pen. The fun part is that your child gets to wield the magical pen inside the game to draw solutions for Max. This iPad game was originally released on the Wii, PC, and Mac.

Presented as a video, the back story is that when Max receives this mysterious pen in the mail, he immediately draws with it. Unfortunately, the first thing he draws is a monster that comes alive and jumps into other paintings Max had on the floor. To keep the monster from mucking up his drawings, Max draws himself into the paintings. So starts this physics-based puzzler about running and jumping through three different worlds. You control Max and want to make sure that you figure out ways to reach the globes of orange ink that power your magic pen. You must also find gold time spheres as well as elusive black ones.

What makes this game so much fun is that you play it the way you want to. When faced with a chasm, you design your bridge. Need to reach a high-up ledge? Should you draw a teeter-totter and drop a stone on top to catapult yourself up, or simply draw stairs? Things get tricky because you have a limited supply of ink. Also, some of the environmental puzzles and platform jumping can get a little tricky, but in a fun way.

I love that creativity is built into playing this game. No two players play it the same way. By making it personal, kids become more invested in the game.

**Best For:** Creative kids who enjoy coming up with solutions to problems.

# World of Goo HD

$4.99 US/$4.99 CAN/£2.99 UK, Ages 8 and up, 2D BOY

Winner of many game-of-the-year awards, this fascinating physics puzzler stars squirming, wiggling, gibberish-talking balls of goo. These balls like to stick together to form structures that wobble and tilt as other goo balls run across their surfaces. When mysterious pipes appear in their world, the goo balls are inexplicably attracted to pipes that suck them up.

A humorous but wispy story line ties these puzzles together. However, it's the inventive and highly engaging puzzle levels that are at the heart of this game. In each, the goo balls need your help to put them together into structures that allow them to reach the pipes. To solve a puzzle level, you must get the minimum number of goo balls to the exit pipe. But this is not always easy because dangers in the environment can wipe out the balls, dangers such as spikes, spinning blades, pits of doom, chasms, and other obstacles. You need to learn how to build bridges, cantilevered structures, towers, and more to solve these puzzles.

When you bring a goo ball near another, it automatically sends out sticky tendrils to make triangulated structures. And as you play, you meet different kinds of goo balls. Some become solid after attached, others can be pulled off a structure and repositioned higher. Some absorb a helium-like gas to make them float, and others look like they're made of water and stretch farther than expected. Some even ignite and cause chain reactions. This is an amazing learning environment because it encourages experimentation with physics principles.

The goo balls blink at you and make noises when excited, which makes them endearing. Some appear in dramatic black-and-white environments. The musical score that accompanies these puzzles varies, depending on the threat to the balls.

Although I love solving these puzzles, the other fun part of this game is the cryptic and witty messages left by the Sign Painter. These serve to provide you hints and also move the story forward. The puzzles get more difficult, so kids may benefit by brainstorming with a parent or older sibling.

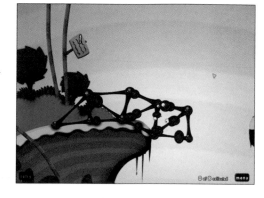

**Best For:** Kids who enjoy Legos and building sets. These sentient building materials shouldn't be missed!

# Bad Piggies

$2.99 US/$0.99 CAN/£1.99 UK, Ages 9 and up, Rovio
Entertainment Ltd

Pigs are flying in this Angry Birds sequel. The egg-stealing swine are back, and this time they are the star of their own game. Have they learned their lesson about taking eggs from birds? No. Somehow they've dragged you into their dastardly schemes as you assist them in constructing a variety of machines to help them navigate crazy environments on their search for the Angry Birds' eggs. Each puzzle involves building some kind of contraption to encase a piggie and then testing out your contraption to see if it can navigate that level's landscape to reach the ending point (while also earning the coveted three stars). The game has 72 levels broken into 2 sets, with 18 additional puzzles unlocked by earning 3 stars in the other puzzles. You can eventually unlock a sandbox mode where you can experiment with building your own bigger contraptions.

In the first set of puzzles called Groundhog Day, the contraptions you build have a go-kart feel to them, sort of rickety and homemade. You drag boxes together, add some wheels and some sort of crazy propulsion, including umbrellas, fans, air bellows, and others; and then you place your determined pig inside. Most scenes have TNT explosives in them, which can hurt or help you, depending on where they send your piggie flying. In the second set of puzzles, appropriately called When Pigs Fly, it's all about flying. There you start with balloons and add more sophisticated propulsion as you progress.

These puzzles have a madcap feel to them that may appeal to some, but not to others. Also, they are harder than the puzzles found in Angry Birds. As a consequence, I set the age appropriateness at age 9 instead of age 6 as for Angry Birds.

TIP

If you get stuck, you can use money to hire a mechanic (they start at 10 for $1.99).

WARNING!

The game contains ads for other Rovio games.

**Best For:** Kids who enjoy tinkering with engineering movable devices and relish a more difficult challenge in their puzzles.

# Scribblenauts Remix

$0.99 US/$0.99 CAN/£0.69 UK, Ages 10 and up, Warner Bros.

Based on an award-winning video game series, Scribblenauts Remix is an inventive puzzle game where you analyze a scene, brainstorm how to solve the problem presented, and then literally write items into the scene for you to use. For example, if you need the lead character Maxwell to cross a chasm, you can write in the words *flying bathtub,* and he can whiz over the expanse in style.

The 50 puzzles all feature Maxwell, whose goal is to find, unlock, or reach a special puzzle-winning star called a *starlite*. A puzzle starts with a hint about what you need to do to solve the puzzle. For example, one puzzle starts with telling you that you need to kick off a beach party. You see Maxwell and two others on a beach. By writing in a surfboard for one and a bucket for the other, the characters become happy and the starlite appears. But you could have written in hamburgers and soda, or a giant crab and a beach ball.

What I love about this app is that it encourages kids to use their imagination to solve the puzzles. There is no one right answer, so kids can get creative. Plus, many of the puzzles can be solved only by experimenting. Hints are available, as is a special identify mode where you can run a magnifying glass over an object to get more information about it. By writing in objects, kids practice spelling; and if they spell a word incorrectly, the app offers them words that are close to what they spelled. They can even add adjectives to their creations so as to conjure up a rainbow dolphin or a colossal winged toaster to ride. Some of the things you can think up are weapons, which can attack, or predators (who eat others), which is why I recommend this app for ages 10 and up.

The app has links to Facebook.

An in-app purchase of $0.99 unlocks a World Pass and 40 new puzzles. It's fun and worth it!

**Best For:** All kids who enjoy using their imagination. My family plays this app on long car trips, with everyone suggesting outlandish solutions to try!

# 14 Girl Power: Heroines, Fashion, and Princesses

## Little Bella's - I Close My Eyes HD

$1.99 US/$1.99 CAN/£1.49 UK, Ages 3–7, Out Fit 7 Ltd.

Little Bella is a little girl with a big imagination. This story app is filled with Bella's fanciful imaginings that occur when she closes her eyes. Telling us these adventures is a charming little-girl voice that narrates the words of Bella's dreams. After each imagining, the app changes from words on the page to full animation that looks like you're watching an animated movie. In this manner, your children watch Bella climb the tallest tree, run so fast that she skims over the surface of the water, turns into a dolphin to frolic in the ocean, and becomes a caterpillar that turns into a chrysalis and emerges as a gorgeous butterfly. There is nothing that Bella can't do.

The tale of girl empowerment is a wonderful one to share with all children, but especially little girls. Bella isn't afraid to imagine herself in outrageous situations, including being a big stomping giant or a slimy slug. Her outlandish imaginings are sure to get your kids giggling.

**Best For:** Little girls; although, all children can be motivated to think big by playing this app. The book doesn't have an autoplay feature, so you may need to remind very young kids to tap to make the story move forward.

# Angelina Ballerina's New Ballet Teacher

$2.99 US/$2.99 CAN/£1.99 UK, Ages 3–7, Callaway Digital Arts Inc.

For girls who love ballet, this book app will make them pirouette with pleasure. It tells the story of a little girl mouse who must adjust to the ways of a new, less rigid ballet teacher. Although she's initially resistant, Angelina learns that her new teacher's novel approach has some positive benefits. This app's video-like animations reinforce the story and are smooth and lovely to watch. The app also has special pop-up glossary boxes that explain and show ballet moves. Plus, kids can put together jigsaw puzzles from the scenes in the book, play an arcade game, and color pictures using a simple paint program.

This is a delightful story about change and how to adjust to it. It's a must for fans of this famous mouse from the books and TV show.

**Best For:** Fans of Angelina Ballerina. It's also good for all girls who are interested in ballet.

# The adventure of the 7Wonderlicious girls

Free US/CAN/UK, Ages 3–7, 7Wonderlicious Pty. Ltd.

This app presents 28 story cards about 7 Wonderlicious girls. Meant to be discussion starters for girls and their parents, each card presents one of the girls doing something helpful. For example, Neela's mother is handy and teaches her how to fix a broken hose. Mimi sees that her pet cat doesn't like walking in puddles, so she picks her up to carry her across the park. That story card reminds readers that healthy girls can help others by carrying heavy things. Other stories feature girls fixing their bikes, exercising every day, being a leader, speaking up when they see someone doing something wrong, aspiring to become an astronaut, working with others to solve a problem, enjoying studying science, and other empowering activities.

Although these story cards don't have animation or interactivity, they are well written to inspire girls to be bold, helpful, adventurous, creative, and confident in who they are.

**Best For:** All girls. These seven wonderlicious girls are great role models for little kids growing up today.

# Pickle's Paper Dolls
$1.99 US/$1.99 CAN/£1.49 UK, Ages 3–7, Playtend Apps LLP

If you're looking for a wholesome dress-up game for your young daughter, Pickle's Paper Dolls is my top choice.

The app provides six lovely dolls from around the world to dress up. The dolls hail from the United States, Argentina, Ethiopia, England, France, and China. Girls select a doll and then have their doll try on more than 200 items from the closet. The dress-up items are sorted into categories, and girls scroll sideways to select the item they want to try. In addition to tops, bottoms, dresses, shoes, and accessories, the app also lets girls personalize their model's eyes and hairstyle. Before snapping a photo to save in the iPad's photos, girls can select an international background for their doll.

You can find hundreds of dress-up apps in iTunes, and many are free, but they constantly bombard your kids with requests to buy new clothes. Worse, many of the dolls are over-sexualized. What sets this dress-up app apart from others is that it enables little girls to enjoy the process of dressing up dolls without distractions from ads. The clothing items are all in the closet to try on — you just tap the item. And you have plenty of age-appropriate clothing options that vary greatly.

I also selected this app because it provides dolls that represent different races. Little girls can see beauty represented by dolls from around the world. If your iPad is connected to an AirPrint-enabled Printer, you can print your creations, cut them out, and play with them away from the iPad.

When you first start the app, go to the settings button in the app. From there, find the "Childlock" option. By turning on Childlock, you turn off the button that leads to other apps by this publisher, e-mailing, in-app purchases, and printing. This is an excellent feature, so activate it before handing your iPad to your child. You can always deactivate Childlock if you want to use any of those features.

**Best For:** Little girls interested in exploring fashion.

## Princess Fairy Tale Maker - by Duck Duck Moose
$1.99 US/$1.99 CAN/£1.49 UK, Ages 4–9, Duck Duck Moose

Girls can produce their own fairy tales using this simple story-creating app. They select the setting, the characters, and record their own voice telling the tale. Then they can share their creation with family and friends.

From the home page, storytellers choose to start with a premade fairy tale scene or a black-lined coloring page. If they choose the fairy tale scene, they can select from 32 premade scenes that range from castles to clouds to the deep sea. What's cool about these scenes is that they're animated. If you set your story in the clouds — the clouds move across the sky. Kids can also select a blank scene or a photo from the iPad's camera roll.

If you start with a coloring page, you can use a simple art program to color it. This app has 32 coloring pages, some inspired by classics such as Cinderella and Red Riding Hood; but others let their heroines explore the moon or rescue a sleeping prince. You can use crayons or pencils, as well as patterns and stickers. You can even use animated patterns and overlays to do things like fill the sky with stars that sparkle.

After you've set the stage, you can then add characters, scenery, and other extras. Many of these items can be resized by pinching and pulling. Then, it's time for action as you direct your own fairy tale, recording your story as you move the characters around. All of this is saved as a video for later playback. You can even create separate scenes and bundle them to create longer movies.

Little girls (and even little boys) can create and act out anything their imaginative minds come up with. I especially like the magic wand feature that lets younger kids simply tap the scene to automatically fill each area with color. And the role reversal in which the prince is sleeping and the princess rescues him is a great addition.

**Best For:** Girls who enjoy telling their own stories. This app provides just the right tools to inspire storytellers to share their stories.

This publisher has a companion app for boys called Superhero Comic Book Maker HD - by Duck Duck Moose Design.

# Builda the Re-Bicycler
$1.99 US/$1.99 CAN/£1.49 UK, Ages 5–8, Midlandia Press

This highly animated book app stars Builda O. Bobo, an anthropomorphized dog who is the owner of the Bike Factory in the city of Midlandia. She has been very successful because all of the Midlandia residents use bicycles to get around. But the Midlandians have a habit of tossing their bikes into the town dump whenever something goes wrong or — gasp — even as a whim. When Firefighter Sparky comes to Builda requesting a new bike because he has a flat tire, she notices that the dump is now full. Builda has the idea to make the dump smaller by sorting the old bike parts into usable and unusable piles. Instead of building a new bike for Firefighter Sparky, she decides to reuse a tire from the dump. She calls her idea Re-bicycling. When that word is too long to fit on a poster sharing her idea with the community, she shortens her idea to Recycle. The Midlandia community loves Builda's idea about recycling. As the citizens embrace re-bicycling, they discover that they can recycle other materials as well (such as cans, bottles, and paper). Builda becomes a hero of her community and earns the Spirit of Midlandia trophy.

This app has it all: amazing animations on each page, words that are highlighted as read, fascinating characters and illustrations, fun interactive hotspots, and a terrific story.

But even more important are its two vital messages: Recycling is important and one little idea can make a huge difference. Builda is a great role model for all kids, but particularly girls. She's smart and resourceful, and proves to be a leader of her community. As a strong, inventive female character, she is one that little girls can aspire to imitate.

**Best For:** Little girls and eco-conscious kids. The book app even offers discussion questions at the end to facilitate kids' focusing on how they can help in their communities.

This publisher creates thoughtful book apps, so if you liked this one, you might enjoy Be a Buddy, Not a Bully about anti-bullying.

# Pixeline and the Jungle Treasure HD

$3.99 US/$3.99 CAN/£2.49 UK, Ages 8 and up, osao

Pixeline is one of those rare games starring a girl. She's plucky, adventurous, and on a hunt to find treasure in the rainforest. This 2D side-scroller game plays like one of Nintendo's *Mario* games. Pixeline travels through three game worlds and many different terrains, from rainforest to ruins to swamp. In the rainforest, Pixeline is investigating the rumors of jungle treasure guarded by shape-shifting spirits.

As Pixeline runs sideways, she occasionally encounters furry-looking baddies that can be dispatched by jumping on their heads. You control Pixeline by using two onscreen buttons, one for running and one for jumping. This game's environments are full of floating platforms (which makes it a *platform puzzler* in gaming vernacular), chasms, and other perilous terrains; so learning how to time Pixeline's jumps is one of the key play mechanics. You also need to use logic to figure out how to get to where you need to go. The game's tutorial is good, so if your daughter has never played this type of game, this is a good one to start with.

With 23 levels, this is a game girls can enjoy for quite some time. It's about collecting coins, finding hidden keys, unlocking chests, and dispatching pesky baddies. You have a certain number of lives, as indicated by hearts, but you can earn more hearts by collecting silver coins. It also uses a fun, shape-shifting mechanic in which Pixeline gets to become three different jungle animals. By using these animal abilities, she can fit into tiny spaces or approach enemies in different ways. I include Pixeline in this chapter because it's a nice break from the dress-up and ballet apps. Here is a heroine who is fearless and loves adventure.

**Best For:** Girl gamers. This is a traditional platform puzzler with lots of exploring, jumping, and timing.

# 15 Learning Apps: Language Arts

## Reading Raven HD

$3.99 US/$3.99 CAN/2.49 UK, Ages 3–7, Early Ascent, LLC

Reading Raven HD is a phonics-based learning game. It teaches reading as part of an adventure, so kids enjoy the process of learning how to read! The app has five sequential lessons, each with a different setting, ranging from visiting a circus to blasting into outer space. The lessons offer a variety of different learning games, each incorporating the theme of the setting. The games focus on letter and word tracing, letter and word matching, word beginnings, spelling, word identifications, rhyming, and more. The app also asks kids to read aloud, and it records their sounds for playback. Kids earn cute items to decorate Reading Raven's treehouse.

These sequential reading lessons do a great job of introducing kids to phonics and sight words in a wide variety of fun games. For example, while at the circus, kids play games with tight-rope walkers and trained lions to match words. The app is careful to offer clear pronunciation of individual sounds and blending, picture associations, the ability to hear an item's name when tapped, and positive feedback delivered in children's voices. Parents have lots of options deciding what they want their kids to study, nicely hidden under a child lock (only an adult can activate).

**Best For:** Kids learning to read, as well as those already starting. You can jump in to any of the lessons.

# Reading Rainbow
Free ($9.99/mo; $29.99/6 mos.) US/CAN,
Age 3–9, Reading Rainbow

Featuring LeVar Burton, the original host of the long-running PBS television show of the same name, this reading service on the iPad is a way to constantly provide quality books for your child to read. The books can be read aloud with light animation and interactivity. The service tracks your child's age, sex, and interests to make recommendations based on that information. The hundreds of books available are found on floating islands in the sky, with each island reflecting different interests. One island includes books about action, adventure, and magical tales. Another focuses on animals. Two others are called Genius Academy and My Friends My Family. Kids can carry five books at a time in their personal backpack, and those can be read even when the iPad is not connected to the Internet. In addition to reading, kids can play some reading-related games. And as with the TV show on which this service is based, kids can watch videos starring Burton acting out roles or taking kids on field trips.

Although this app is free to download, the free version allows your child to read only one book. To use this service, parents need to sign up for a $9.99 monthly subscription or $29.99 for 6 months. Parents receive e-mail reports about the minutes read. The service also provides parents with discussion questions based on the books read, and it makes suggestions for new books based on what your child has read.

I include this reading service because LeVar Burton and his team do an excellent job of providing good books read by exciting, professional storytellers. Burton himself reads about 15 percent of them. When I interviewed Burton about his service, I was impressed with how passionate he is about sharing the love of good storytelling. But, this service isn't perfect. The books do not highlight the words when read, a flaw I hope this book service corrects because highlighting helps kids learn to associate the spoken word with the written one. And these books are just calling for more fanciful animations, so I hope that the books eventually get more interactivity.

**Best For:** Families who use their iPad as the equivalent of going to the library. This makes hundreds of books available for children to enjoy.

# LetterSchool
$2.99 US/$2.99 CAN/£1.99 UK, Ages 4–6, Boreaal

LetterSchool is an interactive adventure that makes learning to write letters fun. Its four-part process is both effective and highly entertaining. The app introduces a letter, shows it being drawn, lets kids trace it, and then asks kids to write it on their own. But this isn't your typical paper and pencil exercise.

When kids choose a letter from the alphabet-filled screen, the app introduces the letter's name, shows a toy object that starts with that letter, and speaks the object's name slowly so that kids can hear the letter's sound. Nothing unusual there — tons of apps do that. What happens next is the interesting part.

Three buttons appear on the bottom of the screen, and the first one bounces. After touching it, a big letter pops up onscreen, with dots showing where you change directions when writing it. When you tap the first dot, something surprising happens: It may be that a rocket flies down the path that shows how to draw the letter, leaving sparkling stars in its wake. Or, it could be that the letter is drawn as a row of candies. This magical ink makes the learning fun.

But that's not all. When kids tap the second button on the bottom of the screen and start to trace a letter, they are again met with the magical ink. What appears under their finger might be a line of green grass or maybe railroad tracks. After kids trace the letter, a silly animation appears, such as a lawn mower cutting the grass ink or a train driving down the ink tracks. These animations reinforce how to draw the letter. When kids tap the last button on the bottom of the screen, the writing activity commences, using white paint or chalk. The app adjusts its guidance, depending on how much help your child needs.

With two levels and options for three styles of writing (D'Nealian, Zaner-Bloser, and HWT (Handwriting Without Tears)), covering both letters and numbers, this app offers a lot to practice. The only thing missing is an option for left-handedness, but it's coming. The constantly changing, sleek animations, coupled with fabulous sound effects keep kids interested.

**Best For:** Children who need practice writing their letters and numbers. With its fun and delightful animated ink, this app is a great choice for reluctant learners.

TIP

Other good handwriting choices are iWrite Words (Handwriting Game) in Chapter 3 and Touch and Write in Chapter 24.

# Noodle Words HD – Action Set 1

$2.99 US/$2.99 CAN/£1.99 UK, Ages 4–7, NoodleWorks

If you're looking for a fun way to increase your child's vocabulary, you should download this app. With the help of two adorable animated bugs named Stretch and Squish, your child plays — yes PLAYS — with 18 words. A cute bee teaches your child how to play and then presents your child with a box of words. Tapping the box makes the words rise one at a time onto the screen.

Touching a word makes it animate in a way to reinforce its meaning. When playing with the word *dance,* the letters sway and sashay around the screen. Stretch and Squish also dance to reinforce the concept. If you shake the iPad, the music changes. For the word *sparkle,* shiny confetti shoots out of the letters when you tap them. For the word *grow,* a flowing vine grows out of the word, while Stretch and Squish each get bigger if you tap them. The word *spin* actually physically spins in a circle, creating enough of a breeze that if you drag it near the bugs, you can see them being buffeted by the wind.

My favorite word to play with is *surprise.* Every time you touch the word, it does something unpredictable and, well. . . *surprising.* Your child will laugh out loud at the antics of this word as it tries to sneak up on the unsuspecting bugs to *surprise* them.

For emergent readers, this app makes learning new words fun. It helps with comprehension by presenting meaningful but silly animations that reinforce the definition of the word. By playing Noodle Words, kids are exposed to new words in a context that can help them understand and retain their meaning.

**Best For:** Kids who are just starting to read. This app uses humor and creativity to construct a zany learning environment for kids. Don't miss this one.

Mom, Pop and Peg had a hat.

# Bob Books #2 – Reading Magic HD
$3.99 US/$3.99 CAN/£2.49 UK, Ages 5–7, Learning Touch

This is the second app in the Bob Books series based on the popular book series that has taught millions of kids to read — including my son Peter. This app presents 12 scenes to read, with more than 50 words to learn.

Kids see a very simple drawing made with black ink on white paper. A sentence is on the bottom of the page. A character in the drawing or an object wiggles, trying to get your child to touch it. When he does, the reading begins.

The object touched now fills the page with just one word shown below it in shaded letters. Strewn around the page, kids see bold letter blocks to drag and drop onto the shaded letters. If kids touch a letter block, the app makes that letter's sound. When all of the letters are in their correct spots, the app makes each letter sound in order and then reads the word. Kids are rewarded when the object fills with vivid color, and that image now appears in the main reading page. Kids continue to select, spell, and learn to read each of the main words on the page until the whole sentence can be read. The page transforms into vibrant color and animation.

The app lets kids work through four levels of reading. The one described above is Level 1. Level 2 requires kids to drag the letters in order; Level 3 doesn't show the visual clues; and Level 4 adds extra letters to the page.

Learning phonics and how to read the 50 words becomes fun because the sentences are silly. In one, a dog sits on a hat and a cat. In another, a dog and a pig are driving cars. The levels allow kids the support they need at first, and then gradually remove it as they gain confidence.

**Best For:** Early readers. This app provides kids support so that they feel comfortable trying to sound out words.

 The first Bob Books app is equally as good, and I review it in Chapter 4.

# The Opposites

$2.99 US/Free CAN/Free UK, Ages 7 and up,
Mindshapes Limited

The Opposites is a word game that makes the process of learning antonyms fun. Presented as a girl and boy being snarky with each other, one says a word and the other counters. The words float about their heads into a contained space. The object of the game is to clear the words by tapping pairs that are opposite. If you can't match up the pairs before the space fills up with words, you lose the level and have to try again. Occasionally, a word is highlighted, and if you make its match, you earn more time between new words appearing.

The app offers ten levels of words, and players can study them in the in-app dictionary before taking on a level. In Level 1, kids match words such as fat and thin, bad and good. By Level 5, you're handling words like optimistic and pessimistic, and malevolent and benevolent. Word masters who reach Level 10 face the words aggravate and appease or compulsory and voluntary.

The competitive, combative way that the tween girl and boy deliver the words to each other makes this game amusing. And it's empowering to correctly match the words (which turn green) and see them disappear. If kids don't want to cram before playing the game, that's okay because enough time is built in to let you learn as you go. Mismatch two words — no big deal — they just turn red for a short time and stay onscreen so you can try again.

**Best For:** Learning words and expanding kids' vocabularies in a game format. SATs coming down the line? No problem!

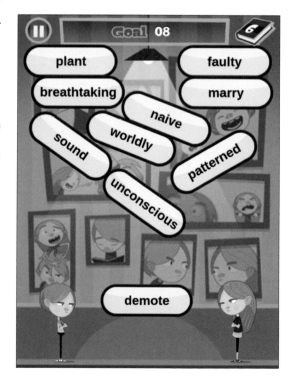

# Word Mess

$0.99 US/$0.99 CAN/£0.69 UK, Ages 8 and up, Masala Games

This fast-paced word game tests visual perception, rhyming ability, and general knowledge of words by presenting three different types of games. All are set to funky, upbeat techno music that helps you get in the word-finding zone.

In one type of game, the screen fills with about 25 words scattered in all different directions and colors. The challenge is to find all of the copies of a specific word (such as *drinks*) nestled among other words. As time passes, more words appear to create more of a "word mess." The second game is about finding all of the words that rhyme with a target word, such as *band,* in the middle of the jumble of words. You look for *land, sand, bland,* and others in that rhyming family. In the third game, you look for vocabulary words that relate to a topic, such as the word *fish* or *beach.* For the latter, you look for the words *sandcastles, water, volleyball,* and so on. In each of the three games, you're rewarded points for speed, the number of words found, and whether you used a hint.

These three games can be enjoyed in two ways: Quick Play or Challenge. In the former, you decide which of the three types of games you want to play. In Challenge, the type of game you play is controlled by the app. This mode also introduces a new game called a Bonus Round, which sends you hunting for the odd word in a cloud of identical words. The Challenge mode ends when you fail to find all of the words in the time given.

Although Word Mess presents a jumble of words onscreen, its clean design and simple rules make it a pleasure to play. This is one of those learning games in which kids will be begging to play "just one more game."

**Best For:** All kids. This is a word game that feels accessible to everyone. Unlike crosswords or Scrabble, kids can expand their vocabularies without feeling intimated by the gameplay or their opponents. For younger kids, it could be a fun app for a parent to explore with the child, each tapping words together on the same screen.

# Shakespeare in Bits: Romeo & Juliet iPad Edition

$14.99 US/Free CAN/£10.49 UK, Ages 12 and up,
Mindconnex Learning Ltd.

"O Romeo, Romeo, wherefore art thou Romeo?" He can be on your iPad in an amazing app that makes the bard accessible for kids. In this Shakespeare in Bits version, kids can watch two and one half hours of an animated version of the play, while reading the unabridged text shown alongside of the video. With Kate Beckinsale and Michael Sheen voicing the leads, the performance helps kids to understand the play. The sometimes difficult word constructions can be translated by simply touching them in the text. The app also provides biographies of the characters and a character relationship map. Kids can access section notes, summaries, and analyses, as well as a map to jump to any scene they want.

The concept of breaking Shakespeare into bits works well to help tweens and teens understand this classic play. I particularly like that kids can listen to this fully voiced and acted play while watching the words being highlighted as the action unfolds. They can pause the production to tap the colored phrases of the Elizabethan poetry for translation into contemporary, recognizable phrases (*piteous overthrows* becomes *misfortunate setbacks*). The app even has a place to take notes as you watch. This amazing blend of classic literature with new technology works so well that I believe even the bard himself would be impressed.

If you think your family would like to explore more of Shakespeare in Bits, check out A Midsummer Night's Dream, Macbeth, Hamlet, and Julius Caesar. You can opt to download the free Shakespeare in Bits app, and then purchase Romeo & Juliet from within that app as an in-app purchase. The price is the same, but all of your plays are found within the same app. Because this app is geared toward older children, the connections to Facebook and Twitter aren't troubling the way they are with apps for younger children.

**Best For:** Tweens and teens studying or interested in Romeo and Juliet. This app makes watching the play compelling and poignant.

# 16 Learning Apps: Math

## Motion Math: Hungry Guppy

$2.99 US/$2.99 CAN/£1.99 UK, Ages 3–7, Motion Math

If you're looking for a fun way to teach your child number recognition and beginning addition in a game-like setting, this is the app for you.

Kids play this game by feeding numbered bubbles to a guppy fish. The app divides its content into three difficulty levels to accommodate children of different ages.

On the first level, kids learn that the guppy has dots on his side to indicate what kind of bubble he eats. Kids practice combining two one-dot bubbles to make a two-dot bubble to feed the guppy that has two dots on his side. The levels eventually introduce bubbles and guppies with one, two, three, four, or five dots. Level two mixes dots with numbers. Level three is completely numbers. Periodically within a level, kids win color pearls to feed to their guppy. The pearl allows them to customize their guppy's color.

Through this clever mechanism of feeding the guppy, kids learn counting and simple addition. Kids as young as 3 can play because no reading is involved.

**Best For:** Introducing numbers and addition through play. Kids find this cute guppy irresistible.

 This is the first in a suite of apps from Motion Math. The next one is Motion Math: Hungry Fish, which covers harder addition, subtraction, and even negative numbers.

# Little Digits
$1.99 US/$1.99 CAN/£1.49 UK, Ages 3–6, Cowly Owl Ltd

From the moment I opened this app, I could see that these developers understand kids. Their corporate logo is a pair of owl eyes that fill the screen and blink. Nice! But their app is even better. Little Digits brilliantly uses iPad technology to teach early counting, addition, and subtraction.

By simply placing their fingers on the screen, kids learn to count and do simple addition and subtraction. For counting, the screen first fills with a zero that's been turned into an animated character with eyes that blink and a mouth that opens. If your child puts a finger on the screen, the zero character disappears and is instantly replaced with an animated 1. Add another finger, and the screen becomes an animated 2, and so on to 10. This simple but charming method of connecting the number of fingers touching the screen to the numbers shown is highly effective. Because the numbers are animated, kids delight in experimenting to see what happens next.

The same is true of the addition and subtraction exercises. Here, the app asks kids to solve the simple math equations by placing the correct number of fingers on the screen. For addition, they can solve 5 + 4 by placing five fingers from their left hand on the screen and then adding four more from their right hand. All of the digits on the screen celebrate after your child solves the equation.

Little Digits works so well with kids because its method of teaching numbers is intuitive. The app uses a child's voice to announce each number, but there is also an option to record another voice. This technology dazzles kids by showing them that the iPad knows how many fingers are touching the screen. This is a fun app for a parent and child to explore together.

For this technology to work, you need to turn off multitasking gestures on your iPad within the Setting app. Don't worry, the app explains this procedure to you.

**Best For:** Preschoolers who are learning to count. It also works well with young kids who are exploring addition and subtraction up to ten.

# Eddy's Number Party! HD

$2.99 US/$2.99 CAN/£1.99 UK, Ages 4–6,
Scientific Learning Corporation

This math app teaches preschoolers and kindergarteners about numbers. In this app, you play counting games while throwing a birthday party for Eddy the dog. Kids count balloons to take to the party. They choose gifts with the right number of squiggles on the wrapping paper; and they match numbers to their spotted representations to find party favors and gifts. Kids also listen to dogs bark and associate the number of barks to a written number. And they visually track party hats to find a hiding ladybug. In this party atmosphere, kids earn stickers to arrange into a fun scene.

What makes this math app so good is its support system and the way it automatically adapts in difficulty. The app watches how your child responds to its educational material and adjusts its content accordingly. It offers hints when your child is stuck and even activates helpful demos at crucial times. For example, in the counting balloons game, the bottom of the screen shows several dogs with numbers on their collars. A set of balloons floats in. Kids count the balloons and then drag the bunch to the pooch with the same number on its collar. If they're having trouble with this, the app suggests they count each balloon. If they still don't get it right, the app counts the balloons for your child — showing the number on each balloon as it's counted. This built-in support is rare in children's apps and makes this app rise above the hundreds of other counting apps.

The app provides parents with a separate Grown-up Central area, accessed only by answering a multiplication problem. In this area, you can track your child's progress and see the research behind these games.

**Best For:** Kids beginning to learn their numbers. This app does a good job of going beyond just counting to associate numbers with numerical amounts. You cannot select which of the activities you want to play, so kids don't have the option of jumping into their favorite games.

# Intro to Math, by Montessorium
$4.99 US/$4.99 CAN/£2.99 UK, Ages 4–6, Montessorium, LLC.

Presenting the Montessori method, this app uses virtual math manipulatives — rods, dot counters, sandpaper number cards — to help kids recognize numbers from one to ten. The app teaches numerical order, how to write the numbers, and that these numbers represent a quantity. It also introduces the concept of even and odd numbers.

By working through the five activities, kids learn that numbers can be represented by rods, dots, or a written number. They copy sandpaper numbers where their tracing makes a grainy sound.

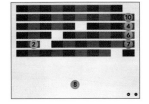

This is a very hands-on way to learn numbers. With helpful voice-over and accompanying musical sound effects, this app creates a safe environment in which to experiment with number concepts.

**Best For:** Families looking for the Montessori method of teaching math.

 # Park Math HD – by Duck Duck Moose
$1.99 US/$1.99 CAN/£1.49 UK, Ages 4–7, Duck Duck Moose

Learning early math concepts becomes fun with the seven different activities found in Park Math HD. This app features engaging cartoon characters and simple navigation. Kids play games to practice addition, subtraction, counting, patterns, ordering, and comparing amounts.

Hosted by a blue bear wearing skates and a backpack, the app moves kids around the park to play new activities. For example, at the swing set, players join in counting the number of times the purple rabbit swings. The blue bear speaks the directions and he also provides feedback. If kids drag the wrong item to complete a pattern, the bear says "oops, try again;" and he applauds when they're correct.

These activities can span preschool, kindergarten, and first grade by adjusting the three difficulty levels. By combining upbeat background music, an engaging playground setting, and friendly animals to play with, Park Math HD delivers math learning that's full of kid appeal.

**Best For:** Preschoolers, kindergarteners, and first graders. Set the level of the app to match your child's abilities.

# Math Bingo

$0.99 US/$0.99 CAN/£0.69 UK, Ages 7–12, ABCya.com

Practicing math facts is something all elementary students have to do. With Math Bingo, this practice seems fun. Kids answer addition, subtraction, multiplication, and division facts to earn Bingo Bugs that cover their correct answers on a Bingo card. The math questions appear at the top of the screen. Kids tap the correct answer on the card and a cute animated bug appears to cover the spot.

The bingo card usually has more than one square with the correct answer. Kids need to use logic to figure out which correct answer to select that most likely helps them to complete a pattern of five in a row (horizontally, vertically, or diagonally).

Kids play until they win Bingo. Their score is determined by the time it took minus points for every wrong answer. If you achieve a high score, you receive a Bingo Bug like the ones that appear on the card. But now you can play with the bugs by touching them (they make funny, high-pitched sounds) or tilting the iPad to make them slide. You can also play an arcade game with the Bingo Bugs in which you use a slingshot to shoot them up into a grid of blocks to try to earn points by bumping into the most blocks possible.

Kids can choose to drill a specific type of math (addition, subtraction, multiplication, or division), or they can select a random game in which all four operations show up. Each game is offered on three difficulty levels.

This math app presents a bright, clean interface. In between Bingo rounds, kids hear upbeat, fast-paced music, but the music stops after kids move into the math rounds. Winning cute Bingo Bugs whenever you better your score motivates younger players. Because kids need to learn math facts, this is a way to make the learning fun. The app can accommodate 30 players, so teachers can also use this fun game in a classroom.

**Best For:** Kids who need to drill math facts. The Bingo-game format makes the drilling seem less like work and more like fun.

# Super 7
$0.99 US/$0.99 CAN/£0.69 UK, Ages 7 and up, No Monkeys

This fast-paced arcade game makes doing math fun. Kids see gems with the numbers from one to six float onto the screen from all sides. When gems touch each other, their amounts add together and create a bigger gem with a higher number. The goal is to draw paths to connect two or more gems whose sum equals seven. As the game continues, more gems enter the space, at a faster pace, and some include computations or special powers. In addition to madly doing math computations in your head, you also have to keep gems that add up to more than seven from colliding. If and when they do, the game is over.

What is amazing about this simple math app is that it feels like a retro arcade game. You just happen to have to do a ton of fast math in your head to play.

**Best For:** Kids who like fast-paced arcade-style games. This is a game that hones math skills without kids really ever thinking about it.

# Oh No! Fractions
Free US/CAN/UK, Ages 8–14, diLuNa

If you have a child who is having trouble visualizing fractions, download this free app.

Kids see two fractions onscreen. Between the two fractions, kids select less than or greater than. After selecting an answer, kids tap the I'm Sure button to see whether they are right or wrong. But then, the cool feature of this app becomes available. Tapping the Prove It button displays the two fractions as bar graphs so kids can easily see which is greater.

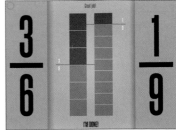

This free app is simple and effective. By allowing kids to compare fractions side by side, kids can more easily understand fractions and their size relationships.

**Best For:** Kids needing extra help with fractions.

# DragonBox+

$5.99 US/$5.99 CAN/£3.99 UK, Ages 7 and up,
WeWantToKnow AS

This clever game looks like another earn-three-stars puzzler. Kids jump in to play with a magical DragonBox, which sparkles and makes munching sounds. They start to learn the rules of this game without realizing that they're really learning how to make algebraic equations!

So you might be saying to yourself, how can a 7-year-old learn algebra? That's the beauty of this app. It teaches kids algebra under the guise of teaching them rules about playing with the DragonBox. No mathematical symbols or numbers are introduced until kids have been sucked into this fun and clever puzzle.

Kids see a play space divided into two trays. The DragonBox is on one side and a few animal cards are on the playing table. Kids learn rules about how to remove cards from the table to isolate the DragonBox. For example, they're taught that all cards have a night image and that when those two cards are laid on top of one another, they both disappear in a vortex. What kids don't realize is that they're learning how to isolate $x$ in an algebraic equation.

The pacing is just right for kids in these puzzles, and the tutorials are fabulous. Kids younger than 7 can reason through these puzzles, but the tutorials have to be read, so if you want to try it with a younger child, be around to help. Kids can create a profile so that more than one child can explore these puzzles.

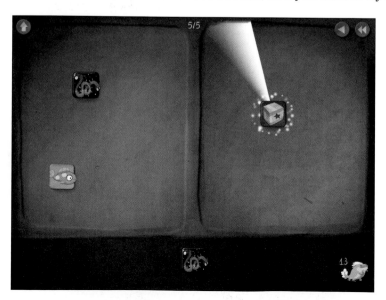

**Best For:** Kids who have the focus to concentrate on a brainy puzzle. What is nice about this app is that you don't have to know any math to play it. It teaches you everything you need to play.

# Numbers League
$3.99 US/$3.99 CAN/£2.49 UK, Ages 6–14, Bent Castle Software

Kids become superheroes in this clever math app set in Infinity City, a comic-book-style universe. Their assignment? Thwart a team of super villains who are wreaking havoc on the town. How do they do it? By using their math skills! Players even get their name in the headlines of the Infinity City Times newspaper!

Your child leads a team of superheroes known as The Numbers League. Each bad guy is vulnerable to one number, and each hero at your disposal has a powerful number. When you pit a hero against a villain where their numbers match, the hero defeats the villain and sends him to jail.

Heroes are depicted on cards, but before you create one, you spin a slot machine–like device that brings up different heads, bodies, and legs — each worth different amounts. You can lock in any of these body parts and spin two more times to get the numbers you want. A hero's powerful number is the sum of his or her parts.

When taking on villains, you can deploy more than one superhero at a time, adding up their powerful numbers so that their sum equals the villain's vulnerable number. In some of the five game versions, you can also earn superhero device cards that can change your heroes' sum (using addition, subtraction, or multiplication, depending on the game).

Kids can play this game alone until all of the villains are defeated, or as a turn-based game against up to three others.

This game oozes comic-book fun with spinning headlines, hilarious one-liners, and great-looking heroes and villains. Gameplay is accompanied by jazzy, mood-enhancing music. The tutorial is top notch, teaching kids as they play. And options abound, letting you set the math at different levels, provide hints or not, and choose a timed or untimed game. This is a masterful math app.

**Best For:** All kids. This app's superhero-themed environment can motivate even the most reluctant kids to stretch their math muscles.

# Math Doodles

$2.99 US/$2.99 CAN/£1.99 UK, Ages 7 and up,
Carstens Studios Inc.

Three different math games await your kids' reasoning skills in this clever app. The first, called Sums Stackers, was originally released as a standalone iPhone app. Kids see three stacks of counters (you can choose how they're represented: as dice, numbers, fingers, and so on), and below each stack is a target number. The goal of the game is to move the counters around on the three stacks so that the counters match the target number. The second game, Connect Sums, presents a 4 x 4 array of numbers. Using the 16 numbers, kids are challenged to combine them in ways so that their sum equals a series of displayed target numbers. In the third game called Unknown Square, kids must deduce what missing numbers belong in the 3 x 3 array of numbers, where you are given information about the sums of the vertical columns, the horizontal rows, and diagonal lines of numbers. This type of puzzle is also known as a *magic square*.

This app was developed by a dad who is both a mathematician and an artist. The presentation is full of whimsy, with artful borders and counters that look like they belong in a cereal bowl. But at its heart, these games challenge kids to think about math in different, playful ways.

I am impressed by the thoughtful options presented in these games. All of the puzzles can be tackled on an easy or hard setting. Kids can decide whether they want to play a timed or untimed game. And there are 24 different value representations.

**Best For:** Kids who can add and who enjoy math games. These are wonderful puzzlers.

 If your kids like the challenge of these math puzzles, they may like Symmetry Shuffle, another math game from this same developer.

# Move the Turtle.
# Programming for kids
$2.99 US/$2.99 CAN/£1.99 UK, Ages 10 and up, Next is Great

When my older son was about 7, he went to a summer camp that taught computer programming using a software program called Logo. He loved the challenge of learning how to program the little turtle so that it would draw a sneaker with laces tied. Your child can now enjoy the process of learning to program a turtle to draw things on a virtual chalkboard by using this app.

The app has three areas to explore. Kids should start with the Play area because it teaches them how to program the cute little turtle to draw things on the chalkboard. Kids work their way through 27 lessons, broken into 3 chapters. The lessons also set forth challenges, so kids have an opportunity to apply what they just learned to solve tasks and puzzles. They learn how to move the turtle forward, make it turn, change its ink color, repeat procedures, transport it to another area on the board, and much more. They also learn how to repeat steps to create a mini-program, including one that draws a square. The Compose area provides a blank slate on which to program the turtle to do things. This is an open-ended programming space. Kids can also explore the Projects area to get ideas of how to program more complicated tasks, like drawing a fractal tree or flowers.

I have set the age appropriateness to 10 because this app's directions are not particularly detailed — you must experiment a fair amount to figure out the tasks set forth in the Play area. It's a nifty app for older kids to explore if they are interested in computer programming, but if you want to try it with kids younger than 10, I would be around to brainstorm with them. This is a great way to teach kids logical thinking. Children must plan ahead to figure out how to make the turtle do their bidding. It's an app that requires trial and error, which means kids invest in their own learning. And when that happens, the learning sticks!

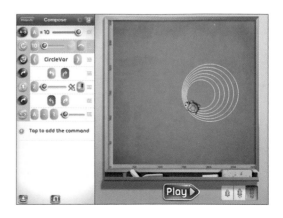

**Best For:** Kids interested in logic and computer programming. This app is a good way to introduce kids to beginning programming.

# 17 Learning Apps: Reference

## Apps Covered in This Chapter

▶ BrainPOP Featured Movie

▶ Barefoot World Atlas

▶ Geo Walk HD – 3D World Fact Book

▶ Khan Academy

## BrainPOP Featured Movie
Free US/CAN/UK, Ages 9 and up, BrainPOP

This exciting reference app offers a free educational animated movie every day. Topics vary, and fall within the categories of science, social studies, English, math, arts and music, engineering and tech, and health. The amusing duo of teenager Tim and his robot Moby host these short films. They have a knack for taking dense subjects and making them exciting. After watching the movie of the day, which might be about the international space station, Yo-Yo Ma, or digital animation, kids can take an interactive quiz about the topic just screened.

Although the busy interface takes some getting used to, if you visit it often, you start to cut through the clutter. In addition to the free movie of the day, more than 20 others are archived, also offered for free. More than 750 movies are available; but if you want immediate access to them all, you need to purchase a subscription.

I like that the movies are closed-captioned to allow kids to read as well as hear the video. And the quizzes are a great way to reinforce the learning. Download this free app and open it regularly for a burst of educational movie magic.

**Best For:** Curious kids ages 9 and up.

 For younger kids, try BrainPOP Jr. Movie of the Week, also free.

# Barefoot World Atlas

$4.99 US/$4.99 CAN/£2.99 UK, Ages 5–10, Touch Press

Kids spin this globe virtually to explore the world. Sprinkled across its surface are icons and animations enticing your touch. See a killer whale swimming below you? Touch it and the app presents you with a photo and a paragraph filled with interesting facts about these whales. You can have BBC TV presenter Nick Crane read the paragraph aloud. Then it's off to spinning the globe again, perhaps this time to the Great Pyramids in Egypt, which (the text informs you) were constructed from more than 2 million blocks of limestone. Next you might choose the Rubik's Cube hovering over Hungary, and if you tap it, you learn that it was invented in the 1970s by Ernő Rubik.

As you turn the globe, the music changes to reflect the area of the world you are exploring. As you zoom in, more icons, flags, and names of locations appear. Plus, the app provides you with other ways to explore its wealth of information: by regions and the countries therein; alphabetically by country; or by features (such as animals, topographical features, peoples, and so on). You can even bookmark your favorites. If you permit the app to use your location, it will calculate your distance to the places you're exploring.

With this app, kids no longer spin a globe and dream about faraway places; now they can see what those places look like and learn facts about them as well. I love that this app puts kids in charge of learning — *they* decide what they want to discover.

**Best For:** Explorers. This app puts the world in the palm of your hand. Just tap to go adventuring.

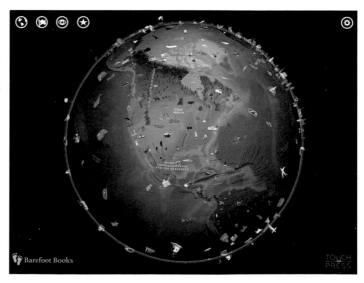

# Geo Walk HD – 3D World Fact Book

$2.99 US/$2.99 CAN/£1.99 UK, Ages 8 and up, Vito Technology Inc.

This reference app opens to reveal a slowly spinning globe. Small rectangular images float above the world. Tap one and the image enlarges to become a flashcard: On one side is a spectacular photograph; on the other, a paragraph of information about the subject in the photo. You can explore a total of 566 cards, covering the categories of places, animals, plants, people, and events. For example, kids can learn about Big Ben, emperor penguins, Coco de Mer palm trees, Albert Einstein, and the Japanese earthquakes of 2011. This app encourages kids to explore the world by presenting them with inviting and intriguing photographs, coupled with short paragraphs of zippy information.

I selected this app because it presents information in kid-sized bits. Geo Walk HD makes exploring our vast world exciting. The app doesn't show videos, but it does have exciting photos. It presents the information in a variety of ways to create this sense of going on an adventure. In addition to spinning the globe, kids can explore the cards themselves, arranged on a circular plane in interesting geometric formations that kids can scroll through. Plus, the app sorts the cards into lists so that if you want to simply learn about famous people, you can. You also have an option of placing a star on a card, so that it is easy to find. The learning can be reinforced by playing a fun trivia game in which kids are asked to answer questions that can be answered by selecting the correct image from the cards displayed.

 The app offers three in-app purchases to buy more cards. And it contains links to Facebook, Twitter, e-mail, and Wikepedia.

**Best For:** Kids wanting to journey around the world. Your adventure is just a tap away.

# Khan Academy

Free US/CAN/UK, Ages 10 and up, Khan Academy

This reference app is a way of viewing more than 3,200 educational videos produced by the brilliant Salman Khan, a hedge fund analyst turned philanthropist. He started making his whiteboard videos as a way of tutoring his cousins remotely. When his YouTube channel went viral, he quit his job and founded the Khan Academy.

This app gives you free access to videos explaining a wide range of topics in math, science, finance and economics, humanities, and test preparation. Elementary school students can enjoy video lessons on things like fractions and decimals. For middle- and high-school students, Khan Academy covers algebra, geometry, and beyond. The videos explain science by focusing on individual concepts such as mitosis or photosynthesis. Sal has a way of breaking down complicated topics into learnable bites.

If your kids want to track their progress in watching the videos, they need to sign in by creating an account or using an existing Gmail or Facebook account. Because kids under 13 can't have a Facebook account, parents might want to help with this. Still, registering isn't necessary; you can just search through the categories to find what you want.

Khan Academy is a great resource for kids who are struggling with an academic subject. Because this app is free, it's a good place to start before you decide to hire a tutor. It's also a great way for kids interested in a specific topic to explore ideas. The videos can be rerun; and most offer closed-captioning so you can read along as you watch and listen.

**Best For:** Older kids looking for help or more information in the areas of math, science, computer science, finance, humanities, and test prep.

# 18 Learning Apps: Science

## Rounds: Franklin Frog

$4.99 US/$4.99 CAN/£2.99 UK, Ages 3–6, Nosy Crow

Little kids can learn about the life cycle of a frog by joining Franklin Frog at his home near a pond. This life science app is told in a book format, with your child interacting with Franklin throughout. Your youngster becomes Franklin's friend.

Franklin explains what he eats, how he can swim and breathe underwater, and where he hides in the winter. But even better, your child can help Franklin: Swiping over the frog makes him jump. Touching a buzzing fly makes Franklin shoot out his sticky tongue to grab it.

This book presents the concept of a life cycle in a way that a child can understand. Your child protects Franklin and his mate's eggs and then helps one of the little tadpoles grow up until the book starts over with a new frog named Fraser. This cycle repeats one more time with a frog named Fletcher before another Franklin is born. By the story's repetition with new characters in the lead, it shows kids how the life cycle of a frog is "round."

**Best For:** All young children. This book is a magnificent way to show kids the life cycle of a frog.

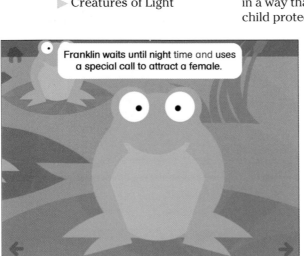

Franklin waits until night time and uses a special call to attract a female.

# Sid's Science Fair

$2.99 US/$2.99 CAN/£1.99 UK, Ages 4–6, PBS KIDS

Hosted by the cartoon star of the PBS show *Sid the Science Kid*, Sid invites your kids to visit a science fair and play three games with other characters from the show. With Gabriela, your kids control a virtual magnifying glass to closely inspect Gabriela's collections of coins, butterflies, and such to find matching details for those shown magnified on the side of the screen. With Gerald, kids explore time-lapse photography to see how objects change over time. Before they can place the photographs into Gerald's time machine, kids must put the photographs in order so that they are sequential when you speed them up to create a movie. With May, kids learn what data is and arrange collections on charts, sorting by attributes such as color, shape, or design.

These three science games are easy to understand and engaging to play. Sid and his friends provide friendly support as kids explore the games they like most. Each game has multiple levels because the characters brought many collections to the science fair. By playing this app, kids start to think like scientists. They study collections to look for details, chart data to see the results, and order things to create accurate sequences.

**Best For:** All preschoolers and kindergarteners. This app makes exploring science entertaining.

# The Strange & Wonderful World of Ants

$1.99 US/$1.99 CAN/£1.49 UK, Ages 4–12, Amos Latteier

Presented in a book format, this app introduces your child to a close-up look at the world of ants. Through its 26 pages, it imparts facts about all kinds of ants. Kids learn that some ants take care of aphids because they produce a sweet substance the ants like to eat. Other ants cut leaves to feed to a fungus they like to consume. The app introduces ants whose heads are so big that they block the entrance to the colony and thus keep out enemies. Some ants (such as army ants, which are constantly on the move) don't have time to build a colony; instead they sleep by making a big ball to protect the queen and the larvae.

Each of the 26 pages starts with a collage-like scene onto which an ant picture appears. When you touch a page, a realistic-looking ant appears. If you tap him, you meet E.O. the Ant. E.O. offers his individual perspective on each page, frequently pointing out how humans and ants do similar things. For example, "Both people and ants eat fungus. Don't forget that mushrooms are fungus," explains E.O.

All of the factual information about ants is fascinating; but what makes this app so good is that it has a slider button on each page that allows kids to adjust the amount of information they want to read. When set on the easiest reading level, the app is read out loud by a reader who projects just the right amount of respect and awe at what ants can do. When you set the slider to the middle or hardest reading level, you or your child need to read the book yourselves. Scientific words appear highlighted and are explained in a glossary at the end of the app. Interested kids also find other free ant resources at the end of the book that are linked to the Internet, so that tapping them opens them on the iPad's browser. This is a "wonderful" resource for kids.

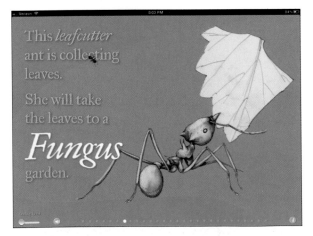

**Best For:** Any child. This book's presentation appeals to both nature-lovers as well as kids who couldn't care less about insects.

# Bats! Furry Fliers of the Night

$2.99 US/$2.99 CAN/£1.99 UK, Ages 5–12, Story Worldwide

This science app takes kids into environments where bats live. It teaches kids about bats by presenting fascinating facts within interactive sequences. Displayed in a book format and broken into seven chapters, the app lets kids learn about different kinds of bats, where they live, and what they eat.

The stunning visuals make you feel as if you're standing outside in the dark. Slide your finger up the screen, and it appears you are walking further into the night; swipe upward and you focus up into the starry sky, where bats are visible as they fly in front of the moon. If you tap the bat, the scene changes to an annotated image of a bat, identifying its body parts. This presentation quickly engages even the most reluctant learner.

Accompanied by realistic nighttime sounds, kids also adventure into scenes where they must tap cave entrances to find bats. Some are roosting in barns, others under bridges, or hiding behind leaves. Each time you find one, a card with a photo and some information pops up onscreen.

This app even provides kids with an interactive echolocation demonstration where they can screech like a bat to create the sound waves shown onscreen. In another scene, tilting the iPad lets your child control the bat's flight.

This app should be used by others as a model of how to present nonfiction to kids. On every page, it immerses players with new things to do and discover. The navigation welcomes exploration by providing an easy way to jump into chapters of interest. And the unique bat spinner — which kids turn to find out more about a specific kind of bat — is masterful. Plus, this app is gorgeous to look at!

**Best For:** Kids interested in nature. The presentation is so compelling that kids who are afraid of bats might be calmed after investigating this app.

These nighttime furry fliers are bats!

^ A big brown bat opens its mouth as it hunts for insects.

# The Magic School Bus: Oceans
$7.99 US, Ages 5–10, Scholastic Inc.

In this interactive science exploration app, Ms. Frizzle, the beloved teacher in *The Magic School Bus* book series by Joanna Cole, drives her fantastical bus into the ocean.

Your child joins Ms. Frizzle's class as they take a field trip — under the sea! Presented in a book format with cartoon drawings and speech bubbles, kids can find tons of information on each page. The story, which mixes factual information and zaniness, is read aloud as the words highlight. Touch a student's speech bubble to hear what he or she says, watch 11 videos, scrutinize more than 25 photos, and play games — this app offers so much for your child to do!

Taking Ms. Frizzle's famous phrase of "take chances, make mistakes, get messy" to heart, this app presents kids with an open exploration format. When something bubbles on the page, your child can interact with it. Some bubbles lead to interactive science explorations, such as a chart showing the underwater food chain of fish. Arrange the different-sized fish in order from largest to smallest and the food chain springs to life. In another exploration, your child follows arrows on the screen to mimic the different ways that animals swim.

This app teems with interactive bits of science. Kids can learn amazing facts, including that a squid can grow to be 46 feet long! The videos interspersed throughout mesmerize viewers by showing sea urchins crawling on the sea bottom and flounder fish swimming with both eyes on the same side of the head. Even the app's fun match-three-type arcade game is sea-life oriented.

The app uses more than 20 voices and sound effects to make your child feel like she is surrounded by other kids. If you're going to go swimming with whale sharks, it's better to do it with friends — even virtual ones.

 Scholastic offers a free, Lite version of this app that lets kids explore 3 of the 41 pages. If you're hesitant, start there.

**Best For:** All kids! By plunging into the deep with "The Friz," your kids will be awash with aquatic facts.

# Pettson's Inventions
$1.99 US/$1.99 CAN/£1.49 UK, Ages 5 and up, Filimundus AB

Pettson is an inventor, and he needs your child's help putting together his wacky, Rube Goldberg–type machines. In 25 puzzles, kids drag objects from a side bin into the emerging contraption. Budding inventors puzzle through how to build showers out of wooden tubs and pipes, connect grooved planks to gears, and tap into the energy created by a windmill.

Pettson's Inventions makes learning about science and engineering fun. Kids get hands-on time with gears, gadgets, and thingamabobs. But the zany goals of each puzzle are what make this app a hoot to explore. In one puzzle, you're designing a shower for a bird, in another a gadget for cleaning a pig. You even invent a contraption to make an old lady laugh. After you successfully design an invention and meet Pettson's objective for you, he rewards you with a gear or gadget to use to build the final cat-flying machine.

What I love about these puzzles is that they're silly, off the wall, and utterly engrossing. You won't get any hints, but each gizmo, gadget, and wild animal found in the side tray goes somewhere; so trial and error is the key to finding the solution. It is also a good idea to flip the "On" switch of the contraption before it's completed just to see how things start. In some, the first thing that happens is that the window opens, which frightens another character, who then jumps, and starts a chain of events. These puzzles slowly get more complicated, but they build on the knowledge you gain in the earlier, easier puzzles.

You can choose the option to have unneeded parts appear in the side tray to make finding the correct pieces harder.

**Best For:** Kids who like creating crazy inventions and playing board games like Mouse Trap. This is the virtual equivalent of that famous board game, only you play it by yourself.

## This is my body – Anatomy for kids

$1.99 US/$1.99 CAN/£1.49 UK, Ages 6–12, urbn; pockets

This anatomy app offers kids a peek inside the body of a child to see how it works. Using an innovative navigation system, kids peel back each layer of the body to see what lies underneath. The app keeps this complicated subject simple, and makes the exploration engaging by adding games, hidden stars to find, and hands-on activities. It delivers a "wow" experience.

Kids start by deciding which of eight racially diverse children they want to investigate. Next, by pulling down a ribbon at the top of the screen, they take off one layer at time. First, kids learn about the parts of the body. Then they move to learning about the skin, the senses, and the systems of the body, including digestive, respiratory, circulatory, muscular, nervous, and skeletal. Within a given layer of the body, ribbons on the sides of the pages reveal more information — up to 5 or 6 extra pages. To return to the main page, just tap the triangle at the top of any page.

For each new human body system revealed, the little girl narrator suggests an activity. For the respiratory system, she asks you to hold your breath as a timer counts. With the skeleton, the narrator asks you to shake the iPad and then put together a puzzle of the skeleton parts.

I am amazed at how much fun this app is to explore. Its clever presentation of running your finger down from the top of the screen to peel back a layer of the body impresses me the same way Jonathan Miller's clever pop-up book, *The Human Body,* did the first time I opened it. This app is innovative and jam-packed with kid-friendly information. It makes a dense topic easy to understand.

1 SKULL
2 SPINE
3 RIBS
4 PELVIS
5 SHOULDER
6 COLLARBONE
7 UPPER ARM
8 FOREARM
9 HAND
10 THIGH BONE
11 KNEE CAP
12 LOWER LEG
13 FOOT

MENU

 By default, this app has no nudity (the models wear underpants), but parents can allow it by adjusting the app's preferences from within the iPad's Settings app.

**Best For:** Kids in elementary school. However, even older children find this app fascinating; the app has special Little Smarty-Pants sections just for tweens that have more detailed information in written form, not narrated.

# Bobo Explores Light

$4.99 US/$4.99 CAN/£2.99 UK, Ages 7 and up,
Game Collage, LLC

This is one of my all-time favorite apps for kids because it combines exciting science learning with humor and whimsy. Kids meet an adorable little robot named Bobo and then join him on a journey to discover the wonders and scientific properties of light. With Bobo, they fly to the sun to learn about solar flares, watch lightning strike in slow motion, explore deep-sea fish to learn about bioluminescence, and even play with the concept of reflection by shooting lasers at mirrors.

The app covers 15 subjects, from photosynthesis to telescopes to the human eye, and makes these topics fun. Bobo introduces videos, awe-inspiring photos, fun facts, and hands-on explorations. One of the most magical pages starts with a blighted forest. When kids touch the page, light shines on that spot and things start to grow. Dead brown areas magically turn into live green as vines and leaves appear, eventually revealing a riot of colorful flowers. And your finger directs all of the growth. It's a mesmorizing demonstration of photosynthesis.

This app works well across many age categories because it puts the readers in charge of how much they want to explore. Each topic page offers three extra drop-down pages for kids to pursue. Bobo is both a source of exciting information (by casting holographic diagrams and images, or setting up hands-on experiments) and humor (like when he burns a marshmallow while trying to roast it over a fire). This app also has a brilliant navigation system, enabling players to jump easily to any page in the book app from within any other page.

**Best For:** Kids who can read. Younger children can enjoy many parts of the app if they have a parent or older sibling to read it to them.

This book app makes science interesting, even for children who show no real interest in the subject. By discussing topics that appeal to all kids — like why do glow sticks work — it makes difficult topics accessible.

# Amazing Alex HD
$2.99 US/$2.99 CAN/£1.99 UK, Ages 8 and up, Rovio Entertainment Ltd

For all Rube Goldberg wannabes, this app is for you! Alex is a little boy with a great little engineering mind. He has devised a set of puzzles for your child to solve using things around his house, yard, treehouse, and even in his classroom.

In each puzzle, players try to reach a goal by dragging objects found in Casey's toolbox to a play space and then manipulating them so that they can accomplish a goal. Typical goals include getting some tennis balls into a laundry hamper, and figuring out a way to pop helium balloons. Puzzles can be solved in a variety of ways — there is no one correct answer. In addition to attaining the goal, players get a higher score if they can collect the three stars found in the puzzle.

When my kids were young, they used paper towel cores and wrapping paper tubes to create tracks for marbles to run. They would duct tape these homemade tracks on our wood paneling. These puzzles remind me of those contraptions.

These puzzles challenge your kids to think like an engineer and problem-solve like a scientist. Experimentation is the key to success. Players must make minor adjustments to perfect their solutions. I really like that kids can even build their own puzzles: They can learn from Alex's puzzles to improve their own. Kids can even share their puzzles via e-mail (the recipient must also have the app) or send them to Rovio for posting on their website. The sharing option can be toggled off in the app's settings. Kids can also download and try to solve puzzles made by others. Don't worry; there is no communication with strangers.

This app uses Game Center for sharing and viewing solutions to Alex's puzzles and also has ads for other Rovio games, which take you out of the game.

**Best For:** Kids who love making contraptions and building with materials like Legos. This is a great app to explore after finishing Pettson's Inventions (reviewed earlier in this chapter) because it's more challenging.

# Science360 for iPad

Free US/UK, Ages 8 and up, National Science Foundation

This free science resource from the National Science Foundation opens to a bright collage of photos inviting your child to explore. Tap any photo that piques your interest, and it opens to reveal a topic or some ongoing research. Some of the images lead to videos such as "Science of NFL Football," in which you explore the Pythagorean Theorem to understand how football players determine the angle of pursuit when trying to catch a runner. Other images might lead to research about emperor penguins or the way the carnivorous sundew plant creates small adhesive balls to catch insects.

This app offers hundreds of images and videos to investigate, with new content added weekly. You can scroll through the images or use a keyword to search (by touching the surface with two fingers). If you like a topic, the app allows you to save it as a favorite so you can easily return to the image.

If you find an image you want to share, the app offers the options of using Twitter, Facebook, or e-mail. For older kids already using these services, this is fine, but for younger kids, you might want to talk about these options.

Some explanations are easy for kids to understand, whereas others can be too complex; but with so much to explore, kids are bound to find many items that interest them.

**Best For:** Budding scientists. This is also a great app to explore to entice reluctant learners because the images are stunning and inherently fascinating.

**Studying Sundew Plant Adhesive (Image 2)**

January 19, 2012

A sundew plant. Sundew plants are carnivorous, consuming insects by capturing them with small adhesive balls on the ends of their tentacles. Mingjun Zhang of the Nano Biosystems and Bio-mimetics Lab at the University of Tennessee is studying the adhesive properties of sundew plants on the nanoscale, which may lead to improvements in medical replacement operations such as hip replacements. In a paper published in the Journal of Nanobiotechnology , Zhang's group reported that the naturally occurring nanofibers and nanoparticles from the

# Star Walk for iPad – interactive astronomy guide

$4.99 US/$4.99 CAN/£2.99 UK, Ages 8 and up,
Vito Technology Inc.

If you take your iPad out at night and point it skyward, this app identifies what you're seeing. It takes star-gazing to a whole new educational level.

The app can tell you what constellation you're looking at and even give you the history of its name. When the app displays the planets in the sky, tapping on the "i" next to the planet's name pulls up an article and photo of that planet. The interstellar map of the sky also tracks stars, satellites, deep space clusters, and the moon. If you tap the moon, the app gives you general information, as well as a gallery of photos, including ones showing astronauts planting a U.S. flag on the moon's surface.

I like that the app provides a special night mode, to reduce the light that comes off the iPad so you are better able to see the stars. Also spectacular is the Picture of the Day section, which provides stunning photos such as the photo below of the Andromeda Galaxy shown in infrared as a swirling mass of blue and pink. The app provides active links to the Internet source for the photos. Another interesting feature is the ability to track the changes in the sky by moving a timeline slider found on the side of the nighttime viewing screen.

To allow this app to work, you need to let it use GPS to track your location and more accurately present the stars in the sky. It also uses augmented reality where, by using the rear-facing camera, it sees what you see and then superimposes information on that image.

This app allows you to e-mail, tweet, and share on Facebook directly from within the app.

**Best For:** Kids who are interested in astronomy. This app will broaden their . . . horizons!

# Creatures of Light

Free US/CAN/UK, Ages 10 and up,
American Museum of Natural History

This magnificent, free science app focuses on the topic of nature's bioluminescence. It shows how some animals use light to make themselves glow with bioluminescent substances, how plants produce glowing colors, and even how we can use these naturally occurring florescent proteins as research tools to explore topics such as how the brains of fruit flies work or how plant roots grow.

Produced by the American Museum of Natural History, this app is broken into six chapters. Kids can learn about bioluminescence in fireflies, fungi, beetles, land snails, and even special earthworms that live in Australia. They can see images and videos of creatures that live in the sea and deep in the oceans. My favorite shows a dolphin swimming among glowing dinoflagellates, which makes its outline sparkle as it swims. It's magical to watch.

For those interested in the science behind these glowing creatures and plants, the app contains explanations and offers many hands-on explorations using sliders and other interactive things to tap. Kids can learn how some marine creatures absorb one color of light and then emit another glowing one. It also contains videos of scientists explaining the subject matter.

Cleverly, the app is accompanied by gentle, flowing music, which serves to enhance the magical reality of this little-seen area of science. This is a treasure trove for kids interested in science and the wonders of the world. And it's free, so why not try it?

**Best For:** Kids curious about the world around them; and a must-have for kids who love science. It doesn't provide narration, so kids need to be old enough to read and absorb this interesting information.

# 19 Learning Apps: Social Studies

## Painting with Time
$0.99 US/$0.99 CAN/£0.69 UK, Ages 5 and up, Red Hill Studios

This inventive app shows kids how things change over time. Kids alter scenes by using their fingers to paint with time instead of color. Before swiping a finger across the screen, your child can select from tubes of paint labeled in units of time. For example, to alter a landscape scene, kids can choose to paint with fall, winter, spring, or summer. When kids move their fingers over the scene, it magically transforms to the season indicated on the tube of time paint.

Players can transform a man growing a beard by selecting from tubes representing 10, 20, or 30 days of time. Likewise, they can watch a young woman age, a glacier retreat, and the tides come in along the ocean. Kids can explore 14 scenes, using time as their paint.

Funded in part by a grant from the National Science Foundation, this app helps children to think about time from a different perspective. They can also explore slicing photos into different times, so that they can line up all the different images on the same photograph. The app includes a written tutorial on how to capture change using photographs.

TIP If your child enjoys exploring this app, check out the sequel, Painting with Time: Climate Change.

**Best For:** All kids. This app cleverly turns the concept of time into something that children can see and understand. It's simply brilliant.

# Ansel & Clair's Adventures in Africa

$4.99 US/$4.99 CAN/£2.99 UK, Ages 4–10, Cognitive Kid, Inc.

This is one of my favorite educational apps for the iPad. It allows kids to go on an adventure with an inquisitive alien who crash-lands in Africa. As the alien learns about Africa, so does your child.

Presented with high quality graphics and gorgeous animations, the story involves helping the alien Ansel and his robotic sidekick Clair to find the missing parts of their spaceship. Ansel and Clair's mission is to film Africa, so your kids help with that part too, using a virtual camera to capture photos of the African animals they encounter.

Kids travel with Ansel and Clair to three geographic regions of Africa: the Serengeti Plains, the Sahara Desert, and the Nile Valley. At each region, kids encounter animals and vegetation unique to that area. If your child taps an animal, he is told facts about the animal and given an opportunity to take its photograph. Kids can also transform things in scenes, such as changing day to night in the desert and switching seasons while on the Serengeti.

This app is so good because Ansel acts as your kid's always-curious guide. Kids who want more information can tap the screen to explore more topics. I also like the way this app incorporates facts seamlessly into the game play. Kids learn about the life cycle of a frog by rearranging the events to find the correct order. They play games that reunite babies with the parents, and visit an Egyptian pyramid by navigating a maze.

Because the text is spoken aloud, even nonreaders can learn. Kids hear original, African-influenced music. And they'll love the opportunity to take photos they can share with you in their own travel log. Don't miss this app!

**Best For:** All kids. This app has it all: a fun story, exciting interactions, great characters, ability to control how much you learn, and the feeling of contributing via taking photos.

# Presidents vs. Aliens

$0.99 US/$0.99 CAN/£0.69 UK, Ages 8 and up, Dan Russell-Pinson

This trivia game tests your kids' knowledge of the current and past U.S. presidents. The hook that makes this drill-the-facts game fun is that it's tied into an arcade-style game of flinging balls at floating aliens that fill the screen.

Here's how it works: A group of aliens appears onscreen. Next, kids must answer a multiple-choice question about one of the presidents. If they answer the question correctly, they earn a ball to fling at the aliens to knock them off the screen. What's silly is that the ball has been imprinted with a president's face. It's wacky fun that serves to encourage kids to learn more facts about the presidents.

The app has a separate section where kids can go to review flash cards for each president. Players can also decide what kind of questions they want to answer, choosing from the following categories: pictures of the presidents, political party, before and after their term of office, historical events, nicknames, quotes, and general facts.

If players get three correct answers in a row, they earn a crazy power-up. These power-ups vary, but include the ability to fling three presidents at one time, and to throw an invincible president that can fly through obstacles shielding the aliens. Because the power-ups are so much fun to use, they motivate kids to learn their presidential facts. The game ends when the player has knocked all of the aliens off the screen. If you answer enough questions correctly during that round, you earn a president card. The goal is to collect all 44 president cards.

As players collect more and more of the president cards, two more bonus games unlock. In one, you tap presidents who are floating in space; and in the other, you place the presidents in order.

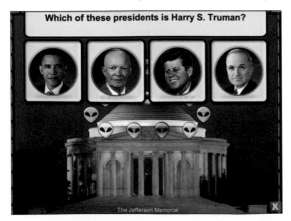

This app is a perfect example of how combining a simple zany arcade game with factual information can make learning fun.

**Best For:** Kids interested in U.S. history and, in particular, the past presidents. The fun gaming aspect of this app may convince kids who don't like history to give it a try.

# Stack the Countries

$1.99 US/$1.99 CAN/£1.49 UK, Ages 8 and up,
Dan Russell-Pinson

Kids can travel the world by playing this app. Similar to Stack the States (reviewed later in this chapter), this app teaches kids facts about countries by having them play a trivia game and by asking kids to balance countries on top of each other to create a stack.

This game is broken into a series of rounds. To win a round, kids must earn countries by correctly answering multiple-choice questions and then balance the earned countries on top of each other so that the worldly pile reaches a goal line drawn onscreen.

Kids can select regions of the world about which they want to be quizzed. They can also choose the categories of questions, covering capitals, continents, languages, border countries, cities, landmarks, flags, and country shapes. The app even provides kids with a Learn section of interactive maps and flash cards so that they can study before attempting the questions.

This visually appealing app uses famous world landmarks as a background for playing the earn-the-country rounds. Also fun is the way the animated eyes on the earned countries follow your hand movements and seem to interact with other countries in the stacks. Figuring out the best way to rotate a country and deciding when and where to drop it on your stack takes some thought. Stack correctly and you earn a country; misjudge and you lose a country you've won. Don't worry — that's part of the fun!

In addition to the main stacking game, the app also has two bonus games that unlock after you play for a while.

**Best For:** All kids old enough to read and understand maps. This app expands kids' world view and helps them understand the geography of our planet.

# Stack the States

$0.99 US/$0.99 CAN/£0.69 UK, Ages 8 and up, Dan Russell-Pinson

This app makes learning U.S. geography a blast! The core game brilliantly combines a fun stacking game with answering factual questions about the 50 states.

Kids play this game by correctly answering multiple-choice questions about the states. For example, answer a question about Minnesota and you earn an animated version of that state to place on your pile. By answering enough questions correctly, you can place states strategically on top of each other to create a stack. (You can rotate the states to better balance them.) When your stack gets high enough (typically three to five states) to reach the goal line, you win the round. Win a round, and the app awards you with a randomly chosen commemorative state for your map collection. If you win enough commemorative states, four bonus games unlock, including one that tasks you with tapping where a state belongs on a blank map of the U.S.

In the main stacking game, the animated states with their adorable, expressive eyes steal the show. They're so much fun to play with that your kids will be begging for just one more game. You'll be amazed by how much information your kids pick up about the 50 states. Plus, there's a Learn section for kids who want to review the facts. The app cleverly puts kids in control of their learning by letting them select the game's categories of questions. If your child has an upcoming quiz about state capitals, set the questioning to cover those facts. Need

to know each state's flag? This game has got you covered! Kids even learn from their wrong answers because the app is careful to show the correct ones. In between rounds, players see high resolution photos of famous U.S. landmarks. I also like that kids need to use logic and some geometry to balance the states on top of each other.

**Best For:** Kids who love geography and even kids who don't. This fun gaming format makes learning state facts exciting.

If your kids like playing this game, download Stack the Countries (review on the previous page) for a broader world view.

# Ansel & Clair: Paul Revere's Ride

$4.99 US/$4.99 CAN/£2.99 UK, Ages 8–12, Cognitive Kid, Inc.

This is the third Ansel & Clair app, and like the first two (reviewed earlier in this chapter and in Chapter 11), it is an outstanding learning adventure. Alien photographer Ansel and his robotic sidekick Clair visit Earth, this time traveling back in time to 1775 to meet Paul Revere. Ansel wants to learn about what happened to start the American Revolutionary War. With Clair acting as the guide, your kids join Ansel to relive exciting moments in history.

This adventure focuses on meeting Paul Revere and following his famous ride to warn of the British soldiers coming. Across more than a dozen interactive scenes, kids meet and speak with historic figures such as Paul Revere, Samuel Adams, John Hancock, and others. In addition, kids solve rebus puzzles (which use pictures in place of words), answer pop quizzes, create a travel log of the photos they take within the game, and play minigames such as the Boston Tea Party game, in which kids toss tea chests into a whale's mouth.

As with the previous Ansel & Clair apps, Clair offers deeper understanding for those who want it. By tapping her Clairvision icon, additional historic information is available. To keep this information interesting, the app cleverly presents it in a question and answer format between Ansel and Clair.

This app is fascinating to explore and makes the American pre-Revolutionary War period come alive by transporting kids back in time to talk with and meet the key historic figures.

Kids can send the photos from their travel log using e-mail on your iPad. Also, the app shows Paul Revere's famous engraving of the Boston Massacre, which depicts death to Boston citizens with small red splashes of blood. The home page has a button advertising other apps from this developer that leads to iTunes.

**Best For:** All kids who are studying the Revolutionary War in school or who are history buffs.

# 20 Monsters & Aliens

## Elmo's Monster Maker HD

$3.99 US/$0.99 CAN/£0.69 UK, Ages 2–5, Sesame Street

Elmo of *Sesame Street* hosts this fun make-a-monster app. He calls forth five of his monster friends that don't have eyes, noses, or hats — they're just furry bodies with mouths. Kids can design a monster by first selecting a specific monster and then tapping the face to scroll through a selection of eyes. Kids then add a nose and a hat, using the same process. After creating a monster, kids can make it dance or invite Elmo to play with it. Kids can also take a photo of their newly designed monster, which automatically shows up in the iPad's photo collection. From there, it can be easily e-mailed to friends and family.

**Best For:** Because of its simple interface and limited choices, this app works great with kids in the 2–5-year-old range. If your kids are older, they will enjoy the greater selection found in Create a Monster HD, reviewed later in this chapter.

# Another Monster at the End of This Book . . . Starring Grover & Elmo!

$4.99 US/$0.99 CAN/£0.69 UK, Ages 3–6, Sesame Street

This book app is a sequel to the outstanding The Monster at the End of This Book . . . Starring Grover!, which is one of the apps on my 10 Favorite Kid Apps list (see Chapter 27). Your child joins Grover from *Sesame Street* and his buddy Elmo in exploring a book that promises to end with a monster on the last page. In a typical Grover response, the blue furry monster is afraid of meeting a monster at the end of the book, and he spends his time cajoling the reader and coming up with schemes to prevent the turning of pages. In contrast, curious, intrepid Elmo can't wait to meet the monster. He encourages your child to keep turning pages and provides tips about how to overcome the obstacles built by Grover.

This book app is hilarious because Grover's antics are so over-the-top. By speaking directly to the reader, the monsters make your child feel like he is a part of the book-reading adventure. And by participating in freeing the pages by wiping away the glue that Grover applies or by removing paper clips, kids feel in control. The book highlights the words as read, to help beginning readers.

**Best For:** Kids who enjoy the monsters on *Sesame Street*. This book is also good for children who are fearful; it helps them learn how to deal with their own fears by watching Grover and Elmo.

## Go Away, Big Green Monster! for iPad

$2.99 US/$2.99 CAN/£1.99 UK, Ages 3–6, Night & Day Studios, Inc.

This app brings a popular children's book by Ed Emberley to the iPad. In the first half of the book app, kids build a big, scary, green monster by adding a part of the monster's face with every turn of the page. The monster takes shape as readers add the monster's eyes, nose, mouth, ears, scraggly purple hair, and a green face. Delightfully, in the second half of this book, kids make all of those scary features disappear by changing the background color so that you can no longer see a particular monster part. For example, by changing the background to green, the big, scary monster's green face disappears. This book app can be read aloud by author Ed Emberley, or by a child's voice (my favorite because it's just the perfect combination of wonder and determination), or you can hear it sung, or you can read it yourself.

The simple act of slowly building a scary monster and then making it disappear puts kids in control and changes the way they look at the creature. With this control, kids are willing to touch the monster and giggle as its eyes blink or its ears twitch. Even when the monster gnashes its big white teeth it seems funny — not scary. This is a monster that kids will love to play with.

**Best For:** Young kids who enjoy monsters but might be secretly scared of them. This book shows them that monsters aren't all that scary and that they can control the monsters.

# I'm Not Afraid

$2.99 US/$2.99 CAN/£1.99 UK, Ages 3–6, Flying Rabbit Studios

This book app by Eric and Nathalie Lee features an intrepid little boy and his pet monster. Told in rhyme, the monster, who appears to be afraid of lots of things, asks the boy if he is afraid of many common fears of young children. These include bugs and creepy critters, the dark, thunder and lightning, loud sounds, and — most importantly — monsters! In each situation, the little boy explains why these otherwise scary things don't scare him. And when it comes to monsters, the boy isn't afraid of them because he made them up. The graphics remind me of Maurice Sendak's *Where the Wild Things Are,* but simpler.

The words highlight as spoken or the narration can be turned off. This book app has only light interactivity so that kids will focus on the important message of overcoming fears.

**Best For**: All kids, and especially those with fears.

# Monster Melody Mash Lite – Animated Monster Music

Free US/Free CAN/Free UK, Ages 2–12, Tui Studios

This free app welcomes musical exploration by presenting six brightly colored monsters on a black screen. When you touch one, it starts its unique musical riff that blends with the other six. Kids can experiment with creating music by turning the monsters on and off with just a touch of their finger. One of the monsters has eight eyes, each of which plays a different note. Kids can compose their own melodies using these eyes and have the other monsters accompany them with percussion and harmony.

**Best For**: All kids. It's a magnificent musical mash-up, and it's free!

The paid version ($1.99) adds only two extra scenes, which are fun, but may be a tad expensive for what it offers, especially because you can't save your compositions.

# iLuv Drawing Monsters HD – Learn how to draw 20 cute monsters step by step!

$0.99 US/$0.99 CAN/£0.69 UK, Ages 4–8, MyVijan LLC

A cute, animated tiger with a child's voice acts as your tutor when you first launch the instructions section of this drawing app. The tiger shows you how to use your finger (or stylus) to copy the gray lines presented. He also explains how to undo actions, use an eraser, choose your colors, add stickers, change the background, and save your masterpiece. Under the Learn to Draw section, you can select from 20 monsters. By tapping one, you see light blue lines waiting to be traced. A voice explains that you start with the body. After completing a body part, more lines to be traced appear. When the outlining is done, you get to decide how you want to color your monster. Then you can save it to an in-app drawing book or to your photos, print it, or e-mail it to your friends and family.

Because all of the instructions are both shown and spoken, this is an easy app to use with young children. The collection of the 20 monsters is cute, and only a tad bit fierce, so young children will find them fun, not scary. This app makes it easy for kids to learn to draw monsters by showing them the step-by-step process and giving them confidence to draw on their own. It even has blank pages on which kids can experiment. They can combine monster features they've learned to draw in new and creative ways.

 This app automatically connects to your e-mail for sending finished drawings and it has a "More Apps" button on the title page that leads directly to iTunes.

**Best For:** Young children who don't have confidence with drawing. But it's also fun for kids who love to draw because it might give them new ideas. Kids need to be old enough to be able to close all of their lines so that the fill feature works without filling the whole painting with just one color.

 The other apps in this series are also great. See iLuv Drawing Animals reviewed in Chapter 5.

## Cozmo's Day Off – Children's Interactive Storybook

$3.99 US/$3.99 CAN/£2.49 UK, Ages 4–10, Ayars Animation Inc.

This book app follows Cozmo the alien as he wakes up and heads to work. Kids can explore his bedroom, which is full of things that, when tapped, respond. A one-eyed monster follows you around the room, the radio can be turned on or off, and a toy spaceship can whirl around and hover over the alarm clock as it tries to beam the time-piece aboard. And all of that action is just on the first page! Each of the ten pages has marvels to find and explore, including embedded jigsaw puzzles, and a whack-a-mole-type game at the fueling station for Cozmo's rocket ship. When Cozmo finally makes it to work, after riding inside a suction tube, he discovers he has a day off.

More than 100 interactions are what make this app fun. Many of the hotspots feature multiple animations, so something different happens when you touch the same spot repeatedly. The zany, out-of-this-world setting is irresistible as kids tilt, touch, and swipe to see what new surprises are hiding in this alien world. Every page offers unique musical accompaniment. But the pièce de résistance is the ability to slide the narrator's voice from a fast-talking, high-pitched alien to a slow-talking ogre (and everything in between). No matter where you set the voice, the narration is spoken in rhyme.

**Best For:** Astronauts in training. Kids who love to imagine a world filled with friendly aliens will be over the moon with this app.

# Monster's Socks

$2.99 US/$2.99 CAN/£1.99 UK, Ages 4–7, Jordan & Martin

Monster's Socks is a book app about a cute little monster who has lost his favorite socks. The monster, who lives in a box, travels over the meadow, into the forest, over the sea, and then up to the moon to find his missing socks. Along the way, your child helps the monster by using left- or right-arrow keys on the bottom of the screen to move him around, stopping each time the monster walks into a yellow circle. When the monster enters a circle, more of the story's narrative appears. Your child's involvement continues throughout, including pulling a bridge across a stream, and shaking apples from a tree so that the hungry monster can have a snack.

This adventure story is fun, and the visual style of this book adds to the experience. The landscapes combine realistic backdrops with craft products to create a fun, quirky vibe. By pulling tabs on the screen, the book also works like a pop-up book. The scene of the monster crossing the ocean in a boat is awesome, with waves crashing around the boat and sea creatures jumping out of the water to talk to the monster. This app teaches kids kindness by having them help the furry guy. Better yet, kids are put in control of when and what direction the monster moves.

**Best For:** Young children who love to participate in a story while it's being read. This is a good book for antsy kids because they need to participate to move the story forward. Because this little guy is anything but scary, this app's a great pick if your child is afraid of monsters.

# Even Monsters Get Sick

$.99 US/$0.99 CAN/£0.69 UK, Ages 4–8, Busy Bee Studios

This is a book app about an adorable monster named Zub and a boy named Harry who helps him. Harry's friend Mona thinks her pet monster is boring. She offers Harry a trade of three stickers, two sticks of gum, and a skateboard for Zub, the no-fun monster. Harry jumps at the offer because he loves monsters, and your child helps by dragging the traded items across the screen to Mona.

Harry tries all sorts of fun things to get a rise out of Zub, including taking him to the movies, giving him ice cream, and sitting on a jumpy ball. Only after all of these playful things fail to make Zub happy does Harry realize that his monster is sick. After calling a doctor, Harry nurses Zub back to health by soliciting your child's help in using a seesaw to catapult cans of chicken soup into the monster's giant maw. When Zub gets better, he turns out to be the best monster ever. He helps Harry make a rocket ship out of bottle caps; he teaches Harry how to play musical video games; and he even tells Harry spooky stories. When Mona wants to make a trade to get Zub back, Harry turns her down, noting that Zub is the best hugger in the world.

In addition to a charming monster story, this book app has playable mazes and 24 pages filled with fun, touchable hotspots waiting for you to find them. In the scene where Harry offers a sick Zub an ice cream cone, if you touch the wall clock, the cuckoo flies out to lick the cone. It's charming. This book can be read to you by a perfect little boy voice or you can explore it by yourself. The words don't highlight when read.

**Best For:** Kids who are afraid of monsters and those who adore them. Zub teaches kids that anyone can get sick and that although he was afraid of doctors, he learned that they can be very helpful.

The next day he helped me make a rocketship out of bottle caps!

# Create A Monster HD
$0.99 US/$0.99 CAN/£0.69 UK, Ages 5 and up, justfun llc

This easy-to-use app encourages your kids to create the coolest-looking monsters. With a simple double-touch system, players can choose a body from an array of choices at the bottom of the screen. Then they add as many body parts as they want, choosing from a wide range of eyes, noses, mouths, ears, antennae, and other extra appendages. Kids can change the colors of each part as they see fit. A completed monster can be saved to an in-app gallery for showing later, revisited for further additions, or cloned to take your creature in a new direction. Kids can also frame it as in the illustration below and print it out.

They can e-mail it, or share it on a parent's Twitter or Facebook account.

Create A Monster is more sophisticated than the Elmo's Monster Maker app reviewed earlier in the chapter. You control what attributes your monster has and how many to add. You also have the ability to size and rotate each part's placement. The app has a symmetry tool if you want to use it. This freedom allows you to do things like place eyes on top of antennae or add extra teeth inside of mouths. The best part of the app is that when you add any eye, it starts to blink.

**Best For:** Older monster-loving kids (ages 5 and up) who enjoy experimenting with making dazzling-looking, high-definition monsters. Kids need to be proficient with pinching and pulling so that they can resize the parts and figure out how to rotate items added.

## Save the Aliens
$1.99 US/$1.99 CAN/£1.49 UK, Ages 8 and up, Alchemy Games

Save the Aliens is a match-three puzzler with a unique spin. Instead of matching colored gems on a grid, this game presents the gems within three rotating rings that fit inside a circle. You play by rotating the rings to align the jewels, which makes them disappear. With a story about an alien world soon to be destroyed by a supernova, players work furiously to line up gems to match a series of three-gem codes before time runs out. Creating a code means an alien is rescued and transported to the safety of the waiting mothership. If the gems you need to make a code aren't present, you must clear out gems by matching three of the same color so that your rings refill with new gems.

Presented with excellent tutorials and plenty of animation, this brightly colored app starts out easy, but slowly increases in difficulty. It stays fresh with the introduction of special gems that, when combined, do things like add time or blow up all the gems of one color. This game has 4 planets that need saving, with a total of 84 levels. Kids can even earn 38 special achievements.

The title page has links to Facebook, Twitter, the developer's website, and Game Center.

**Best For:** Kids who like timed puzzles in which they have to think and act quickly. These aliens are adorable, and by rescuing them, you become the hero or heroine.

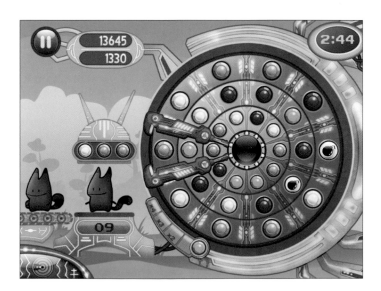

# 21 Music

## Musical Me! HD — by Duck Duck Moose

$1.99 US/$1.99 CAN/£1.49 UK, Ages 3–6, Duck Duck Moose

Musical Me! HD creates an inviting and whimsical way for kids to explore music. Through five activities involving cute animals, kids learn about musical notes, rhythm, pitch, and percussion instruments. Budding musicians play games in which they listen to musical notes and then copy what they hear, or create songs by tapping birds flying by to create a rhythm. Kids can also tap the screen to play percussion instruments, including a drum, cymbals, triangle, and even a baby duck. In another activity, children rearrange musical notes on a staff to experiment with composing a song. The silliest activity involves moving animals around the screen as they dance and rock out to various songs.

With two of the activities offering three difficulty levels, this is an app that can grow with your child. The app offers different instrumental options, from hearing someone sing to listening to a violin, piano, or electric guitar. The developers at Duck Duck Moose use high quality music in all of their apps; this one contains 14 different songs.

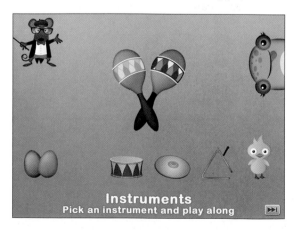

**Instruments**
Pick an instrument and play along

**Best For:** Introducing young children to music. Its light-hearted manner makes this musical exploration lively and fun.

TIP

If your kids enjoy this app, this developer has several others that showcase musical nursery rhymes, including Itsy Bitsy Spider, Baa Baa Black Sheep, and Old MacDonald (reviewed in Chapter 2).

# A Jazzy Day – Music Education Book for Kids

$4.99 US/$4.99 CAN/£2.99 UK, Ages 3–7, The Melody Book

Looking for a fun way to introduce your kids to musical instruments and the sounds they make? This app's for you.

The main part of the app is a story about two kids (anthropomorphized kittens) and their hip-cat father who is taking them to see a big jazz band. Told in 15 pages, this cute story has light animation. As the kittens in the story learn about jazz, so do your kids.

On the way to a concert hall, the father explains the various parts of a big jazz band. Kids meet a raccoon playing the bass, a fox beating the drums, a goose on the piano, and a squirrel strumming the electric guitar, as well as lots more animal musicians. Kids control the music by tapping each musician whenever they stop. From the horn section, kids meet four mice playing trombones. Kids can touch each mouse to make them jive together.

The father uses colorful language to explain how the instruments work together to make jazz. He likens jazz music to having a musical conversation in which one section asks a question and another answers. He explains that when jazz starts to *swing,* it means the music makes you want to dance. The last page of the book lets kids hear a short, fully orchestrated jazz piece. It's pretty spectacular.

In addition to the book, the app has a separate page where kids can tap 12 instruments to hear their sounds, including: bass, drums, guitar, piano, vibraphone, trumpet, trombone, alto saxophone, baritone saxophone, tenor saxophone, flute, and clarinet. Kids can then play a game about identifying which instrument is making the music they hear. You can even take a photo with the kittens and send it to your relatives. Cute!

The sound quality in this app is impressive, and the story mode makes learning about the instruments fun. Being able to touch the musicians throughout the pages to have them play engages kids in creating the music.

**Best For:** All kids. This is an excellent introduction to jazz and may start your kids on a life-long journey of enjoying music.

The TROMBONES are lower and more mellow. They're played by using a slide instead of pressing valves like on the trumpet.

# Little Fox Music Box – Kids songs – Sing along

$2.99 US/$2.99 CAN/£1.99 UK, Ages 3–6,
Shape Minds and Moving Images GmbH

As the title implies, this app makes you feel like you've just opened a magical music box. Inside, kids can explore three scenes filled with interactive hotspots. Each features a different song. Additionally, kids can conduct their own music in the Fox Studio, a room filled with music-making devices. This app is a feast for exploring fingers!

With the "London Bridge" song, kids see a whimsical representation of a London street where the bridge is missing. Here a whale pops out of the river, a pirate ship sails by, an animal-filled hot air balloon floats over-head, and cartoony pedestrians pass along the street — kids can explore a lot of zany animations. Likewise, the scene depicted in this rendition of "Old MacDonald" is the wackiest farm I've ever seen. The pig is in a bathtub, the cow is in love with the donkey, the squirrel drops acorns on the sleeping farmer's head, and the fox is disguised as a sheep. It has a madcap feel to it because these animals are cheeky and mischievous. "Evening Song" is a gentler composition, so the animations are calmer, but equally magical. Here kids find animals snuggled up for the night in hidden tree hollows or caves in the mountains. Players can even use their finger to paint the Aurora Borealis across the sky.

In addition to these three fabulously interactive songs, which can be shown with the words highlighted karaoke-style, the app also provides kids with an open-ended musical creation room where every object you touch makes a different sound. Kids can conduct a chorus of singing frogs, an ensemble of tweeting birds, a trio of teapots, a quartet of hang-ing ladles, and other musical giggles. This is a place to have fun and create your own music.

Between the three song pages and the musical studio, kids have lots of ways to enjoy songs and explore musical con-cepts in a whimsical manner.

**Best For:** All young children. This app creates an irresistible musi-cal fantasy world that just beck-ons your child's exploration.

# Toca Band
$1.99 US/$1.99 CAN/£1.49 UK, Ages 3–10, Toca Boca

This app creates a musical playground where kids can experiment by moving 16 different characters onto a stage to create music. Each character creates its own sound and rhythm, but its musical riff varies, depending on where it's standing on the stage. The result is a fascinating musical mash-up.

Every character is quirky, but each resembles something that makes sound. For example, the grandmotherly lady is an opera singer, and the pair of frogs belongs in the percussion group. Others creating percussion sounds include a tap-dancing spider, a teeth-chattering pickle, a dancing alarm clock, and a chef using his pots and pans. However, the rapping blue ball wearing sunglasses and a melodic cat who has singing balls within its mouth steal the show. This band is like nothing you've seen before. And all of the characters are endearing.

The placement of the characters onstage also affects the music. You have three rows with eight positions to fill. Musicians placed in the back row of the stage are louder and more upbeat, carrying the performance. You can move one character into the coveted yellow starlight; and when you do, it rises up for a close-up, which allows you to play it by touching it. The ballerina Dancy Nancy, when placed in the starlight, magically appears on top of a playable piano.

Although these musical creatures are all contributing to just one song, it's so infectious and changeable that it's irresistible. This app encourages families to explore it together. No one can resist jumping in to try to change the tune.

This app has a For Parents section on the home page that provides you tips about how to best use this app with your child. You can make this icon (and the icon about other Toca news) disappear by going to the Settings app on your iPad, scrolling down to Toca Band, and then toggling these two options off.

**Best For:** All kids. This is an amazingly creative app that makes exploring music an imaginative process.

# My Musical Friends HD

Free US/CAN/UK, Ages 4–8, Melody Street LLC

By turning musical instruments into cartoon friends, this app acquaints kids with the instruments of the orchestra. The app introduces 19 different musical friends, who belong to families, including strings, woodwinds, percussion, brass, and pluck (piano and harp). Each instrument appears one at a time, and is shown in three ways as it starts to play: first as a cartoon with a silly name (Benson Bass or Porter Piano); next, after kids touch it, as an image of the real thing; and finally, after kids touch it again, as a photo of someone actually playing that instrument. Onscreen are two buttons. By tapping the Did You Know button, kids hear something funny about the cartoon friend, but it may also weave in a true fact about the instrument. The Fun Fact button tells kids something specific about that instrument — for example, that bassoons have 7 feet of tubing. Also, some buttons allow you to play the instrument.

By combining whimsy and fact, this app makes learning about each instrument fun. The anthropomorphized versions of the instruments are very cute, and each has a distinct personality. For example, Tiberius Tuba sports a dashing mustache and wears black boots. His Did You Know fact reveals that he is cool, calm, and in control, but that he is also the lowest and loudest sounding member of the brass family. By providing budding musicians with five buttons on the bottom of the screen to hear and play each instrument, the app lets kids continue to explore the sound of the instrument even after it has stopped playing its introductory ditty.

The home page has a button that leads kids out of the app to the iTunes store.

**Best For:** Introducing young kids to the instruments of the orchestra and the sounds each instrument makes. By turning the instruments into cartoon characters with distinct personalities, the app lets kids have fun learning about their new friends.

Publisher Melody Street LLC has two other free apps featuring these animated musical instruments. I recommend that you download Mozart Interactive and Melody Street HD — they are both cute.

# Stella and the Startones

$1.99 US/$1.99 CAN/£1.49 UK, Ages 4–10, Bohem Interactive

Stella and the Startones presents a series of musical landscapes that respond to your kids' touches. Kids can start by running a finger over a giant globe representing the night sky. Musical tones and interludes play as their fingers move over the constellations. Linger on a specific constellation, and a new landscape opens, featuring a fictional character created from that constellation's configuration. Every touch produces a musical tone and most objects and notes can be moved around within the landscape.

The 21 characters, each presented in an open sand-box-like environment where there are no rules, offer different musical styles including Samba, Modern Jazz, Caribbean, and more. This app is unique because it provides a way for kids to appreciate the pure joy of exploring a responsive, unusual musical environment. The app has more than 500 interactive elements.

**Best For:** Kids who enjoy exploring music in a totally unstructured way, which works for some kids and doesn't for others.

# Pluto Learns Piano HD

Free US/CAN/UK, Ages 4 and up, Pluto Games, Inc.

This nifty music game teaches kids how to play the piano by inviting them to play a side-scrolling game, moving a penguin over bubbled notes on a musical staff floating in the sea. Kids need to avoid incorrect notes (indicated in a different color) and animals like whales who are also float-ing in this musical ocean. In another game, players use a piano keyboard to play a song by following highlighted keys. In either game, you earn up to three stars for playing well. Collect enough stars, and you can unlock one of 19 new songs to play.

The app begins with two starter songs, but you can purchase song packs inside the app instead of unlocking them through practice. You can also purchase a feature called Practice Mode, which lets kids see the musical notes when they are playing on the piano. In essence, it teaches kids how to read music. You can buy all 17 songs and the Practice Mode for $29.99.

**Best For:** Families looking for a playful way to learn how to play the piano.

# 22 Puzzles

## Magic Garden with Letters and Numbers – A Logical Game for Kids

$1.99 US/$1.99 CAN/£1.49 UK, Ages 4–8, Alexandre Minard

By connecting water pipes, kids help bring this magic garden to life. In this garden, flowers, letters, and numbers bloom. You find the pipes on a puzzle grid. Kids start at a pond and connect the pipes closest to it by tapping each grid square to rotate the pipes so that they connect to the water source. When the water finally reaches its objective — flowers, numbers, or letters — the flowers bloom, the letters pulse, and the numbers sparkle. Each puzzle presents a maze that kids need to figure out by rotating the pieces on the grid. The app has 108 puzzles in all, with 36 each covering flowers, numbers, and the alphabet. The faster kids solve the puzzles, the more stars they earn.

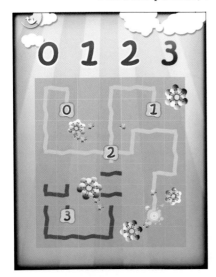

This is a gentle logic puzzle with a nice, artistic design, intuitive controls, and flowing music. Tapping to rotate a puzzle piece is simple, but connecting the pipes in the right order requires logical thinking. The app offers a good tutorial in the beginning, but it's not read aloud, so parents may need to read it to younger children to get them started. I also like how the app celebrates the completion of a puzzle with a rainbow and clapping. Kids get a real sense of accomplishment by working through these visually pleasing garden mazes.

**Best For:** Teaching young children logical thinking. These puzzles ramp up very slowly in difficulty, and celebrate kids' accomplishments.

# My First Tangrams HD – A Wood Tangram Puzzle Game for Kids

$1.99 US/$1.99 CAN/£1.49 UK, Ages 4–7, Alexandre Minard

Tangram puzzles originated in ancient China and involved seven geometric shapes. This collection of puzzles for kids still uses geometric shapes, but has more than seven pieces.

The app provides kids with four different modes. In the first, kids solve 32 puzzles in which the outline of the shape is shown in the solution area. Wooden blocks are found at the bottom of the screen, and kids drag the pieces to place them on the puzzle. In the second mode, again with 32 puzzles, only one shape's outline is shown; but kids can see what the final product should look like in a small picture in the upper-right corner. The third mode lets kids create their own puzzles to share with others. In the fourth mode, you can try puzzles made by others.

This puzzle has a clean, simple interface. You hear music as you play, but you can turn it off. Kids know when they have moved a puzzle piece into the correct place because the piece makes a dinging sound, it gets bigger, and then it settles into place. When players finish a puzzle, they hear applause, and confetti gently falls from the top of the screen.

I really like the setup of these puzzles. The first mode is the easiest, showing kids what the puzzle should look like. The second mode is more challenging because kids have to study the diagram and copy it. At no time do you have to rotate the shapes, which can be hard for little fingers to do. I also love that kids can get creative and make their own designs using these geometric shapes, and then send their puzzles to the developer for sharing. The developer screens all puzzles submitted before posting them for others to try.

**Best For:** Young kids who enjoy puzzles. These slowly get progressively harder. Designing your own puzzles to share can also be exciting and rewarding.

**I SPY Spooky Mansion for iPad**
$3.99 US, Ages 5–12, Scholastic Inc.

Based on one of the original *I SPY* books by Jean Marzollo and Walter Wick, this delightfully spooky app lets kids play seek-and-find puzzles inside and around a creaky old mansion. When kids enter the mansion estate, they get locked in! The only way out is to play the 21 puzzles filled with hidden objects to earn the 7 keys needed to unlock the gate and escape this mansion.

After choosing one of seven locations on a map, players are whisked to an object-filled scene. A riddle is spoken and shown in writing at the bottom of the screen. You hunt for the objects described by the riddle. When you find and tap the objects in the picture, their words turn red, indicating that part of the riddle is solved. Spooky music accompanies your search.

These *I SPY* puzzles are fun because the scenes are filled with fascinating things. The puzzles challenge kids to think about words in different ways. For example, one of the riddles asks kids to find two shoes — one is a human shoe, but the other belongs to a horse.

Because many of the pictures are so crowded with items, it's helpful that the app allows you to zoom in and out by using the pinching and pulling-open motion.

**Best For:** Kids with perseverance. These puzzles can be tricky and they don't offer any hints. However, you can leave an unfinished puzzle and then come back to it, and the app remembers where you were in the puzzle.

 If you're looking for an easier hidden-object puzzle app with hints, try Little Things by KLICKTOCK.

I SPY a red needle, a jar filled with dew,
A swordsman, a skeleton, GHOST, and BOO!

# Rush Hour Free

Free US/CAN/UK, Ages 6 and up, ThinkFun, Inc.

Rush Hour Free, based on the 1996 award-winning puzzle game, uses sliding as its basic movement. Played on a grid, the challenge is to slide cars and trucks forward or backward to create a path for the red car to exit the traffic jam.

This app has a great tutorial and gives you 35 puzzles spread over 4 difficulty levels. The app rewards clever thinking and gives stars for solutions that use the fewest moves possible. The app has hints, an Undo button, and even a Solve button.

Rush Hour is a fun way to introduce logical thinking to kids. These puzzles, even on the Easy level, require you to think ahead before you start sliding the vehicle around. Rush Hour also teaches kids that some challenges can be solved by trial and error.

By keeping track of the number of moves you take to solve a puzzle, the game lets you know if you found the most efficient solution and, if not, whether you bettered your score from the last time you played. This information motivates kids to replay puzzles over and over again until they find the perfect solution.

**Best For:** Kids who like thinking challenges. Kids as young as 6 can play the easy puzzles, whereas the harder ones are better for age 8 and up. When my kids were young, I used this puzzle (in its physical form) to teach them how to plan ahead in games. It's a good way to teach logic, and it can be used as a precursor to chess.

If you want more puzzles, the app offers an in-app purchase to upgrade to the paid version for $2.99, which unlocks a whopping 2,500 levels!

Remember to turn off in-app purchases if you don't want to accidentally upgrade.

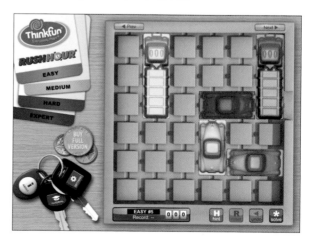

# Doodle Fit

$0.99 US/$0.99 CAN/£0.69 UK, Ages 6 and up, Gamelion Studios

The object of this set of puzzles is to fit a set of oddly shaped geometric blocks into to an outlined frame. Some of the more than 100 puzzles have just one solution, whereas others have two or more. You have no time limit or any requirement to finish the puzzle in the least moves possible; and hints are available. A funky soundtrack accompanies the puzzle-playing.

Since this is a *doodle* puzzle, the blocks appear on paper as if drawn with black crayons. When a piece is moved into the puzzle, it changes color. Players have the option of drawing the shape of the piece anywhere within the puzzle frame and the piece automatically appears. You can also pick up a piece within the puzzle to move it around. You can't rotate pieces. For every two puzzles you solve, you earn a hint. Hints place one piece in the puzzle, and you can use multiple hints per puzzle. The game is broken into four sets of puzzles; and within each set, you unlock the next puzzle by completing the one before it.

This puzzle is good because it lets kids experiment with fitting geometric shapes within a frame. With no time pressure, kids focus on trying new ways to combine the pieces. I like that the difficulty level ramps up slowly and that hints are readily available.

This app has some in-app purchases for new levels, unlimited hints, and the capability to unlock all of the levels without having to earn them. If your child loves this app, the new levels may be worth it. And for dedicated kids who hit a difficulty level that is too challenging, the unlimited hints may be a good way for them to learn. The app has a Facebook button and a pop-up ad for other apps by the developer.

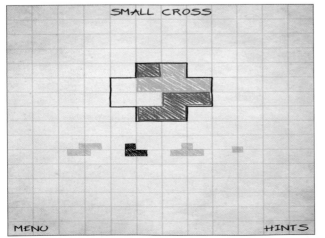

**Best For:** Kids who like shape puzzles, such as tangrams. It's also a good fit for kids who enjoy playing Blokus (reviewed in Chapter 9). This is the perfect app to explore when your kids graduate from doing My First Tangrams HD – A Wood Tangram Puzzle Game for Kids, reviewed earlier in this chapter.

# Blueprint 3D HD

$2.99 US/$2.99 CAN/£1.99 UK, Ages 7 and up,
FDG Entertainment

Among the thousands of puzzle apps crowding the iTunes store, Blueprint 3D HD is unique. Its more than 300 levels challenge kids to make sense out of chaos. Each puzzle presents them with a set of random lines and scribbles onscreen. By rotating the jumble, kids can bring order to the craziness as a familiar object starts to appear. By lining up the lines and dots across multiple planes, and rotating the image so that it faces the correct direction, the puzzle snaps into place, revealing the blueprint of a familiar object, building, or animal. You are scored by how long it takes you to solve the puzzle, winning three stars if you can rotate the blueprint quickly into place.

Blueprint 3D HD divides its puzzles into themed packs. You can discover famous buildings such as the Eiffel Tower and the Statue of Liberty. Other packs cover technology, electronics, space, military, transportation, musical instruments, Christmas, and my favorite: animals. Different musical scores accompany the various packs.

You can solve each puzzle on three difficulty levels, with the hardest level requiring you to rotate different planes separately in the 3D image — a process that is devilishly hard. But the easiest level is fine for ages 7 and older because it provides you with a hint about the location of the top and helps you complete a puzzle when you get close to the answer.

These puzzles are great for challenging your kids to see things in 3D. When your child sees the object taking form, she'll have a great sense of accomplishment, particularly because the puzzle seems impossible at the beginning.

This app has an in-app purchase to buy solutions. It also connects to Facebook and is aggressive about asking you to share the app by gifting it or sharing an e-mail.

**Best For:** Kids who relish a challenge. These puzzles teach kids about perspective. They each have an "aha" moment when everything comes together and kids find the solution. Parents, you may want to try this one, too — it's exciting to explore.

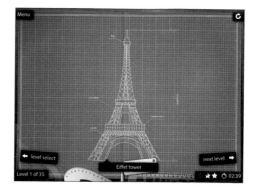

# Joining Hands

$2.99 US/$2.99 CAN/£1.99 UK, Ages 7 and up, 10tons Ltd

This charming set of puzzles has a little bit of story to keep your child motivated. The stars of these puzzles are creatures known as Peablins, adorable round beings who aren't happy unless all of their hands are being held by others. Some Peablins have one hand, whereas others have two, three, or even up to six.

As the Peablins journey through Whispering Woods to find their lost cousins, they need to always hold hands so that they feel safe from the Bogeyman. That's where the puzzle comes in — it's your job to arrange the Peablins and their relatives on honeycomb-like grids so that all of their hands are connected. The grids also contain stars, and you earn them by placing characters on the spots with the stars.

These puzzles are spread over ten episodes in which the Peablins meet new relatives, each with its own quirks and hand-holding appendages. For example, the Brufflins are strong but inflexible. Unlike the Peablins, whose hands rotate freely around their bodies, the Brufflins' muscled arms are set in one position, so you have to rotate them to hold hands with others.

Other than the reference to the Bogeyman, kids don't see anything scary. These puzzles aren't timed, so kids won't feel pressure as they experiment rearranging the characters on the grid so that all are holding hands.

This puzzle app is good because it has simple rules (rearrange the characters so that you leave no hand untouched), but it's also challenging. The levels slowly ramp up in difficulty. By introducing new characters with different characteristics, the puzzles stay fresh. Plus, all of these characters have personalities revealed through their facial expressions. They become riotously happy when you line them up correctly, jumping up and down with joy. When you start a puzzle, the Peablins' world is muted, but when you solve it, the world brightens. It's the characters' bubbly charm and the simplicity of the rules that keep you coming back for more.

 The app contains a rotating ad on the home page that links directly to the app store, or when featuring Facebook, to that social network.

**Best For:** Kids who like puzzles and are also social. Because these characters seem alive, kids feel like they are playing with someone as they flex their puzzle-solving muscles.

# Polymer

$1.99 US/$1.99 CAN/£1.49 UK, Ages 8 and up,
Whitaker Blackall

This puzzle game is played on a grid that can be shifted by moving rows and columns. Each grid piece has a geometrically shaped piece of polymer clay. If the piece has a black dot on the edge, it must be connected to another piece. But there are also pieces without the dot that work as end pieces. The goal is to shift the pieces around until you create a polymer structure that is encased with no black dots on the end. When you succeed, tap the polymer structure to earn points. The bigger the structure, the more points you earn.

Play can be timed — two-, five-, or ten-minute rounds — to see how many points you can earn in that time period. Or you can also explore the Endless Mode in which there is no time pressure. The app has a multiplayer mode, but it's not for players on the same iPad; rather, it uses the Game Center to find other players.

You can also unlock two additional modes: One Polymer, in which you try to build the biggest polymer, with no time pressure; and Bombs, which is just the opposite because it's all about time pressure as you madly try to create polymers that have bombs in them before they explode. The bombs show how many seconds you have left.

Polymer follows the successful pattern of the best puzzles: easy to learn but difficult to master. This is a great puzzle game for kids because it teaches them how to plan ahead. You have to figure out how to move the pieces that close a polymer into the right position so that you can best use them.

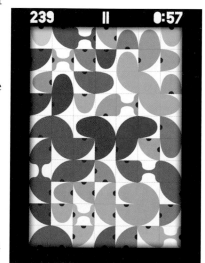

You can earn what you need to play this puzzle without using its in-app purchases. But, it does provide pieces to purchase for players who don't have the patience to earn them. Parents may want to make sure they've turned off the in-app purchases before letting their kids play this puzzle. Also, this app uses Game Center for multiplayer mode, and connects to Facebook, Twitter, and email.

**Best For:** Kids who love the challenge of puzzles that make you think. Because this puzzle has so much movement, it's a good choice for kids who get antsy.

# TwinGo!

$0.99 US/$0.99 CAN/£0.69 UK, Ages 8 and up, Chillingo Ltd

The weather twins, Fuyu and Natsu, have somehow misplaced the stars that appear in the sky. They need your help in playing more than 90 puzzles in which you can find 3 stars each.

These puzzles, spread over four worlds, have a unique shtick: The two weather twins, one a ball of flame and the other a ball of ice, always move in tandem. So instead of moving one character around on the elevated, irregular grid, you have to pay attention to two. That means if you roll one of the round twins one space to the right, the other twin (who may be several spaces away) also rolls one space to the right. You have to be careful that your decisions don't cause one of the two twins to roll off the platform into game-ending oblivion. Spaces with walls are the key to solving these puzzles because they can keep one twin from rolling while you move the other. After collecting the three stars, you must roll the two twins onto colored launch pads to send them catapulting into the next puzzle.

These puzzles are great for teaching kids logical thinking and planning ahead. Figuring out how to use the walled spaces is the key to success, but this logic takes some practice. The game cleverly offers an undo button so that kids can experiment with a series of moves to see if their plan will work. While your kids are busy being brainy, the app supports their concentration with a delightful upbeat soundtrack.

This app has some aspects that can be troublesome. The start page contains links to Twitter and Facebook. You may need to remind kids younger than 13 not to touch those. Also, you can connect to the Crystal gaming network to share scores and achievements, but I would recommend that you don't use that network until kids are teens. Also, the app shows ads for this publisher's other apps, but you can hide them by tapping a button.

**Best For:** Kids who like challenging puzzles. These are fresh and unique.

# Slice It!

$0.99 US/$0.99 CAN/£0.69 UK, Ages 10 and up, Com2uS Inc.

For the mathematically minded, this is a fun puzzle game about slicing geometric shapes into equal areas. For each puzzle, you are shown a shape and then given a certain number of slicing motions. Your goal is to slice the object into a specified number of equally sized shapes. You start by dividing a square or a pizza into equal shares, which seems like no big deal, but you quickly encounter silhouettes that aren't symmetrical. Now the puzzles get interesting. As the shapes get harder to slice, you also encounter obstacles that keep you from slicing all across the page, so you have to be creative about how you separate portions.

With 200 puzzles spread out over two episodes, you've got a lot of slicing and dicing to do. This app also has bonus content and a shortened version called Quick Mode in which you slice up as many shapes into equal parts in a limited amount of time. You also earn hints by solving previous puzzles.

This is an excellent puzzler for older kids because it gets them playing with geometric shapes while just having fun. This isn't one of the thousands of game apps that just kills time — this game gets your kids thinking. Kids have to think outside of the box to come up with ways to use their limited slices in a way to reach the goal. It's challenging, but doesn't move into the realm of frustrating because of its hint system. Plus, trial and error is encouraged, and tips are plentiful.

Kids are encouraged to share their scores on Twitter and to "like" this app on Facebook. The home page has a button to sign up using your e-mail to connect with the Com2uS Hub, which keeps track of global and country rankings. I would recommend that your children don't use these social networking features until they are at least 13. There are also ads on the home page.

**Best For:** Older kids who enjoy brainy puzzles.

# 23 Road Trip Apps

## Apps Covered in This Chapter

▶ Road-Trip-Bingo HD

▶ Mask Jumble Animals

▶ Wonderputt

▶ Mad Libs: On the Road

▶ BRAIN QUEST

▶ Learn the States – USA Capital and Geography Fact Learning

## Road-Trip-Bingo HD

$1.99 US/$1.99 CAN/£1.49 UK, Ages 4 and up, Bright Bunny

For families traveling by car, bus, or train, this nifty app provides a way to play the classic travel bingo game with either one or two players. For one player, the app presents a bingo card full of road signs, vehicles, traffic signs, animals, weather, and things typically found along the road, like street lights and telephone poles. When kids see the items on the card, they tap the picture and a purple marker appears. When they get five in a row in any direction, they win. When playing with two players, you can place the bingo cards either side by side or facing away from each other. The gameplay is the same as for a single player. Both versions can have classical music play as an accompaniment.

The iTunes store has a ton of travel bingo apps. This one rises above the others because it has the option of playing with another person — which makes the game more fun. Also, the icons used on the cards are nicely painted and easy to understand. For example, because kids see a red car as well as a white one on the Bingo card, they understand that seeing just any car is not enough; rather, they must see the correctly colored car.

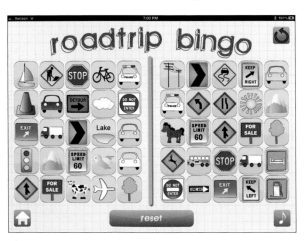

**Best For:** Families traveling. It's particularly fun for siblings. This is a great way to make those miles go by quickly, and it teaches kids to be observant.

# Mask Jumble Animals

$1.99 US/$1.99 CAN/£1.49 UK, Ages 3–8, Piikea St. LLC

When traveling with my kids, I found that if I had saved some special activity for late in the afternoon, instead of having whiny kids, I could buy some peace until dinner. This app is perfect for the late afternoon pick-me-up.

Mask Jumble Animals is a virtual dress-up app that appeals equally to boys and girls. It turns the iPad into a virtual mirror onto which it projects cute animal masks. The app shows your child her face, but then puts a mask on top so that she sees herself looking like an animal. Children can try on the masks of a dog, rabbit, lion, gorilla, elephant, horse, panda, tiger, goat, and cow.

Using real-time face recognition software, the app lines up your child's nose, ears, chin, and forehead inside of a template and then lets kids superimpose animal parts onto their faces. The child makes the animal parts appear on her image by touching her facial features on the iPad's screen. This transformation creates a moment of wonder because kids see themselves wearing an animal mask.

The app asks your child to create a specific animal. If your child touches her nose on the iPad image of herself, she sees it change into an animal's nose. By touching the same spot again, the app cycles through the possible animal noses. By tapping her forehead, chin, and ears, she can build the whole mask of the specific animal. When she does, the app rewards her with sparkles and brings in an appropriate background to take a photo. You can share the photo with others via the iPad's photo collection.

Also fun is this app's virtual strawberry-catching game. When kids are wearing a mask, a strawberry is dropped from the top of the screen. Kids tilt their masked heads so that they line up to bite strawberries. Munching on virtual strawberries unlocks new masks to explore.

This is a simple but hilarious creativity app that makes dressing up on the iPad a breeze.

**Best For:** Families looking for a silly and charming pick-me-up late in the day. This virtual dress-up is almost as good as the real thing and perfect for the confined spaces of travel.

# Wonderputt

$0.99 US/$0.99 CAN/£0.69 UK, Ages 5 and up, Damp Gnat Ltd

Whenever our family goes on vacation, we are always on the look-out for a miniature golf course. Because it's one of the few sports in which I have a shot at trouncing my athletic guys (yes, two sons and a hubby), my eye is particularly eagle-like. That's why I was delighted to discover this amazing course — right on my iPad. It makes a perfect addition to your travel apps.

Breathtaking is the word that comes to mind when you open this app. It's like no other miniature golf course you have ever seen. It's a multi-layered and constantly changing course of greens where you play on top of lily pads in a pool, through a submarine, down a ski slope, and across crosswalks that lead to elevators — all while seeking to attain that elusive hole in one. At the end of one of the holes, a hot air balloon express delivers your ball to the next green. It's over-the-top and cool!

The play mechanics involve simply touching the ball, dragging back to set the strength of a putt, and then releasing, so this is a golf game that's easy to play; however, mastering these wildly original holes can be challenging. Although the app has only 18 holes, they are exciting to explore. I hope the publisher adds more holes and allows us to zoom in; but even so, this is so worth the $0.99.

This app only plays on iPad 2 or newer.

Have fun playing mini-golf on your vacation at the most spectacular course I've ever seen!

**Best For:** All families, on vacation or not. This is a must-have app!

# Mad Libs: On the Road

$3.99 US, Ages 6 and up, Penguin Group USA

Mad Libs booklets were standard fare in my travel toy bag. Now they are digital, and equally as fun to explore as a family. For those unfamiliar with Mad Libs, they are stories with blanks you ask others to fill in, and players try to contribute the zaniest words they can think of to produce a hilarious hodge-podge of a story.

Mad Libs can be filled out alone, but the best way to play them is in a group with one person designated as the reader, who calls out the kind of word needed — usually a part of speech, such as an exclamation, noun, or adverb, but sometimes it's something more specific, such as a color, part of the body, or number. The reader gets to decide which of the suggested words he wants to add to the story. This app has 20 stories to explore, ranging from "A Family Car Trip" to "Your Junk Is Someone Else's Treasure." In the latter, you fill in 18 words to create a funny story selling items at a garage sale.

Our family loved playing Mad Libs on road trips. My sons quickly learned the parts of speech so that they could contribute an adjective or an adverb. In this version, the About section reminds kids what each of the parts of speech means.

A free version is available called Mad Libs, but it has only four stories, and it hits you up to buy a collection such as this one or others called Goofy Mad Libs or Cool Mad Libs. All of the paid versions cost $3.99. Because most families probably want to explore more than four stories, I suggest bypassing the free, ad-filled version and going straight for the good stuff — this app.

After you finish a Mad Lib story, the app offers you the option to e-mail the completed story. Selecting this option can lead kids right into your e-mail application.

**Best For:** Traveling families that like to use outlandish language and have fun telling silly stories.

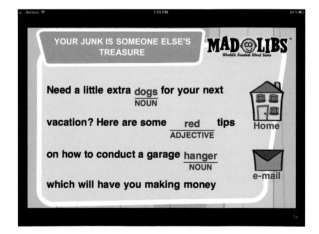

# BRAIN QUEST

Free (with $2.99 in-app purchase) US/CAN/UK, Ages 6–11, Workman Publishing Company, Inc.

When my kids were in grade school, I used Brain Quest cards as part of my standard traveling toy box. This app modernizes these traditional educational travel card sets. Now, the brainy questions, broken into sets for grades 1–5, are all on the iPad — and all the grades are in this one app.

This app is free to download. Your kids select their grade level, and then play an adventure game that moves them forward by answering a set of educational questions. These sets are called *stages*. Depending on the grade level, stages can contain anywhere from five to seven questions. The app provides only the first four stages in each grade level for free. And three kids can play; so if you have only one child using this app, he could sign in three different times to play the same four levels three times (the questions rotate) and get about 75 questions for free.

However, if you're going on a trip, I recommend that you buy your child's grade from within the app for $2.99. If you think you'll use this app across several grade levels, I would unlock the whole app (all grade levels) for $9.99.

This is a game of simply drilling educational, grade-appropriate questions, with little story interludes between rounds. The good news is that the questions are presented in interesting ways. For example, a 1st grade question might ask, "Which day has two "e's" in it?" If your child gets a question wrong, the correct answer is shown. Plus, if the child loses a stage and has to replay it, the app is careful to repeat the questions previously answered incorrectly. Questions cover all subjects and the content is vetted by a panel of educators.

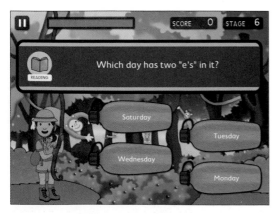

With siblings, this is an app that can be used for a pass-the-iPad game with each child playing his own grade level and then comparing scores after each round. When traveling in the car, my family also enjoys having one person read the questions out loud, and then everyone throwing out answers.

**Best For:** Traveling kids. This app is particularly helpful during summer vacation to help kids counter the dreaded "summer slide."

# Learn the States – USA Capital and Geography Fact Learning

$1.99 US/$1.99 CAN/£1.49 UK, Ages 7 and up, Merge Mobile

Want your kids to learn U.S. geography? Here's an app with three different games that make learning fun. This app doesn't talk to children, so they must be able to read to play.

The most unusual of the games is one in which kids plan the ultimate driving trip by drawing a path for a car to follow. The game challenges kids to drive across three targeted states to win the round. In another game, kids touch the interactive map according to directions, such as "Tap on the state of California." The last game is a multiple-choice quiz in which the answers are shown either as the state or in words. I like that you don't get a penalty for a wrong answer; so kids who don't know an answer won't hesitate to guess and can use the process of elimination to learn. Kids can also opt to study an interactive map that also shows state flashcards by accessing a separate learning section.

I selected this app for two reasons. First, the plan-your-trip-on-a-map game is unique and fun, especially when you get to watch a little toy car motor its way across the country to see if you managed to plan a path that travels over the correct states (the states light up if you're right). Second, it has a reward system in which kids earn one of the 50 state quarters when they are correct.

This isn't the slickest app, nor does it showcase great graphics; but it makes learning geography fun.

The app does occasionally show an ad for other apps by this developer in a way that is intrusive. The ad takes over a page and must be closed.

**Best For:** Car-loving kids and kids motivated by collecting quarters. The game involving drawing a path on the map so that a toy car can follow it is intriguing and is the perfect hook for kids who love cars.

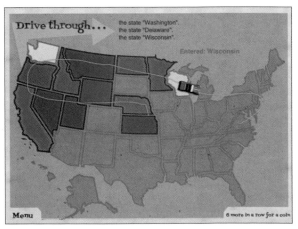

# 24 Special Needs

## Touch and Learn – Emotions

Free US/CAN/UK, Ages 3 and up, Innovative Mobile Apps

Aimed at kids who need help identifying emotions in others, this app presents four gorgeous photos and then verbally (and in writing if you so desire) asks your child to select the photo showing a person expressing the requested emotion.

Although a lot of apps help kids learn to read facial clues and body language, I chose this one over others for the following reasons. First, it's free — which makes it inexpensive to try out. Second, it starts right up on opening so there is no wait to get started. Third, the photos are vibrant and clearly represent the requested emotion, and they show great diversity in both race and gender. And lastly, you can set up the app to provide error-free learning — meaning you can toggle off the error sound.

I am also impressed with the way this app allows parents to tailor the content to best meet their child's needs. For instance, you can select

which of the 28 emotions you want displayed, customize which of the photos appear, and select the reward sounds your child hears. To make this app special and personal, you can record your own voice praising your child, and add photos of loved ones showing emotions.

**Best For:** Children needing extra practice at deciphering emotions on various faces.

# Proloquo2Go
$189.99 US, Ages 2 and up, AssistiveWare

This app creates a voice to aid speech-impaired kids in communication. By touching easily recognizable pictures, kids can have the iPad speak for them. Called an *augmentative and alternative communication (AAC) solution,* the app lets kids talk by tapping the symbols that appear onscreen, or by using the onscreen keyboard, which includes a word-prediction feature. The app can be adapted to fit a wide range of communication needs and adjusted to match different literacy levels. The voices that speak for the user are trained actors — real people, that is, and not a synthesizer — and you can select whether the voice is female or male and adult or child.

When using the pictorial interface, the app can be set up to use one of two vocabulary organizations: Basic Communication or Core Word. Basic Communication is for new users and offers buttons with only one or two words on them. Core Word is more nuanced and lets users select single words to say what they want. For example, in the Core Word system, to ask for an apple, you would first select the I and Want buttons, and then Food, a category button that produces a submenu from which you would select Fruits and then, in another submenu, Apple.

According to David Niemeijer, the founder and CEO of AssistiveWare, 60 percent of the users of this app have autism, Down syndrome, or cerebral palsy. Preschoolers make up 20 percent of users, school age children 60 percent, and adults 20 percent. The cost of the app, which is uncommonly expensive, reflects the ongoing costs of the years of research that went into making this app. The app has been consistently updated for free since it came out, with the most recent update adding children's voices. The app includes 24/7 e-mail support.

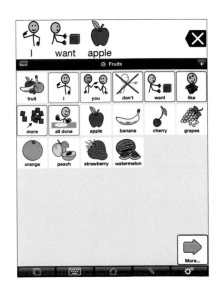

Although there are less expensive AAC apps, this one, recently featured on CBS's *60 Minutes,* is the gold standard. Families curious about its use can go to an Apple Store to try it because it's loaded on the display iPads in the stores.

**Best For:** Kids who need help communicating.

# Zanny – Born to Run

$2.99 US/$2.99 CAN/£1.99 UK, Ages 3–8, Extra Special Kids, LLC.

Part of a book app series written expressly for children with special needs, Zanny features an adorable little boy who is on the go at all times. Delivered in rhyming verse, this story shows Zanny running through a variety of scenes, including breakfast (where the player can zing Cheerios across the screen) and the playground (where he passes up a slide to keep running). Zanny is faster than a chicken, a rabbit, and even a cheetah! Zanny owns lots of shoes, but he doesn't like to wear them, and his buttons are frequently undone. He even moves his legs when sleeping. With hilarious versions of Zanny zipping through each page, this is a fun book to explore with your extra special kid.

The book purposefully shows Zanny's symptoms (and not a disorder) so that both kids who are "typical" but have difficulties and children

diagnosed with a learning disability can relate to Zanny. I really like that the app offers an Extra Special Feelings Game in which kids drag a cartoon expression to the faces of Zanny and his friends. It's a clever way to learn about the facial expressions that make someone look sad, mad, happy, or scared.

**Best For:** All children, but it has particular meaning to those who are extra special.

# Little Lilly's Touch Book

$2.99 US/$2.99 CAN/£1.99 UK, Ages 3–8, Extra Special Kids, LLC.

The second book in the Extra Special Kids series of book apps, this story stars Lilly, a little girl with Sensory Processing Disorder (SPD). Lilly loves to boogie down and cut a rug, but only if she is wearing socks. Lilly explains how she responds to the world in a unique manner, and this helps others understand some of the issues facing kids with SPD.

Written by Pamela Sloane-Bradbury, this is a charming story about how Lilly's sensitive toes think grass is too "prickly" and sand is too "tickly." Any child reading this story comes away with a better understanding of how some kids see, hear, and feel the world differently, but are still unique and wonderful. I adore this story and little Lilly!

**Best For:** All kids, but it is particularly poignant for kids with SPD.

**LetterReflex – Overcoming Letter Reversals & Backwards Writing in Early Childhood Development & Dyslexic Children**
$2.99 US/$2.99 CAN/£1.99 UK, Ages 4 and up, BinaryLabs

Although it's normal for preschoolers to have some trouble with letter reversals and writing letters backward, most have figured it out by early elementary. For kids who are struggling in preschool and for older kids who reverse letters and write some of them backward, this is a good app to check out. It makes learning how to correctly form letters and numbers into two fun games. In the first, kids tilt the iPad so that marbles roll to a specified letter. When they do, the letter re-forms in the center of the screen — thus driving home the correct formation of the letter or number. The second game is an arcade-like game involving flipping letters, numbers, and words to match the yellow ones that are correct. When flipped correctly, the letter, number, or words turn yellow to show that they too are now correct.

The tilt game uses the theory that by learning to tilt to the right and left, kids associate which side the circle belongs on letters such as *b* and *d*. Because it looks like the old-fashioned maze game about tilting the surface to direct the marble, kids think they're just having fun. In the flip game, you can flip as many times as you want until you land on the correct direction. Because you are timed, kids become motivated to study the flipped and upside-down letters so that they can flip them the least number of times.

**Best For:** Kids needing practice with letter reversals and backward writing.

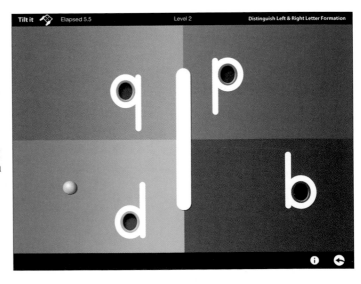

# Injini: Child Development Game Suite Lite

Free US/CAN/UK, Ages 4 and up, NCSOFT

This is the Lite, or free, version of the more hefty Injini: Child Development Game Suite that sells for $29.99. Because this version has eight different, carefully developed games — each of which offers three difficulty levels — start with this free version and see if it meets your child's needs. Designed specifically for children with special needs, this product was tested during development on kids with autism, cerebral palsy, Down syndrome, and others who have developmental delays. The app helps players learn colors, shapes, visual finding skills, matching, patterns, sequences, jigsaw puzzles, and tracing skills in a very deliberate and carefully paced manner.

The artwork is stunning, and the eight games are all fun. I chose this app because it is well thought-out for its intended audience. The tutorials are spoken as well as presented visually, and they start with the eye symbol to indicate it's time to watch. Before a level begins, the app carefully counts backward from three to let players know when to start; when players reach the end, they are presented with a celebratory smiley face. For each activity, a Help button is available to provide a hint or reiterate the goal.

The app is careful to increase the difficulty within a level of the game in incremental ways. For example, in the puzzle game, you start by simply moving a cat to its outline. The cat then animates and makes a sound. After several rounds of this type of puzzling, the level then introduces two pieces to the puzzle. Likewise, in the Find It game, kids first seek one item in a drawer, but gradually a second item is added; and thereafter, one item may be located partially on top of another.

**WARNING!** Because this is a Lite version, a notice at the end of each activity asks if you'd like to purchase the full version. This ad cannot be disabled.

**Best For:** Kids with developmental delays who are learning colors, shapes, matching, sequences and other early learning skills. The app can also be used to practice fine motor skills.

# Touch and Write
$2.99 US/$2.99 CAN/£1.99 UK, Ages 4 and up, FizzBrain

This learning-to-write app is great fun for all kids, but it has some options that make it work well for visually impaired children and children with learning delays. Developed by a special needs teacher and her app-developer/teacher-husband, this app lets kids practice writing by using things like Jell-O, pudding, whipped cream, and other yummies. The writing can appear on more than 28 colored papers, including black for visually impaired learners. In addition to practicing individual letters and numbers, this app lets kids practice spelling words — one letter at a time. Parents or teachers can create a list of words to practice writing, or use the high frequency word lists already provided in the app.

What makes this app work is its whimsy. Kids follow a cute little monster as he shows you how to write by munching cupcakes that decorate the writing pathways. And letting users choose to write with 16 different foods creates high kid-appeal. One minute they are writing using chocolate frosting, and the next it's ketchup! If kids go off track, they just have to repeat the portion of the writing where they deviated, instead of having to start over from the beginning — a nice feature. The ability to add your own word lists means the app can

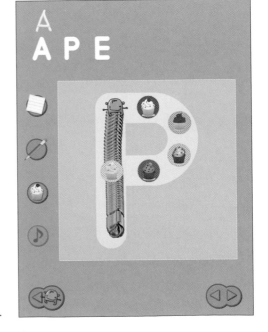

be fine-tuned to appeal to your child's interests. When writing words, the app pronounces each letter when drawn. The completed word shows up in your child's writing and then your kid can pop letter balloons spelling the word. With the ABC Words list, kids also see the object they spelled.

**Best For:** Kids learning to write, spell, and those needing practice on fine motor skills. This app motivates even the most reluctant writers to make their mark.

For other great apps about learning how to write letters, see iWriteWords in Chapter 3 and LetterSchool in Chapter 15.

# Pictello

$18.99 US/$18.99 CAN/£13.49 UK, Ages 5 and up, AssistiveWare

Pictello is an app that lets you use photos and text to create talking books. You can either import the photos already on your iPad, or you can take them directly from within the app for use in your story. You can type up to five lines of text per page, which can be read aloud by a variety of voices, including children's voices. You can also record your own voice. The chosen voice plays every time you tap the photo. The app comes with a simple step-by-step tutorial. It stores your books in an in-app library.

You can use this kind of book in many ways. Because it transfers text to voice, it's a great way for nonspeakers to share information. This app can be used to create books that cover a wide range of things, from teaching social skills to recalling the vacation you just took. Nonreaders can use the books created within Pictello because they are read aloud. This is a great way for a parent to create a fun book for their child, read in the parent's voice. It's also a tool that can be used to teach children how to tell a story because they must select the photos they use and can record their voice if they so choose. And with free downloadable voices in 25 languages, this is an app that can be used to create multilingual recordings.

Users can share with other Pictello owners via Wi-Fi, using the Pictello Sharing Server (you need to create a free account) or using iTunes File Sharing. For non-Pictello users, the stories can be shared as a PDF.

Do you like going on roller coasters?

**I like going to 6 Flags and talking with Bugs Bunny.**

Pictello can be set so that users can't edit the stories. To do this, go to the Settings app on your iPad. Scroll down to Apps and find Pictello, and then toggle Allow Editing to Off.

**Best For:** Creating talking photo stories and visual lessons with both text and sound.

# The Social Express

$89.99 US/$89.99 CAN/£59.99 UK, Ages 6–12,
The Language Express, Inc

This is a set of 16 interactive lessons that helps kids understand and learn about social situations. Presented in amazing full animation, with great emphasis on characters who reveal emotions by using facial expressions and body language, the app introduces your child to four virtual friends: Zack, Emma, Sam, and Katie. By joining these virtual friends, who are also wrestling with social situations, your child is able to explore how to handle typical social encounters. The app teaches kids to look for hidden rules or *Hidden Social Keys* that can help them figure out what to do in a given situation. Some of the hidden rules include using eye contact when talking to others, keeping your body facing the group, observing things about a person before speaking, and more. The app also introduces the concept of using coping strategies as a way of handling difficult situations. The app is meant to be used by a child and an adult working together, with the adult stopping the app periodically to ask leading questions.

This app is incredibly well done, from presenting a fabulous tutorial and printable materials to using movie-quality animation to show video modeling and allowing children to try different solutions — including ones that produce negative results. Because the characters are so realistic looking, kids bond with them. And because these characters are also struggling socially, they make your child feel less isolated while striving to better understand social situations. The app provides kids with easy takeaways, such as start a conversation by asking about something that person is interested in, learn to look at the faces of others to read what they're feeling, and sequence events in your mind so that you can better predict what will happen next.

Although this is an expensive app, it targets a specific need and provides a rich visual-learning solution. Niche apps are frequently expensive because they appeal to a small market. Because the app presents learning in two different levels, it's an app that can grow with your child. Teachers, this app can handle multiple profiles.

**Best For:** Kids who struggle in social situations and have trouble figuring out how to behave appropriately.

# 25 Toy Add-Ons

## Dora Let's Play Backpack – Duo

Free App + Dora Let's Play Backpack for iPad ($39.99)US, Ages 3–6, Discovery Bay Games, Inc

This app-plus-toy combination uses a special add-on device: a plastic version of Dora's friend Backpack. The purple battery-powered Backpack sits on the edge of the iPad and is used by kids to answer questions posed by Dora. The toy Backpack has two colored circles on the top of its head into which kids place tokens to select the correct answers to questions. Dora's questions are divided into the following four games: Let's Pack, Let's Listen, Let's Match, and Say It Two Ways. In each, she asks questions and then presents two pictures sitting on differently colored circles. Kids look at the iPad's screen to see which colored circle has the correct answer and then match that color on top of Backpack to place their token.

Dora's questions teach kids to think about what to pack when getting ready for the beach, camping, and school, and how to identify sounds of musical instruments, the city, and the farm. Dora always answers in both English and Spanish.

This is an excellent preschool/kindergarten app. My favorite game is about matching animals to their geographic locations, which teaches kids about rainforests, deserts, and Antarctica. Also good is the game in which kids match a picture to the word Dora says in Spanish. The toy makes playing this game feel like a board game.

**TIP** The toy can be purchased at Amazon or Barnes & Noble or by going to www.duo-games.com/dorabackpack. Additional packs of questions can be purchased from within the app.

**Best For:** Dora fans and families wanting to learn Spanish.

# Cars 2 AppMATes

Free App + AppmatesToy Car ($12.99) US/CAN/UK,
Ages 4–8, Disney

With special toy cars from the Disney *Cars 2* universe and this free app, your iPad turns into a playmat for exploring Radiator Springs. The technology behind this app-plus-toy combo is pretty amazing because instead of you moving the car around the surface of the iPad, the ground under the toy car appears to be moving. The cars look like they have headlights on, and they leave tracks as they drive over sand. Kids can simply explore this open world, or they can enter races, play mini-games (take-offs of skeeball and Peggle), and go on missions to help other characters. Either way, they earn hubcaps, the currency of this world. With the hubcaps, you can trick out your vehicle, and even buy fuel that sends out colored smoke. Fun!

The toy cars work only when kids place their fingers on the side of the cars, about where the doors are. All the stars from the *Cars* movies are playable, and you hear their voices as you play with them. A single car costs $12.99, and a two-pack is $19.99. They can be found at Target, Toys R Us, Amazon, and other retailers.

Customize with gadgets

**Best For:** Car-loving kids and fans of the *Cars* movies. This app combines playing with the movie characters and just having fun with toy cars.

# Apptivity Hot Wheels

Free App + Hot Wheel Apptivity Vehicle Pack ($10.99)
US/CAN/ UK, Ages 5–10, Mattel, Inc.

This app-plus-toy combination works in a very similar manner to Cars 2 AppMATes. However, with this app, kids need specially made Hot Wheels cars (regular Hot Wheels won't work). The ground under the Hot Wheels car animates to look like you are racing or sailing through the air. This game has more violent content than AppMATes, and thus it may be more appropriate for older children. You can play three games: racing, jumping, and search-and-destroy. Each of these mini-games has three levels.

HOLD THE ULTIMATE DRIFT!

**Best For:** Hot Wheels–loving kids who like speed and high-octane racing.

# Animal Planet Wildlands

Free App + Nuko Cards (pack of 3 for $1.99, or 7 for $3.99)
US/CAN/UK, Ages 7–14, Nukotoys, Inc.

This free app is associated with physical trading cards (called Nuko Cards) that are sold at toy stores and Apple Stores. The app opens to a spectacular 3D world, depicting a fictional Wildlands that resembles a combination of the African Savannah and the Australian Outback. In this beautiful wilderness, kids see wild animals, ranging from elephants and gorillas to giraffes and hippos.

But here is where the magic comes in: Kids introduce the animals on their collectible cards into the game simply by tapping the card to the screen. Voila! One tap and a realistic jaguar is onscreen; double-tap the animal and you now control it. Tilt the iPad up and the animal starts to run. You make it turn by tilting the iPad sideways, and make it stop by leveling it off. It's a thrilling experience. Although the card has some animal facts on it, the in-game version has more. Kids can even watch an Animal Planet video about each animal they own. Players complete quests, make discoveries, and collect puzzle pieces. Each animal can enter a race against the other animals, which is fascinating to watch. Kids can collect a total of 60 cards, with 50 being animals, and 10 providing ways to customize the environment. I activated a card that brought on a monsoon.

This is a great way for kids to learn about animals. By tapping a Nuko card into the game, kids can run in the wild as if they were that animal. It's empowering. The game also teaches kids about the food chain that exists among animals. If you control a predator, you can chase other animals to attempt to earn a takedown. If you're successful, the air sparkles and then the prey simply winks out of existence, and you earn points. All of these animals look and move in a realistic manner. And if you want to see even more realism, you can activate their Animal Planet videos.

 You can purchase additional virtual card packs by first buying NukoBucks with real money as an in-app purchase. Then you can spend the NukoBucks to obtain more Nuko Cards.

**Best For:** Animal lovers and kids who like customizable card games.

# THE GAME OF LIFE ZappED edition

Free App + Board Game ($24.99) US/CAN/UK,
Ages 8 and up, Hasbro, Inc.

This is a technology-enhanced version of the classic board game. For those of you who don't know the game, it's about making decisions in life; some are left to chance and others (like whether you go to college) are up to you. You can play with up to four players. When all players have "lived" their lives and come to the end of the spaces on the board so as to retire, the one with the most money at the end wins.

In this version, you still use the game board, along with little toy cars and plastic pegs representing people in your life. But the iPad sits in the middle of the board to add variety and punch to the game. The iPad becomes a virtual spinner, a way to animate and customize the virtual version of your Peg Person, the source of mini-games which result from landing on certain spaces, and a screen to watch clips from the TV show *America's Funniest Home Videos,* which serve to celebrate life events in the game.

Our family has always enjoyed playing the traditional The Game of Life board game, but, at times, the game dragged on a bit. Not so in this version. The bells and whistles provided by the iPad add zip to the game experience. Graduate from college in the game, and you may see a hilarious video about an excited grad falling off the stage during the diploma ceremony. Land on a Pay Day space, and you can play a game of concentration to earn more money by matching pairs of cards in a limited time. And the customizable Peg Persons are adorable as they add trinkets depending on what happens in their lives.

I actually think this version is more fun than the traditional board game.

**Best For:** Families wanting to play a traditional board game while using their iPad. This version is a blast!

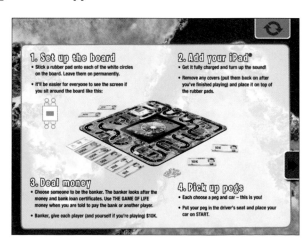

# 26 Ten Favorite Free Apps for Kids

## Monster Hunt – The Memory Game

Free US/CAN/UK, Ages 5 and up, Innovative Mobile Apps

Using monsters who look like they belong in the Disney/Pixar movie *Monsters, Inc.,* this app is a memory game for one to four players. Starting on a grid of four squares, monsters appear briefly and then are shielded. You try to tap the squares where you last saw monsters. As you succeed in memorizing where the monsters are hiding, the grid gets bigger and more monsters are shown. Appropriately ghoulish music accompanies this monster memory hunt, and when you eventually fail, the monsters growl at you with delight.

Although this memory game has no bells and whistles, it's nonetheless very well done for a free app. It has no ads and no in-app purchases — just fascinating monsters to remember. Also good is the ability to play this game in multiplayer mode, taking turns to see who can be the best at remembering.

**Best For:** All kids who think monsters are fun. The monsters provide a great hook to get kids to play a challenging memory game.

# Squiggles!

Free US/CAN/UK, Ages 3–6, Lazoo Worldwide, Inc

This free artistic app creates a no-fail drawing playground where young kids can use their fingers to paint. It presents your child with a scene that needs a squiggle and demonstrates how to draw it. In one scene, she is asked to draw the exhaust of a car. In other scenes, your child's squiggles become the wool on a lamb, a mane on a lion, or nests for birds. Kids can add squiggles onto 14 different pages. After drawing, the player is prompted to hit the Go button, which causes your child's squiggles to magically animate. In the car scene, the squiggle chases after the car as it zooms around. With the lion, his mane jiggles around his head as he roars. Birds lay eggs on the squiggle nests created by your child, and when one big egg arrives, out pops a dinosaur! The app even lets you take a photo and add squiggles to it. Pushing the Go button always creates some silliness.

In addition to these fabulous canvases on which to draw, the app also offers a cute story about a bunny and a monkey who chase jumping beans all the way to the moon. Throughout this interactive story adventure, kids' squiggles are used to create magical things, which reinforce the creative drawing aspect of the app.

This app teaches kids that by using their creativity, drawings can become anything they can imagine. For toddlers, it models how to draw squiggly lines. Whatever your child draws comes alive when she taps the Go button, ensuring that your child feels successful. The Go button also introduces an element of surprise by animating the static drawing in unusual ways. For example, when you add squiggly lines to make cotton candy, the kids holding the candy start to float. This element of surprise may encourage your child to experiment with her drawing.

**Best For:** All toddlers and preschoolers. Success is guaranteed in this app because anything you draw is animated in a cute way. It also allows kids to experience wonder when they hit the Go button.

# Ellie's Wings HD – Free animal coloring game for children

Free US/CAN/UK, Ages 3–9, daniel Sonnenfeld

This free gem lets kids decorate animals' wings by finger painting. What makes it so much fun is that it automatically produces symmetrical drawings. Paint a purple heart on one wing, and it simultaneously shows up on the other wing. The app offers you three different animals to "wing-a-fy," including a butterfly, a bee, and a horse. Each has its own personality and responds to your touch. This is one adorable app.

With nine buckets of paint, three sizes of paintbrushes, animated stickers, and paint splatters, kids can do a lot to decorate these wings. The app's interface is uncluttered and intuitive to use. Kids can tap a camera button to take a photo of their creation and it's saved both in the app and the iPad's photos. The buckets of paint make their own sounds so kids can create a musical scale by tapping them. This app doesn't miss a beat.

I also love the whimsy in this app. If you put a flower sticker on a wing, it opens and closes. Likewise, the stars twist and magical lights blink. And each character responds to your painting by making sounds and expressions. You can even tickle their bellies to make them laugh. But my favorite moment occurs when placing the spider sticker — which turns out not to be a sticker at all. The real spider inevitably surprises the animal whose wings you are decorating by climbing down the wing and out of the picture. It's hilarious!

 The title page contains an ad to purchase three other animals; when touched, it takes kids to iTunes. However, families that like this free version might want to purchase the upgrade.

**Best For:** All kids. Drawing symmetrical wing patterns is fascinating, and these characters are delightful to play with.

# Alien Assignment

Free US/CAN/UK, Ages 4–8, Fred Rogers Center at Saint Vincent College

This free, fun app sends your child on a scavenger hunt to take photos using the iPad. An alien family called the Gloops has crash-landed on Earth, and they need your child's help fixing their spaceship. The Gloops' on-ship computer needs photos of items so that it can figure out how to replicate things to fix the ship. Your child becomes the photographer for the computer.

The alien kids' requests for photos cover a wide range of topics. They may ask your child to take photos of something heavy to help the computer fix the spaceship's Gravity Stabilizer, or something that turns in order to fix the spaceship's steering wheel. You can play this game over and over again and get new requests each time: something you clean with, something you use when it rains, something blue, something that smells stinky, something with words on it, and so on.

By playing this app, kids learn to solve problems and think creatively. They must reflect upon everyday objects in new and different ways. Another great aspect of this app is that it's meant for a child and parent to explore together. After kids take the requested number of photos (you can set it to be between 4 and 20), they are asked to "show your grown-up" the photos. This provides you an opportunity to interact with your child and talk about why they chose the objects. Don't be surprised when your little photographer comes up with a solution that you would never have thought of! When you approve the photos, kids get to see the spaceship repaired and then they can start another episode.

**Best For:** All kids old enough to operate the iPad's camera. This app encourages kids to think about objects in ways different from their ordinary use and to look for details. You don't need to worry about the photos using up the iPad's memory — they disappear when the game is over.

 If your kids like this one, check out another photo adventure from Fred Rogers Center called Out-A-Bout.

# Let's Color!

Free US/CAN/UK, Ages 4–10, Lazoo Worldwide, Inc

This drawing program presents a series of pages on which something is already drawn, accompanied by a verbal prompt to draw something specific on the page. Kids add to the page using their fingers and an easy paint program that features a marker, crayon, chalk, a squirt bottle, and stickers, as well as a basic color palette. When they are finished creating, they push the prominent Go button on the page and watch as their drawing becomes animated. It's as if their painting comes alive.

The app's 18 pages feature things like a person holding a hose with the prompt asking the child to draw what is coming out of the hose. If your child draws stars, stars shoot out of the hose. If he places a sticker of a robot by the end of the hose, it shoots out robots. Some of the pages contain funny situations, such as the one in which a person, an animal, and an elephant all drink out of a big cup at the same time. Kids are asked to fill the cup, and whatever is drawn in the cup gets miniaturized as it's slurped into the transparent straws leading to each character.

From the home page, kids can also watch a short animated movie about how three animals friends use their imaginations to go on an exciting adventure.

Under the parents' section, you can purchase 16 more pages for $1.99. You can also hide this in-app purchase from kids. I love the way Lazoo handles this in-app purchase option and wish more companies would follow suit.

**Best For:** All kids. Kids who are hesitant about drawing are encouraged to try because the animation part is so magical. And for kids who like to draw, this is heaven.

# Toontastic: Play, Create, Learn!
Free US/CAN/UK, Ages 5–10, Launchpad Toys

This app makes this chapter because it's a magical tech-creation tool. Although I review it in Chapter 10, it's so outstanding that I wanted to share more about it here. Toontastic harnesses kids' natural attraction to technology to teach them how to tell stories. By breaking down the parts of a story and having kids create a scene depicting each part, kids learn by doing. The app cleverly incorporates music to create emotional tension in a scene. Then it mashes together all of the scenes to create a unique video cartoon.

I am also a big fan of this app because it encourages kids to use their imaginations. For more years than I can count, I started, ran, and coached my sons in a creative problem-solving program called Odyssey of the Mind. It too was about using your imagination to tell stories (as well as using creativity to solve problems). I think it's important for kids to practice being creative thinkers when they are young. That way, when they get older and enter the workforce, they will be comfortable tapping into their imaginations to solve problems. Toontastic provides kids with the practice they need to be creative thinkers.

The other outstanding feature of this app is that it encourages kids to watch cartoons created by kids around the world. Kids can see how other cultures tell a story and can observe that we all share a common bond.

Although I warn of the in-app purchases in my original review (this is a free app that monetizes by selling add-on playsets), some of the playsets are worth it: They can provide more inspiration. You can purchase packs with historic figures, monsters, wildlife, sports, pirates, castles, space rangers, and more.

**Best For:** All kids. Use this free app to get creative and tell stories!

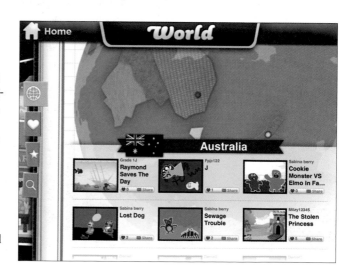

# LEGO Creationary
Free US/CAN/UK, Ages 5–10, The LEGO Group

For Lego lovers, this is a game that tests how quickly you can figure out what specific object is being built using Lego bricks. The game starts with a roll of the die to determine the category of the item being built (nature, vehicles, buildings, things, and two random options). Four objects appear in the four corners of the screen, within buttons for tapping. In the center, the Lego-building starts in a fast-action video. The goal is to tap the correct object in the corner button before the object is completed. This game can be played alone or with up to four. If you're playing alone, you are trying to win 15 rounds in a row. Multiplayer consists of three rounds where the iPad is passed around with each person guessing one time per round.

You'd think that this game, with its simple premise and easy controls, would be easy to win. It isn't. The building is superfast so that kids need to use observation skills, imagination, and knowledge of Lego-building to be successful. It may take a few rounds before you start getting better. The game comes with three puzzle packs: Standard, Winter, and Summer. Turning off some may help make the gameplay easier. The game gets harder the longer you play. And you earn more points for guessing quickly. This creates fast-paced Lego craziness — which is perfect for kids who always have some Legos in their pockets. (My sons did!)

Obviously, The LEGO Group created this game as a form of marketing. When my kids were in their Lego-mania stage, they had already bought into the brand (hook, line, and Lego-formed sinker!). Downloading this app could be the catalyst for a discussion about the clever ways that toy companies market to kids.

**TIP** For families who own the Creationary board game, this app also acts as an assistant by providing a timer, scorecard, and a way to log in your creations using the iPad's camera.

**Best For:** Lego aficionados who enjoy high adrenaline fun. This game is a clever way to hone kids' observation skills and test their quick thinking for predicting answers with very little information.

# Awesome Eats

Free US/CAN/UK, Ages 6 and up, Whole Kids Foundation

Here is a fast-paced sorting game involving anthropomorphized fruits, vegetables, and whole grains. Awesome Eats makes learning about healthy eating fun. Each level has kids moving food characters from one conveyor belt to another so that they end up in the correct box at the end. Because the conveyor belts can be going in opposite directions, and some stop mid-course and change direction, this game can get frenetic. On the harder levels, kids must navigate around obstacles riding on the conveyer belts and chase off poaching birds. Players score more points when they stack characters on top of each other —not easy when everything is moving so fast! In between each of the 32 levels, the app presents kids with interesting nuggets of information about good nutrition.

This free app is one of my favorites because it is a hoot to play. It teaches kids about healthy eating, and it doesn't contain ads or in-app purchases. Whole Kids Foundation, a nonprofit organization connected to the Whole Food Markets, produced this app as part of their mission to "engage children in making good food choices." Boy does it! Don't be surprised when you kids start making suggestions like adding fruits to fizzy water for a refreshing drink.

**Best For:** Boys and girls who enjoy quick challenges. This game is unusual because it's packed with fast action but without any violence, making it a wholesome media snack.

# Scribble Press
Free US/CAN/UK, Ages 6 and up, Scribble Press

This free app lets kids write and illustrate their own books, and then share them on the iPad, or, if you permit, on the moderated Scribble Press servers so that other kids can read their work. You can also decide to share your child's book with friends and relatives via an e-mail link, Facebook, and Twitter. The app can save the book in a format that lets it reside in your iBooks bookshelf.

This app provides 50 story templates to help your child on her path to becoming an author. The templates provide a framework for kids in which some of the story is already written, and all they have to do is add in their own details. The categories range from writing an autobiography, to aliens, to school and beyond. Under the humor category, kids can explore topics such as My Dog Ate My Homework, I am a Secret Super Hero, and The Craziest Dream. You can start with a blank book, or you can alter any of the text already written in the templates.

In addition to the writing, kids are encouraged to add their own artwork or photos. The program comes with a complete art studio featuring markers, stamps, and stickers.

I am very impressed by how easy it is for kids to create their own books. And the final product looks professional, with a border around the cover. When kids see their own book in your iBooks bookshelf, they'll swell with pride.

 To use all the options this app offers, parents must first sign in using an e-mail account and create a password. With kids younger than 13, you have to agree to the Scribble Press privacy policies if you want to let your budding author share his writing with the world.

 Your kids can also download other kids' books, which Scribble Press screens; but you may want to review these before letting your kids read other kids' work. Also, the app has in-app purchases for new templates and art supplies as well as the ability to order your book as a printed product.

**Best For:** Kids interested in writing and creating stories. This app makes it simple.

# Sushi Monster

Free US/ CAN/UK, Ages 7–12, Scholastic

This free app allows your child to practice addition and multiplication in a setting that's way more fun than doing math worksheets. Kids solve equations so that they can feed the ravenous Sushi Monster and thereby earn stars and eventually trophies.

The game takes place in a circular cafeteria with the ravenous Sushi Monster in the middle. On one counter around the monster, plates of sushi with numbers on them arrive. Kids feed the Sushi Monster by combining the numbered plates to meet the target number shown around the monster's neck. Because you can arrive at a target number multiple ways, kids must also consider the other target numbers that are shown in that group (between two and five). They need to plan ahead; it's possible to create the right answer for the early target numbers and then be unable to complete the later target numbers because they've used up all of the necessary numbers.

This app offers practice in addition and multiplication. There are seven addition levels and five for multiplication. A level consists of four rounds, during which you try to reach a total of 14 target numbers. If you're successful, you earn three stars for that level. If you fail, you receive fewer stars. Collect enough stars and you earn a trophy.

Part of the FASTT Math Next Generation program from Scholastic, this game was devised to help children increase their math speed by using it for ten minutes a day. The artwork of this math app is bright and colorful. The Sushi Monster reminds me of Cookie Monster from *Sesame Street* in the way he inhales the sushi. Kids love watching this monster madly eat all the sushi available.

**Best For:** Kids who need to drill their math facts (and most kids do!). Because this drilling is presented as a fun game, most kids won't mind practicing math for the recommended ten minutes a day.

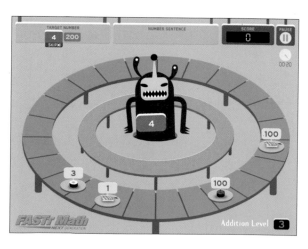

# 27 Ten Favorite Kid Apps

## Elmo Loves ABCs for iPad

$4.99 US/$4.99 CAN/£2.99 UK,
Ages 3–5, Sesame Street

This is one of my Ten Favorite Kid Apps because it uses the iPad well to teach preschoolers. It offers a wide range of entertaining videos that seamlessly appear throughout; varied interactivity from tapping to tracing to swiping; a set of fun games; an art activity; and a variety of musical variations on the alphabet song. I find I pull out this app when someone hasn't seen an iPad before, to show what is possible for young children.

I also love how Elmo makes your child feel included. He looks out of the app and talks directly to your child as if he is right there. And his responses further this fiction, as he looks down at where he has asked your child to touch. When your child responds to the requested touch, Elmo again appears to see what your child has done and offers praise.

Parents can add their own personal objects to appear as alphabet cards. Each new card needs a photo, a video, a title, and a sound recording of that title. You can add cards of your child, grandma, or even your pet dog. It's very exciting when Elmo uses a photo of your child in the alphabet activities. I also like that parents can track their child's progress in a well-designed parents section.

**Best For:** All preschoolers learning the alphabet. Elmo is just the best!

# The Monster at the End of This Book . . . starring Grover!

$3.99 US/$3.99 CAN/£2.49 UK, Ages 3–7, Sesame Street

If you have a *Sesame Street* fan in your house, don't miss this app! This adaptation of the classic children's book not only does the beloved book justice, it actually makes it better.

This story shows Grover at his paranoid best. He sees the title of this book and focuses on the part about a monster at the end and goes, well . . . ballistic. At first he coaxes and wheedles your child to not turn the page; but when that fails, the fun begins.

Grover's inventive attempts to keep you from turning the page are so much fun because kids have to do something to foil him. By knocking down the brick wall he builds to keep you from the pages or untying the knots of the ropes he has brought in, kids move the story forward and cause Grover to go into more over-the-top hysterics.

Contributing to the fun is the way the sound and musical score enhance all of Grover's antics. Just before Grover pops up on the page to emote about your turning the page, you hear a giant "Boing" sound. And when he is so overcome by emotion that he and his words fall off the page, kids hear a musical scale going down, coupled with a tinkling sound. It's magical.

The words on the page also emote by getting bigger for emphasis and changing colors as they are read. And you can tap the words in red ink to hear them read again.

**Best For:** All young kids. This is a top-notch delivery of a classic children's book in which the addition of sound, animation, and interactions greatly enhance the already charming book.

# Toca Band
$1.99 US/$1.99 CAN/£1.49 UK, Ages 3–10, Toca Boca

Of all the music apps I discuss in Chapter 21, Toca Band is the most exciting for kids to explore. This app opens with an empty performance stage and 16 wacky-looking animated musicians vying for your attention. Because the stage has only eight performance spots, you must drag and drop characters to the spots to hear them perform. Each musician delivers a unique sound; but no matter what combinations you put on the stage, they harmonize and complement each other because they are all playing parts of the same song. The combinations produce radically different results, which encourages your child to experiment with the different musicians.

However, you can do more with this app than simply move crazy-looking musicians onto the stage. Where you place them also affects how they play. If you place one in the front row, it plays in a way that supports the others. But if you move it in the back of the three rows, it plays like a headliner. And if you place one in the coveted starlight spot in the back row, it becomes a soloist and takes over the screen. When playing a solo, the character becomes interactive, so kids can do things like make the chattering pickle-like guy knock his teeth together faster or slower, depending on where you touch him. And don't miss Stikk Figga (see Figure on this page), the adorable rapper dude, who produces different sounds and beats as you tap his sunglasses.

With its wonky characters, simple controls, and fabulous arrangements, Toca Band makes playing music fun. Kids instantly feel empowered because they always produce great-sounding music.

**Best For:** All kids. This is one funky fun app!

# Faces iMake – Right Brain Creativity

$1.99 US/$1.99 CAN/£1.49 UK, Ages 4 and up,
iMagine machine LLC

I sing the praises of this collage-making app in Chapter 5, where I discuss the best art apps. Faces iMake makes the list for my Ten Favorite Kid Apps because it teaches kids to think outside of the box.

With this app, kids can create faces using pieces of fruit, toys, candy, musical instruments, tools, school supplies, buttons, letters, and more. They start with a base face shape, and then drag and drop items from the app's tray of objects to use. Does that banana look like a mouth to you? Try it! You can use the pinch-or-pull method to make the object smaller or bigger. How about some candy for eyes? Sweet! And licorice for hair? Groovy!

The app comes with five highly motivating video lessons. But you can also turn to the world for inspiration by visiting the FaceWorld section in which the app connects to a gallery of faces submitted by users from all around the world. You can post your own creations there. And you can download ones you like, modify them, and repost them. With FaceWorld, the world becomes your collaborator.

With the addition of FaceWorld, the app now allows you to share via Facebook or e-mail, and it can send you to a place that can turn your creation into a puzzle for $14.99.

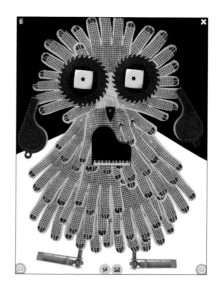

I am keen on the creation part of this app because it helps kids to think about new ways to express themselves. And the international art gallery of sharing and collaborating on art in FaceWorld is cool. But parents should monitor their kids' use.

If your children want to share a creation in FaceWorld, remind them to not use their real name.

**Best For:** All kids, regardless of their interest or talent in art. Everyone can have fun using Faces iMake.

# Ansel & Clair's Adventures in Africa

$4.99 US/$4.99 CAN/£2.99 UK, Ages 4–10, Cognitive Kid, Inc.

I remember when I first opened this app and started to play: I was blown away. I was so impressed with how it combined a playful story with solid learning activities that I immediately featured it in my weekly column in *USA Today*.

I introduce you to this app in Chapter 19: an adventure app where you meet an adorable alien named Ansel and his sidekick robot Clair. Ansel and Clair have come to our world to photograph it. Unfortunately, their spaceship has broken apart, spreading parts all over the continent of Africa. Your kids join the alien duo as they explore and learn about three different parts of Africa: the Serengeti, the Sahara Desert, and the Nile Valley. In each location they interact with and learn about the different animals that inhabit that region.

The best learning apps for kids make the process of learning fun. Ansel & Clair have figured this out so well that they should be used as the gold standard for other apps. Ansel's natural curiosity and naiveté lead him into funny situations with the animals. For example, not knowing that the lion is fierce, he tries to pet it and has to jump back when the lion roars. This provides Clair an opportunity to explain that although related to friendly house cats, the lion is a "big cat" that's a fierce hunter. Another way this app keeps the learning fun is to introduce five clever games. In one found on the Serengeti, kids play the Fur Ball-a-tor game in which they drag a furless animal under a chute that delivers a colored fur ball. The game ends with a graph showing the number of animals that were correctly given their fur. Nice.

Another thing this app does well is involve your child in the learning. Kids pull the clouds across the scene to change the seasons in the Serengeti. They drag Ansel's camera to take photos, and those photos create a travel log for the players.

**Best For:** All children from 4 to 10. This app is packed full of learning and fun!

# The Fantastic Flying Books of Mr. Morris Lessmore

$4.99 US/$4.99 CAN/£2.99 UK, Ages 5 and up,
Moonbot Studios LA, LLC

I gush about this app in Chapter 7. When people ask me for the best iPad app for kids, I usually say this one. This app has it all: a powerful story (moving enough to make me tear-up when I read it), an art style that is both unusual and beautiful, and interactions that enhance the story and charm me with their innovation.

This story about a book-loving man who is transported to another reality where books are alive creates some wonderful moments of imagination. As the caretaker of these fantastical books, Morris realizes that he can't keep the books in order because the tragedies need to visit the comedies to be cheered up. To maintain their health, he feeds the books ABC cereal. When Morris gets lost in a good book, the app creates an animated sequence where you steer a flying Morris through a stack of words that whiz past you on each side. This is a fantasy world that is well thought out and fully developed.

The words used in this story create verbal images to match the spectacular visuals of the app. The books "nest" in the library. When the books get excited, the library fills with "the fluttering of countless pages." Morris can hear "the faint chatter of a thousand different stories." All of these superb phrases are read by a narrator who makes you feel cocooned in his mellifluous voice.

An allegory about life, this story is poignant as well as entertaining. Kids see it as an adventure to a magical place where books are alive. Adults see it as a story reminding us that life is finite, but that our journey — or story — is what matters.

**Best For:** All ages. This fabulous book is so special that you are likely to remember it for a long time. Buy it yourself, and gift it regularly to friends — both young and old.

The days passed. So did the months. And then years.

# Bobo Explores Light
$4.99 US/$4.99 CAN/£2.99 UK, Ages 7 and up,
Game Collage, LLC

I share with you my excitement about this app in Chapter 18. Bobo Explores Light is one of my Ten Favorite Apps for Kids because it makes learning about science fun. Exploring this app reminds me of going to a great science museum, like the Exploratorium in San Francisco or the Ontario Science Centre.

By having kids discover science concepts with a cute and mischievous robot named Bobo, the app makes kids immediately think of science as fun. Creating a positive attitude about science at a young age can spark a lifelong interest in exploring the wonders of our world and beyond. I read tons of science books and did numerous hands-on experiments with my kids when they were young, and my oldest ended up going into physics. Is there a connection? I'll never know, but I'm sure he grew up thinking science was cool. This app can help your kids think science is cool, too.

With Bobo in the lead, kids can find out about space flight, the Sun, lightning, fire, lasers, reflection, refraction, telescopes, color, and so much more. By putting hands-on experiments into this app, kids don't just read about concepts, they learn about them by doing them. For example, when explaining refraction, kids can turn on a light above a fish tank and see how the light waves bend. Also, whenever possible, the app uses fun visuals to explain concepts. That is why when learning about the human eye, Bobo shines a light in a little girl's eye; and via a hologram, you see how the image of Bobo ends up upside down in the girl's head. The app goes on to explain that the brain flips the image.

I also think the navigation of this app is special. The Table of Contents is presented as a gear, with each chapter a separate cog. Kids have access to this Table of Contents from within each page, making it a breeze to jump around to a subject that interests them.

**Best For:** All kids. Bobo Explores Light packs so much exciting science into one little app that you feel like you got a gift, even though you paid $5 for it. I hope new developers use this as a model of how to create a science app.

# MoMA Art Lab
$4.99 US/$4.99 CAN/£2.99 UK, Ages 6 and up,
MoMA, The Museum of Modern Art

An overwhelming number of art creation apps are in the iTunes store, in part because the iPad offers such an intuitive way to make art. With just the touch of a finger to the screen, kids can start to create. I selected this app as one of my Ten Favorite Kid Apps because it does more than simply encourage artistic creation. This app changes the way that kids look at art.

For many people, modern art is an enigma. It jars them into the age-old question: What is art? This app breaks down some aspects of modern art and then puts your kids in charge of creating something similar. When kids become the artist and experience the thought processes of creating modern art, they start to understand and see it in a different light.

In addition to opening kids' eyes to the beauty and uniqueness of modern art, MoMA Art Lab also does a fabulous job using the technology of the iPad. The open art creation area, where kids employ geometric shapes to create art, is easier to use than trying to produce something similar with scissors, construction paper, and glue. All of the projects in the Activities section make clever use of the iPad. In one, you shake the iPad to create a random collage. In another, you trace the outline for virtual scissors to follow. In the project inspired by Brice Marden's *Couplet IV,* kids create their own shape poem by tracing a line from Marden's work, then selecting words that describe the path of the line and dragging them onto the line. The app then reads the shape poem out loud, using creative inflections. In still another, based on work by Jim Lambie, kids choose three colors to create a special lined tape and decorate a floor using this multicolored tape.

This is a transformative app. Kids can even share their artwork with the MoMA, but only if parents grant permission from within the For Parents section. The default is to not allow sharing. If you want more detail, see my review in Chapter 5.

**Best For:** Broadening kids' artistic horizons.

# World of Goo HD
$4.99 US/$4.99 CAN/£2.99 UK, Ages 8 and up, 2D BOY

I review this game in Chapter 13, recommending it as a great game for kids. This puzzle game makes my list of Ten Favorite Kid Apps because building wiggly, stretchy structures using eye-blinking balls of goo is really fun. Having these sentient building balls automatically triangulate when they get near each other creates a brilliant way of teaching kids about architecture and physics.

To solve these progressively more difficult puzzles, kids practice building strong, wide bases to support tall structures. They quickly learn that counterbalancing is important when you try to cantilever a structure out over a chasm. And because these balls of goo like to travel up these teetering structures and thereby add weight to one side or the other, kids learn to compensate for this imbalance.

This is one of those rare games that keeps mixing it up so that you can't wait to see what the next puzzle contains. By slowly adding new goo balls with different attributes, kids feel constantly challenged and excited. Another reason this game is so good is that it encourages kids to experiment. You can replay puzzles as many times as you want. Plus, many of the puzzles contain Time Bugs, fluttering insects that let you undo your last move.

World of Goo HD offers a dark, visually arresting landscape, creating a world somewhat reminiscent of the Dr. Seuss books. The musical score contributes to this funky vibe and helps to make this world feel alive with emotion. The musical score changes to reflect what is happening in the game. It's brilliant.

The game's method of providing hints, using signs written by the never-present-but-always-amusing Sign Painter, is also another great aspect of the game. This game is one your kids will love, and will be sad to finish. The good news is that they can always play it again, trying new ways to build with their beloved balls of goo.

**Best For:** All kids, teens, and adults who love a good puzzle adventure.

# Cut the Rope: Experiments HD
$3.99 US/$3.99 CAN/£2.49 UK, Ages 8 and up,
ZeptoLab UK Limited

Adorable candy-demanding Om Nom has chomped his way into my and millions of other iPad users' hearts. This adorable green dude has such a fan following that the release of this app rocketed it to the top of the iTunes store. What makes the app so good is that it retains the classic gameplay of the first Cut the Rope app and adds to it in ways that surpass the previous game. In this set of puzzles, Om Nom has teamed up with a benevolent professor who looks a lot like Doc Brown from *Back to the Future*. This quirky professor studies Om Nom's candy-eating behavior through a series of experiments, which the player helps him to run.

The core play mechanic from the original app is still here — cut ropes holding the candy in such a manner that the candy swishes over three stars before landing in Om Nom's open maw — but now you get to play with all sorts of gizmos and gadgets, too. It's an inventive reimagining of the core gameplay, and one that kids love. They get to zap ropes onto the candy at just the right moment to keep it from swinging into candy-shattering spikes. They can control robotic arms, play with suction cups, shoot rockets, and avoid candy-stealing spiders. With more than 150 experiments, it's a blast.

Besides just being a great game with a gradual learning curve, this is a game that will have your kids donning their thinking caps. A lot of experimentation happens within each level as kids discover how gravity, motion, and force affect their solutions. And the introduction of the mad scientist adds a level of wackiness as well as encouragement. For those who loved the original Cut the Rope and for those who have never played it, don't miss the magic that follows little Om Nom around.

This app has ads for the other Om Nom games and connects to Facebook and Twitter.

**Best For:** Om Nom fans and kids just looking for a great physics puzzler. It's a lollapalooza.

# Appendix

## Apps by Age Group

| App | 2 | 3 | 4 | 5-6 | 7-8 | 9-10 | 11-12 | 13-14 |
|---|---|---|---|---|---|---|---|---|
| A Jazzy Day, p. 183 | | X | X | X | X | | | |
| A Monster Ate My Homework, p. 118 | | | | | X | X | X | X |
| A Present for Milo: A Touch-and-Surprise Storybook*, p. 57 | X | X | X | X | | | | |
| ABC ZooBorns*, p. 38 | | X | X | X | X | | | |
| Alien Assignment, p. 219 | | X | X | X | | | | |
| AlphaTots*, p. 28 | | X | X | X | | | | |
| Amazing Alex, p. 162 | | | | | | X | X | X |
| Angelina Ballerina's New Ballet Teacher, p. 127 | | X | X | X | X | | | |
| Angry Birds HD, p. 107 | | | | | X | X | X | X |
| Animal Planet Wildlands, p. 214 | | | | | X | X | X | X |
| Another Monster at the End of This Book...Starring Grover & Elmo!*, p. 173 | | X | X | X | | | | |
| Ansel & Clair: Cretaceous Dinosaurs, p. 100 | | | | | X | X | X | |
| Ansel & Clair's Adventures in Africa, p. 167, 230 | | | X | X | X | X | | |
| Ansel and Clair: Paul Revere's Ride, p. 171 | | | | | X | X | X | |
| Apptivity Hot Wheels, p. 213 | | | | | X | X | X | |
| Auryn - Van Gogh and the Sunflowers, p. 54 | | | | | X | X | X | X |
| Auryn HD - Teddy's Day*, p. 59 | X | X | X | | | | | |
| Auryn HD - Where Do Balloons Go?*, p. 69 | | | X | X | X | | | |
| Awesome Eats, p. 223 | | | | | X | X | X | X |
| Bad Piggies HD, p. 124 | | | | | | X | X | X |
| Bag It! , p. 117 | | | | X | X | X | X | X |
| Balloonimals HD*, p. 15 | X | | X | X | | | | |
| Barefoot World Atlas*, p. 151 | | | | | X | X | X | |
| Barnyard Dance, p. 56 | X | X | X | | | | | |
| Bartleby's Book of Buttons Vol 1: The Far Away Island*, p. 72 | | | | | X | X | X | |
| Bats! Furry Fliers of the Night, p. 157 | | | | | X | X | X | X |
| Beat Sneak Bandit, p. 120 | | | | | | X | X | X |
| Bejeweled HD, p. 106 | | | | | X | X | X | X |
| Bizzy Bear Builds a House, p. 81 | X | X | X | | | | | |
| Blokus HD, p. 90 | | | | | | X | X | X |
| Blue Hat, Green Hat , p. 26 | X | X | X | | | | | |

| App | 2 | 3 | 4 | 5-6 | 7-8 | 9-10 | 11-12 | 13-14 |
|---|---|---|---|---|---|---|---|---|
| Blueprint 3D HD, p. 193 | | | | | X | X | X | X |
| Bob Books #2 - Reading Magic HD*, p. 136 | | | | X | X | | | |
| Bobo Explores Light*, p. 161, 232 | | | | | X | X | X | X |
| Bob's Books #1 - Reading Magic HD, p. 41 | | | | X | X | | | |
| Bo's Bedtime Story*, p. 34 | | X | X | X | | | | |
| Brain Quest, p. 202 | | | | | X | X | X | X |
| BrainPOP Featured Movie of the Week, p. 150 | | | | | | X | X | X |
| Brave Rooney*, p. 67 | | | | X | X | X | | |
| Britannica Kids: Dinosaurs, p. 103 | | | | | X | X | X | |
| Bugs & Bubbles, p. 44 | | | | X | X | | | |
| Bugs & Buttons, p. 40 | | | | X | X | X | | |
| Bugsy Kindergarten Math, p. 42 | | | | X | | | | |
| Builda the Re-Bicycler, p. 130 | | | | X | X | | | |
| Car Toons! HD, p. 85 | | | | | X | X | X | X |
| Carcassone, p. 91 | | | | | X | X | X | X |
| Cars 2 AppMATes, p. 213 | | | X | X | X | | | |
| Cars in sandbox: Construction, p. 83 | | X | X | X | X | | | |
| Cinderella animated picture book, p. 63 | | X | X | X | X | | | |
| Coloring Farm Touch To Color, p. 16 | X | | | | | | | |
| Cozmo's Day Off *, p. 177 | | | | X | X | X | X | |
| Create a Monster HD*, p. 180 | | | | | X | X | X | X |
| Creatures of Light, p. 165 | | | | | | X | X | X |
| Cut the Rope Experiments, p. 235 | | | | | | X | X | X |
| Cut the Rope HD, p. 111 | | | | | X | X | X | |
| Dino Discovery!, p. 102 | | | | X | X | | | |
| Doodle Fit, p. 192 | | | | | X | X | X | X |
| Doodlecast for Kids, p. 93 | | X | X | X | X | X | X | X |
| Dora Let's Play Backpack - Duo, p. 212 | | X | X | X | | | | |
| Dr. Panda's Hospital, p. 36 | | X | X | X | | | | |
| Dragon Box+, p. 146 | | | | | X | X | X | X |
| Dragon Brush, p. 66 | | | X | X | X | | | |
| Draw Along with Stella and Sam, p. 47 | | X | X | X | | | | |
| Draw and Tell HD, p. 46 | X | X | X | X | X | | | |
| Drawing Pad, p. 50 | | | X | X | X | X | X | X |
| Eddy's Number Party, p. 142 | | | X | X | | | | |
| Ellie's Wings HD, p. 218 | | X | X | X | X | X | | |
| Elmo Loves ABCs for iPad, p. 31, 226 | | X | X | X | | | | |
| Elmo's Monster Maker HD, p. 172 | X | X | X | X | | | | |

| App | 2 | 3 | 4 | 5-6 | 7-8 | 9-10 | 11-12 | 13-14 |
|---|---|---|---|---|---|---|---|---|
| Even Monsters Get Sick, p. 179 | | | X | X | X | | | |
| Faces iMake*, p. 49, 229 | | | X | X | X | X | X | X |
| Farm 123, p. 33 | | X | X | X | | | | |
| Fish School HD*, p. 30 | X | X | X | X | | | | |
| Flick Champions HD, p. 116 | | | | X | X | X | X | X |
| Geo Walk HD, p. 152 | | | | | X | X | X | X |
| Go Away, Big Green Monster! for iPad, p. 174 | | X | X | X | | | | |
| Happi Full Throttle, p. 84 | | | X | X | X | | | |
| HappiPets, p. 96 | | | | X | X | X | X | X |
| How Rocket Learned to Read, p. 65 | | | X | X | X | | | |
| How to Draw-Full Version, p. 52 | | | | X | X | X | X | |
| I SPY Spooky Mansion for iPad, p. 190 | | | | X | X | X | X | |
| iDiary for Kids, p. 94 | | | | X | X | X | X | X |
| iLuv Drawing Animals, p. 52 | | | X | X | X | | | |
| iLuv Drawing Monsters HD, p. 176 | | | X | X | X | | | |
| I'm Not Afraid! , p. 175 | | X | X | X | | | | |
| Injini*, p. 208 | | | X | X | X | X | X | X |
| Inside the World of Dinosaurs, p. 104 | | | | | X | X | X | X |
| Intro to Math*, p. 143 | | | X | X | | | | |
| its a small world*, p. 29 | X | X | X | X | | | | |
| iWrite Words*, p. 37 | | X | X | X | | | | |
| Joining Hands, p. 194 | | | | | X | X | X | X |
| Khan Academy, p. 153 | | | | | | X | X | X |
| Kindergarten Reading*, p. 43 | | | | X | | | | |
| Learn the States, p. 203 | | | | | X | X | X | X |
| Lego Creationary, p. 222 | | | | X | X | X | | |
| Lego Harry Potter: Years 1-4, p. 121 | | | | | X | X | X | X |
| Leonard, p. 68 | | | X | X | X | | | |
| Let's Color*, p. 220 | | | X | X | X | X | | |
| LetterReflex*, p. 207 | | | X | X | X | X | X | X |
| LetterSchool*, p. 134 | | | X | X | | | | |
| Little Bella's - I Close My Eyes HD, p. 126 | | X | X | X | X | | | |
| Little Digits*, p. 141 | | X | X | X | | | | |
| Little Fox Music Box*, p. 184 | | X | X | X | | | | |
| Little Lilly's Touch Book*, p. 206 | | X | X | X | X | | | |
| Mad Libs on the Road, p. 201 | | | | X | X | X | X | X |
| Magic Garden, p. 188 | | | X | X | X | | | |
| Make Me Smile!*, p. 21 | X | X | X | | | | | |

| App | 2 | 3 | 4 | 5-6 | 7-8 | 9-10 | 11-12 | 13-14 |
|---|---|---|---|---|---|---|---|---|
| Marble Mixer for iPad, p. 87 | | | X | X | X | X | X | X |
| March of the Dinosaurs, p. 103 | | | | | X | X | X | X |
| Mask Jumble Animals, p. 199 | | X | X | X | X | | | |
| Math Bingo*, p. 144 | | | | | X | X | X | |
| Math Doodles, p. 148 | | | | | X | X | X | X |
| Max and the Magic Marker, p. 122 | | | | | X | X | X | X |
| Memory Train, p. 45 | | | | X | X | X | | |
| Middle School Confidential 2*, p. 77 | | | | | X | X | X | X |
| Miss Spider's Tea Party, p. 62 | | X | X | X | X | | | |
| MoMA Art Lab, p. 53, 233 | | | | | X | X | X | X |
| Monkey Preschool Lunchbox*, p. 32 | | X | X | X | | | | |
| Monster Hunt - The Memory Game, p. 216 | | | | | X | X | X | X |
| Monster Melody Mash Lite, p. 175 | | X | X | X | X | X | X | |
| Monster's Socks, p. 178 | | | X | X | X | | | |
| Moo, Baa, La La La!, p. 14 | X | | X | | | | | |
| Motion Math: Hungry Guppy, p. 140 | | X | X | X | X | | | |
| Move the Turtle, p. 149 | | | | | | X | X | X |
| Munch Time HD, p. 119 | | | | | X | X | X | X |
| Musical Me! HD, p. 182 | | X | X | X | | | | |
| My First App Vehicles, p. 84 | | X | X | X | | | | |
| My First Tangrams HD*, p. 189 | | | X | X | X | | | |
| My Mom's the Best, p. 17 | X | | X | | | | | |
| My Musical Friends HD, p. 186 | | | X | X | X | | | |
| Nick Jr Draw & Play 48 | | X | X | X | X | | | |
| Nighty Night! HD, p. 58 | X | X | X | X | | | | |
| Noodle Words HD - Action Set 1*, p. 135 | | | X | X | X | | | |
| Numbers League, p. 147 | | | | | X | X | X | |
| Oh No! Fractions, p. 145 | | | | | X | X | X | X |
| Oh Say Can You Say Di-No-Saur?, p. 99 | | | X | X | X | | | |
| Old MacDonald HD*, p. 19 | X | | X | | | | | |
| OLO game, p. 86 | | | | X | X | X | X | X |
| One Rainy Day, p. 23 | X | X | X | | | | | |
| Over in the Ocean: In a Coral Reef, p. 39 | | | X | X | X | | | |
| Oz for iPad, p. 76 | | | | | X | X | X | X |
| Painting with Time*, p. 166 | | | | X | X | X | X | X |
| Pajama Sam Thunder and Lightning, p. 115 | | | | X | X | | | |
| Park Math HD*, p. 143 | | | X | X | X | | | |
| Pat the Bunny, p. 20 | X | X | X | | | | | |

| App | 2 | 3 | 4 | 5-6 | 7-8 | 9-10 | 11-12 | 13-14 |
|---|---|---|---|---|---|---|---|---|
| Peekaboo Barn for iPad, p. 24 | X | X | | | | | | |
| Peekaboo Forest, p. 25 | X | X | X | | | | | |
| Peekaboo Fridge, p. 25 | X | X | X | | | | | |
| Peek-a-Zoo, p. 27 | X | X | X | X | | | | |
| Peggle, p. 110 | | | | X | X | X | X | X |
| Pepi Bath*, p. 35 | | X | X | X | | | | |
| Pete's Robot, p. 61 | | X | X | X | X | | | |
| Pettson's Inventions, p. 159 | | | | X | X | X | X | X |
| Pickle's Paper Dolls*, p. 128 | | X | X | X | X | | | |
| Pictello*, p. 210 | | | | X | X | X | X | X |
| PICTURE BOOK FOR KIDS*, p. 18 | X | X | | | | | | |
| Pictureka! for iPad, p. 89 | | | | X | X | X | X | X |
| Piece me DINOSAURS!*, p. 98 | | X | X | X | | | | |
| Pixeline and the Jungle Treasure HD, p. 131 | | | | | X | X | X | X |
| Plants vs. Zombies HD, p. 113 | | | | | | X | X | X |
| PlayART, p. 55 | | | | X | X | X | X | X |
| Pluto Learns Piano, p. 187 | | | X | X | X | X | X | X |
| Polymer, p. 195 | | | | | X | X | X | X |
| Presidents vs. Aliens, p. 168 | | | | | X | X | X | X |
| Princess Fairytale Maker, p. 129 | | | X | X | X | X | | |
| Proloquo2Go, p. 205 | X | X | X | X | X | X | X | X |
| Reading Rainbow, p. 133 | | | X | X | X | X | X | |
| Reading Raven*, p. 132 | | | X | X | X | X | | |
| Road-Trip-Bingo HD, p. 198 | | | X | X | X | X | X | X |
| Rounds: Franklin Frog*, p. 154 | | X | X | X | | | | |
| Rush Hour Free, p. 191 | | | | X | X | X | X | X |
| Save the Aliens for iPad, p. 181 | | | | | X | X | X | X |
| Science360 for iPad, p. 163 | | | | | X | X | X | X |
| Scribble Press, p. 224 | | | | X | X | X | X | X |
| Scribblenauts Remix, p. 125 | | | | | | X | X | X |
| Shake-N-Tell, p. 92 | | X | X | X | X | X | X | X |
| Shakespeare in Bits: Romeo & Juliet, p. 139 | | | | | | | X | X |
| Sid's Science Fair, p. 155 | | | X | X | | | | |
| Slice It!, p. 197 | | | | | | X | X | X |
| SpiroDoodle, p. 51 | | | | X | X | X | X | X |
| Sprinkle Junior, p. 114 | | | X | X | X | X | | |
| Squiggles!*, p. 217 | | X | X | X | | | | |
| Stack the Countries*, p. 169 | | | | | X | X | X | X |
| Stack the States*, p. 170 | | | | | X | X | X | X |
| Star Walk, p. 164 | | | | | X | X | X | X |

| App | 2 | 3 | 4 | 5-6 | 7-8 | 9-10 | 11-12 | 13-14 |
|---|---|---|---|---|---|---|---|---|
| Stella and the Startones, p. 187 | | | X | X | X | X | | |
| Super 7*, p. 145 | | | | | X | X | X | X |
| Sushi Monster, p. 225 | | | | | X | X | X | |
| TempleRun*, p. 109 | | | | X | X | X | X | X |
| The adventure of the 7Wonderlicious girls*, p. 127 | | X | X | X | X | | | |
| The Artifacts, p. 78 | | | | | X | X | X | X |
| The DAILY MONSTER Monster Maker, p. 97 | | | | X | X | X | X | X |
| The Fantastic Flying Books of Mr. Morris Lessmore, p. 73, 231 | | | | X | X | X | X | X |
| THE GAME OF LIFE ZappED edition, p. 215 | | | | | X | X | X | X |
| The Going to Bed Book, p. 22 | X | X | X | | | | | |
| The Magic School Bus Oceans, p. 158 | | | | X | X | X | | |
| The Magic School Bus: Dinosaurs, p. 101 | | | | X | X | X | | |
| The Monster at the End of This Book...starring Grover!*, p 60, 227 | | X | X | X | X | | | |
| The Opposites, p. 137 | | | | | X | X | X | X |
| The Social Express*, p. 211 | | | | X | X | X | X | X |
| The Strange & Wonderful World of Ants, p. 156 | | | X | X | X | X | | |
| The Three Little Pigs Animated Interactive Storybook*, p. 64 | | | X | X | X | | | |
| The Voyage of Ulysses, p. 79 | | | | | | X | X | X |
| The Witch With No Name HD, p. 74 | | | | X | X | X | | |
| This is my body - Anatomy for kids, p. 160 | | | | X | X | X | X | |
| Three Little Pigs and the Secrets of a Popup Book, p. 70 | | | | X | X | X | | |
| Toca Band*, p. 185, 228 | | X | X | X | X | X | | |
| Toontastic*, p. 95, 221 | | | | X | X | X | | |
| Touch and Learn: Emotions*, p. 204 | | X | X | X | X | X | X | X |
| Touch and Write*, p. 209 | | | X | X | X | X | X | X |
| Trucks HD*, p. 82 | X | X | X | X | | | | |
| TwinGo! , p. 196 | | | | | X | X | X | X |
| Ultimate Dinopedia, p. 105 | | | | | X | X | X | |
| Uncolor for iPad*, p. 17 | X | | | | | | | |
| UNO HD, p. 88 | | | | X | X | X | X | X |
| Unwanted Guest, p. 75 | | | | | X | X | X | X |
| Wheels on the Bus*, p. 80 | X | X | X | X | | | | |
| Where's My Perry, p. 112 | | | | | X | X | X | X |
| Where's My Water, p. 108 | | | | X | X | X | X | X |
| Wild About Books, p. 71 | | | | X | X | | | |
| Wonderputt, p. 200 | | | | X | X | X | X | X |
| Word Mess, p. 138 | | | | | X | X | X | X |
| World of Goo, p. 123, 234 | | | | | X | X | X | X |
| Zanny Born to Run*, p. 206 | | | X | X | X | X | | |

*Apps that can be used for special-needs kids*

## Apple & Macs

iPad For Dummies
978-0-470-58027-1

iPhone For Dummies,
4th Edition
978-0-470-87870-5

MacBook For
Dummies, 3rd Edition
978-0-470-76918-8

Mac OS X Snow
Leopard For
Dummies
978-0-470-43543-4

## Business

Bookkeeping For
Dummies
978-0-7645-9848-7

Job Interviews
For Dummies,
3rd Edition
978-0-470-17748-8

Resumes For
Dummies,
5th Edition
978-0-470-08037-5

Starting an
Online Business
For Dummies,
6th Edition
978-0-470-60210-2

Stock Investing
For Dummies,
3rd Edition
978-0-470-40114-9

Successful
Time Management
For Dummies
978-0-470-29034-7

## Computer Hardware

BlackBerry
For Dummies,
4th Edition
978-0-470-60700-8

Computers For
Seniors
For Dummies,
2nd Edition
978-0-470-53483-0

PCs For Dummies,
Windows 7 Edition
978-0-470-46542-4

Laptops For
Dummies,
4th Edition
978-0-470-57829-2

## Cooking & Entertaining

Cooking Basics
For Dummies,
3rd Edition
978-0-7645-7206-7

Wine For Dummies,
4th Edition
978-0-470-04579-4

## Diet & Nutrition

Dieting For Dummies,
2nd Edition
978-0-7645-4149-0

Nutrition For
Dummies,
4th Edition
978-0-471-79868-2

Weight Training
For Dummies,
3rd Edition
978-0-471-76845-6

## Digital Photography

Digital SLR Cameras
& Photography For
Dummies, 3rd Edition
978-0-470-46606-3

Photoshop Elements 8
For Dummies
978-0-470-52967-6

## Gardening

Gardening Basics
For Dummies
978-0-470-03749-2

Organic Gardening
For Dummies,
2nd Edition
978-0-470-43067-5

## Green/Sustainable

Raising Chickens
For Dummies
978-0-470-46544-8

Green Cleaning
For Dummies
978-0-470-39106-8

## Health

Diabetes For
Dummies,
3rd Edition
978-0-470-27086-8

Food Allergies
For Dummies
978-0-470-09584-3

Living Gluten-Free
For Dummies,
2nd Edition
978-0-470-58589-4

## Hobbies/General

Chess For Dummies,
2nd Edition
978-0-7645-8404-6

Drawing
Cartoons & Comics
For Dummies
978-0-470-42683-8

Knitting For Dummies,
2nd Edition
978-0-470-28747-7

Organizing
For Dummies
978-0-7645-5300-4

Su Doku For
Dummies
978-0-470-01892-7

## Home Improvement

Home Maintenance
For Dummies,
2nd Edition
978-0-470-43063-7

Home Theater
For Dummies,
3rd Edition
978-0-470-41189-6

Living the
Country Lifestyle
All-in-One
For Dummies
978-0-470-43061-3

Solar Power Your
Home
For Dummies,
2nd Edition
978-0-470-59678-4

Available wherever books are sold. For more information or to order direct: U.S. customers visit www.dummies.com or call 1-877-762-2974. U.K. customers visit www.wileyeurope.com or call (0) 1243 843291. Canadian customers visit www.wiley.ca or call 1-800-567-4797.